A Strange Whim of the Sea

A STRANGE WHIM
— OF THE — SEA

THE WRECK OF THE
USS *MACAW*

Tim Loughman

UNIVERSITY PRESS OF KENTUCKY

Copyright © 2023 by The University Press of Kentucky

Scholarly publisher for the Commonwealth,
serving Bellarmine University, Berea College, Centre
College of Kentucky, Eastern Kentucky University,
The Filson Historical Society, Georgetown College,
Kentucky Historical Society, Kentucky State University,
Morehead State University, Murray State University,
Northern Kentucky University, Spalding University,
Transylvania University, University of Kentucky,
University of Louisville, University of Pikeville,
and Western Kentucky University.
All rights reserved.

Editorial and Sales Offices: The University Press of Kentucky
663 South Limestone Street, Lexington, Kentucky 40508-4008
www.kentuckypress.com

Cataloging-in-Publication data is available from the Library of Congress.

ISBN 978-0-8131-9622-0 (hardcover : alk. paper)
ISBN 978-0-8131-9624-4 (epub)
ISBN 978-0-8131-9623-7 (pdf)

This book is printed on acid-free paper meeting
the requirements of the American National Standard
for Permanence in Paper for Printed Library Materials.

Manufactured in the United States of America

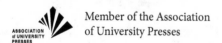

Member of the Association
of University Presses

To Ernest Samed, LeRoy Lehmbecker, Eugene Daugherty,
and Edward Pitta

Such punishment as a court-martial may adjudge may be inflicted on any person in the Navy who . . . through inattention or negligence, suffers any vessel of the Navy to be stranded, or run upon a rock or shoal, or hazarded.

—*Articles for the Government of the United States Navy, Article 8*

It was a mighty big conundrum at one time whether we would ever reach the shore.

—*worker at Midway regarding attempt to return to base camp from dredging site on reef during gale in 1870, as quoted by George H. Read in* The Last Cruise of the Saginaw

It was the sea that got us.

—*Former* Macaw *crew member and Seaman 1/c Joseph Throgmorton*

Contents

Preface   ix
Abbreviations   xiii
Map: Path of the USS *Macaw*   xiv

1. Rough Start   1
2. On the Rocks   18
3. Troubled Waters   27
4. Off to War   38
5. Perilous Passage   58
6. South Pacific   63
7. The Loneliness of the Long-Distance Runner   79
8. Midway   93
9. Emergency Exit   115
10. Business on Great Waters   146
11. Aftermath   160

Appendix   187
Brief Glossary of Nautical Terms   189
Acknowledgments   193
Notes   197
Bibliography   213
Suggestions for Further Reading   217
Index   219

Illustrations follow page 92

Preface

This book is an attempt to the tell the story of the USS *Macaw* (ASR-11), a *Chanticleer*-class submarine rescue vessel that served, briefly, in the Pacific during World War II and came to an untimely demise on the reef at Midway early in 1944. My father, Gerald F. "Bud" Loughman, was the executive officer on the *Macaw*. When the ship went down and its captain, Lt. Cmdr. Paul Willits Burton, USN, died, my father assumed command of a sunken ship and had to handle the attendant burden of paperwork. After he died, my sister found his files regarding the ship, including handwritten accounts of the sinking by the men who survived it, and photographs of the crew, some taken aboard the ship in happier times, some on Midway after it sank. I had talked with my father about the *Macaw*, but it was not until I read those accounts and saw those photos that I conceived a desire to meet some of the men who had been on the ship with him. This being more than fifty years after the war, many of them had died too, but quite a few were still hale and hearty, or at least alive if not so well, and it was my good fortune to contact about twenty of them, most if not all of whom have died since.

Of those men, my most prolific source was one I never talked to, and whom I met face-to-face only once, at his wake. Former Seaman Bob Jacobsen, originally of Garibaldi, Oregon, later Long Beach, California, was having trouble with his eyesight and hearing when I contacted him, and consequently, according to his wife, he was reluctant to talk with me. At age eighty-seven, his frailties apparently embarrassed him. But he could still see well enough to write, so we exchanged letters instead. Over a period of a little more than two years, from July 2009 to September 2011, he sent me sixteen handwritten letters averaging about fifteen pages each, offering a colorful, opinionated, occasionally profane, initially somewhat circumspect and later unrestrained, firsthand account of life aboard the *Macaw* and of his life before and after. This book draws extensively on his letters and on my interviews with his shipmates. Sometimes I paraphrase, but in the interest of better conveying their voices, I generally let Jacobsen and his shipmates speak for themselves, correcting grammar or spelling only as required for clarity. Jacobsen dated some but not all of his letters, so in citations I reference them by number, one through sixteen, rather than by date.

Bob Jacobsen had strong feelings and minced few words. He had some harsh things to say about some of his shipmates. Some of the other *Macaw* crewmen I contacted did too. Jacobsen was less than flattering on the subject of his captain, Paul Burton, in particular. My objective in presenting his and other *Macaw* sailors' personal commentary, positive and otherwise, is to give as full a picture of life aboard the ship as I can. Neither Burton nor anyone else recollected in less than flattering terms in this book is here to defend himself. If any were, or if other voices from the crew were to be heard, a different picture might appear. Bob Jacobsen is no longer here to speak for himself either, but if he were, I think he would agree that, whatever their foibles, all the men he served with risked life and limb in a vital and worthy cause and deserve our thanks.

When I began this project, my ignorance of things nautical was as boundless as the sea itself. That ignorance now has bounds but remains vast. Any errors of fact in this account, regarding seafaring or anything else, are on my account alone.

When my siblings and I were kids, my father would often tell us on the way to church on Sunday to pray for Samed, Lehmbecker, and Daugherty. He referred to them by last name only. This instruction made an impression on me not only because he repeated it so often but also because he never, so far as I recall, asked us to pray for anyone else, relatives included. Nor did he ever explain back then who Samed, Lehmbecker, and Daugherty were, or why he wanted us to pray for them. Nor do I recall that any of us ever asked. My father's instructions to us in the postwar years tended to have a curt, imperative military flavor, and I think perhaps my sister and brothers and I all figured he would construe any questions in response to his prayer order as a sign of reluctance to comply with it. Or perhaps because we couldn't be bothered to pray for people who meant nothing to us, we all just preferred to ignore the order and figured the less said about it the better.

My father died on December 28, 1998. By then, having sat him down with a tape recorder, I knew basically who Samed, Lehmbecker, and Daugherty were and why they had been in at least *his* prayers every Sunday, and I'd gotten his recollections (not always entirely accurate) of a very ordinary ship, and of the extraordinary events that transpired within and about it the night of February 12–13, 1944. The *Macaw* died a violent death, but the violence that destroyed it was that of nature, not man. The story of the *Macaw* is a war story almost completely devoid of war. Some of the ship's crew had been in combat, or would be later, but unless you count one sort of passive, glancing brush with it in which the *Macaw* played the role more of possum than participant, the ship itself never really was. Nor, apparently, was Samed, Lehmbecker, or Daugherty. They seem to have been sailors about as ordinary and workaday in their ways as the *Macaw* was in its, and they had, the three of them, even less direct contact with the Japanese than the *Macaw* did. But there was something extraordinary inside them, and they would show it when their paths and the ship's converged.

There was a fourth man in their party that February 13, Edward Anthony Pitta. Because he alone of the four had the good fortune to survive that day, my father may not have known his name, or known of him at all. If he had, perhaps we would have been instructed to pray for Pitta too. He certainly deserved our prayers every bit as much as his companions did and may have needed them more. All four of them are gone now, as are all the men they risked death trying to save the morning of February 13, 1944, and most if not all of the shipmates of those men. May they all rest in peace.

Tim Loughman
Morro Bay, California
October 2021

Abbreviations

1/c	first class
2/c	second class
3/c	third class
ASR	Auxiliary, Submarine Rescue (i.e., submarine rescue vessel)
CAP	combat air patrol
Capt.	Captain
Cmdr.	Commander
exec or XO	executive officer
jg	junior grade
Lt.	Lieutenant
NAS	Naval Air Station
NOB	Naval Operating Base
USN	United States Navy
USNA	United States Naval Academy
USNR	United States Naval Reserve
USS	United States Ship

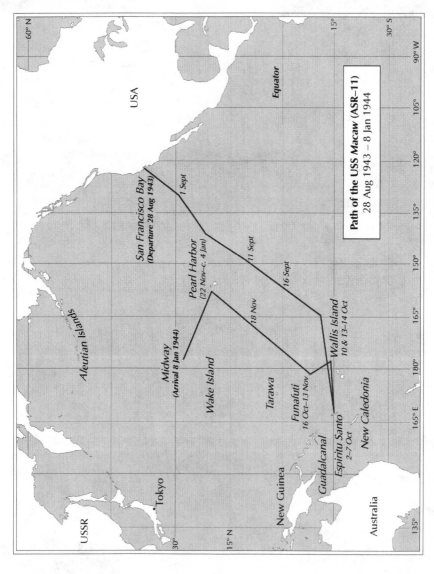

Path of the USS *Macaw* (ASR–11) 28 Aug 1943–8 Jan 1944. Map by Richard Gilbreath

1

Rough Start

The USS *Flier* (SS-250), a newly commissioned *Gato*-class submarine, left Pearl Harbor on January 12, 1944, on what was supposed to be its first war patrol and arrived four days later off Midway, a lonely North Pacific atoll whose roughly twenty-three-mile-long coral reef encompassed a vital submarine refueling depot among other facilities and 2.4 square miles of some of the most bitterly contested dry land in the world.

The *Flier* had been expected at Midway that morning, but head seas the sub had encountered on the way from Hawaii put it several hours behind schedule. Those head seas were not the only source of resistance the sub had met with in its brief career. Built, fitted out, and commissioned in the Groton/New London naval/industrial complex at the mouth of the Thames River in Connecticut, the *Flier* set out for the Pacific the day before Thanksgiving 1943. Approaching the Panama Canal on the surface about five days later, the *Flier* narrowly survived a bombardment of thirteen shells from an armed US merchant vessel, which had mistakenly identified the sub as German. A fortuitous rain squall that shrouded the sub from view may have saved it on that occasion. A subsequent squall would prove less helpful.

A month and a half after that first brush with disaster, the *Flier* drew up tardy but intact to a rendezvous point about two miles off the south reef at Midway and began conversing by semaphore with the signal tower on Sand Island, the larger of the two scrubby, low-lying islands, both just inside the south wall of the lagoon, over which the Battle of Midway had been fought a little more than a year and a half before. Things were violent again at Midway when the *Flier* arrived, but the perpetrator of the violence this time was Mother Nature. Conditions that day were extraordinarily rough.

Since 1940 Midway had been home to NOB (Naval Operating Base) 1504, which by January 1944 encompassed a submarine base, a naval air station, a PT base (PT standing for patrol/torpedo boat), and a cable station. The submarine base served primarily to refuel and otherwise service submarines setting out on or returning from war patrols in the western Pacific. Brooks Channel was the passageway into and out of the lagoon for submarines and surface vessels alike.

From high above, the outer reef at Midway describes a puffy, rounded sort of triangle, the base having a moderate southwest-to-northeast tilt. Brooks Channel is a trough, gouged out before the war, about a mile and a half long, 400 to 500 feet wide and 30 to 38 feet deep, that runs due north and south through the base of the triangle, between Sand and Eastern Islands and into the heart of the lagoon. During the war it was lined at irregular intervals with buoys, six or seven odd-numbered black ones on the left (or port) side for incoming vessels, three or four even-numbered red or white ones on the right (starboard) side, about half of them equipped with 40-candlepower lights that flashed—odd green, even red—every four seconds.[1]

Toward the back, or northern, edge of the lagoon, more than two miles from the entrance to the channel and directly in line with it, stood the channel range lights, a pair of unblinking 15,000-candlepower beacons, the near one seventeen feet above the water, the far one fifteen feet higher and 533 yards farther back, which incoming vessels would use to "take the range," lining themselves up with the lights so as to head straight up the middle of the channel.

That was what arriving vessels were supposed to do, and usually they did, more or less. But as the crews of various ships that had visited over the preceding few years could attest, the channel was not always easy to negotiate. It was wide enough, as long as the helmsman could see where he was going. But when the surf was up or visibility down, the primary challenge the channel posed to an incoming vessel was getting into it. One part of the problem involved currents. The current at the mouth of the channel tends to run south, the channel serving as an avenue of egress for water that pours into the lagoon over a low stretch in the reef on the northwest side. At the mouth of the channel, where it empties into the sea, the current tends southeastward, and that current tended frequently during the war to shove incoming ships close to or onto the coral fringing the entrance's eastern flair.[2]

Another part of the problem involved navigational aids. The buoys that marked, or were supposed to mark, the entrance to the channel, could be hard or impossible to see—hard in a rain squall, impossible when missing.

Brooks Channel flares more or less like a bell where it opens onto the sea. As of January 1944, there should have been four buoys marking the entrance, Nos. 1 and 3 on an inbound vessel's left, 2 and 4 on the right. Buoys 1 and 2, both blinkers, were the first to greet incoming vessels, flanking the approach to the channel from about three hundred yards offshore. Buoys 3 and 4 should have stood sentry just inside the entrance, by its western and eastern sides respectively, but when the *Flier* arrived that day, buoy 4, the inshore eastern marker, was nowhere in sight.

Even when the buoys were present and accounted for, they could be misleading if out of position, as one or both of the two offshore buoys, Nos. 1 and 2, may have been that day. And even the range lights, as bright as they were, were of little use when blocked from view, as one reportedly was that day as well.[3]

Sea conditions at Midway tend to vary seasonally, winter bringing the roughest. Waves build as they approach the channel and break to either side of it. It is critical, and not always easy, for a vessel entering the channel to maintain steerageway. If you have ever ventured beyond the breakers at the beach and then swum or surfed back in, you have experienced being lifted and thrown by waves, and perhaps by the time you emerged from the surf, you were surprised to find how far laterally along the beach you had traveled. The same sort of thing can happen to a ship trying to enter Brooks Channel. As one wartime Midway harbor pilot put it, "In passing the entrance buoys, the surf as it breaks tends to lift and throw the vessel if she does not maintain sufficient speed to over-run the surf." If the surf overruns the vessel, the direction from which the water presses against the rudder shifts from fore to aft, the rudder loses its bite, and control of the ship passes largely or entirely to the sea. The results can be disastrous.[4]

A wartime naval document outlined the procedure for getting into Brooks Channel and underscored the hazards:

> From three miles due south of the entrance, steer a northerly course directed between Sand and Eastern Islands until the channel is distinguished, when approach can be made on the entrance ranges. Pilots are available upon request to the Signal Station on Sand Island. Vessels requiring such services should heave to in the vicinity of the 100 fathom curve until the pilot boards. (As a rule, the Commandant requires all vessels to have a pilot).

Enter channel on range, course 000° True [i.e., due north]. Because of winds and the westerly set of the current outside the reef, caution must be exercised on entering. Leeway and drift should be anticipated and sufficient speed to control the vessel maintained at all times. At the entrance of the channel the current is stronger and variable and has a southeasterly set.[5]

The hundred-fathom curve is a contour line, as on a topographic map, marking a depth of six hundred feet. The hundred-fathom curve at Midway lies about one and a half miles off the mouth of Brooks Channel. The *Flier* "hove to" on the surface at about 1400 (2:00 p.m.) a mile or so outside that curve, and within about fifteen minutes, as a three-man anchor detail awaited orders on a gun platform behind the conning tower, the sub was instructed by the signal tower on Sand Island to "Stand by for pilot."[6]

This was an instruction its captain, Cmdr. John Daniel Crowley of Springfield, Massachusetts, was probably happy to comply with. Crowley, a US Naval Academy graduate, class of 1931, was well versed in handling submarines, having spent much of the first two years of the war commanding an antiquated S-boat in the frigid waters off the Aleutians, and he had studied charts of Midway. But neither he, his navigator, nor his officer of the deck had ever negotiated the channel there before, and this was a rough day for a maiden run, with winds out of the southwest around 35 mph, "extremely large quartering seas," a strong eastward set (or current) at the channel entrance, and heavy ground swells in the channel itself, along with occasional rain squalls that made it difficult to see. On the Midway Naval Air Station's 0-to-7 State of Sea scale, on which 0 represented calm, conditions that day rated a 6. The *Flier*'s executive officer later estimated the waves that day at twenty feet.[7]

To minimize the round trip the small craft delivering his harbor pilot would have to make, Crowley testified later, he proceeded to bring the *Flier* in almost two miles closer to shore. It was a thoughtful move and arguably catastrophic. A motor launch started out with the pilot but never got out of the channel. Someone aboard it thinking better of the undertaking, it did a U-turn inside the channel and headed back into the lagoon. A little while later *YT-188*, a yard tug, emerged. Normally, the craft delivering the pilot would draw abreast of the sub, but that afternoon the seas were too big for that maneuver. The pilot himself and both vessels' hulls would be at risk. So, with the wind making vocal communication, even by megaphone, unintelligible, the tug signaled by semaphore: "Follow me." The *Flier* would have a guide, but Crowley and his men would have to navigate the channel themselves.[8]

Having, by his own account, cut the length of his approach to the channel by more than half, Crowley began it about half a mile south of buoys 1 and 2. With the sub's fathometer (an instrument for measuring water depth) under continuous monitoring and its air intake valves closed against the threat of "pooping," or of seas breaking over the stern and swamping them, he proceeded on battery power at 10 knots, or two-thirds speed, trailing the tug at a distance of about a thousand yards. He said later that he had planned on entering the channel at a full 15 knots but opted for the lower speed for fear of overtaking the tug. He might have done better to stick with his original plan. Just about as the *Flier* passed between buoys 1 and 2, a rain squall obscured the view from the bridge, a massive swell hit the sub, and it yawed sharply to port. A brief, desperate struggle to control the sub ensued, during which it lurched left and right and back to the left, struck the reef, lifted off, and smacked down onto it again.[9]

Crowley ordered "all ahead full" in the hope of propelling his boat over the obstruction, and about as he did so he received a report of a fire in the maneuvering room. A toolbox, jarred loose from its wall mount, had crashed to the floor, and a screwdriver had popped out of it and shorted out a pair of motor terminals, sparking a fire in a pile of rags.

The fire was extinguished promptly enough, the only casualty a brief loss of power to the port propeller, but when he got the initial report, Crowley had reason to fear the loss of his entire power supply. He didn't know how long it would hold out. What he did know was that "all ahead full" was getting the sub nowhere and that it couldn't stay where it was, projecting backward out to sea, broadside to endless ranks of big breaking waves, any one of which could swamp and sink it, drowning its crew within sight of dry land. He had to make some workable shift with the power he had while he still had it. He lightened the sub by blowing out the contents of various fuel and ballast tanks and ordered, "Starboard ahead full, port back full, left full rudder" in an effort to swing the boat about to port—perhaps to spring it free, but failing that, at least to turn it into the waves and pin it there with an anchor to minimize the threat of capsizing.[10]

The ship responded to this urging, effectively pivoting counterclockwise while alternately lifting off and falling back onto the reef and getting swept eastward along it. Nothing about the *Flier* that afternoon was easy to control. Once the sub began turning, it turned too far, swinging past due south to about 150 degrees true, by which point it had started to present its starboard side broadside to the waves coming in from the southwest. So Crowley coaxed it back to the right to about 205 degrees true, and then the three men of the anchor detail—Torpedomen James Cahl, Clyde Gerber, and Kenneth Gwinn—were dispatched at last, along with Firemen and line handlers George Banchero and Waite Daggy, from the after gun platform to the bow to do the topside work of releasing the bow anchor. Another torpedoman, Joseph Lia, who had gotten permission to go topside just to get some fresh air, gamely accompanied them. With waves washing right over the deck, it was dicey going. Only one of the men, Banchero, wore a life belt, a piece of equipment submariners venturing onto the deck frequently went without for fear of its snagging on something in the event of a sudden dive and trapping its occupant outside the hatch.

Clinging to one or the other of a pair of steel cable lifelines strung along rows of stanchions on either side of the deck, the six of them made their way to the forward gun platform, where the two lifelines merged into one. Cahl and Lia hung onto that, Cahl with one hand—he was holding a wrench in the other—as they proceeded to the anchor gear near the nose of the boat, their companions meanwhile retreating back toward the bridge in compliance with an order from an officer that Cahl and Lia apparently failed to hear. Moments later a huge wave surged over the boat, breaking Cahl's one-handed grip on the lifeline. Lia lost his footing but managed to hang on to the line. As the wash of the spent wave drained from the deck, he found himself alone. He shouted, "Man overboard!" and spotted Cahl treading water off the portside with both hands raised pleadingly and a hopeless look on his face as the current bore him away from the sub.

The next wave drove up under the starboard bow, cocked the vessel at an angle Crowley later estimated at 35 to 40 degrees, knocked many if not all of those inside it off their feet, and almost broached it. By this point Gerber too had been swept overboard, and Daggy smashed against the conning tower and down onto the deck. Responding to a call for a strong swimmer, Banchero stripped down to something like bathing attire, leapt in with a cork life ring and his life belt, and swam off toward Gerber. Lia jumped in too, also wearing a life belt now and tethered by a line to the sub, but he could make no headway toward either Cahl or Gerber and was soon hauled back aboard.

The waves, meanwhile, yielded occasional glimpses of Cahl to the men on the bridge. By about the time Banchero jumped in, Cahl had vanished. Soon both Gerber and Banchero were lost from sight too.

Fireman James Alls, originally of Tams, West Virginia, was in the forward engine room when the *Flier* grounded. His presence there was not strictly legal. Like hundreds or thousands of other patriotic adolescent American males born toward the end of the 1920s, Alls had enlisted at age fifteen, having crudely altered the date of birth on his birth certificate on a typewriter at a Western Union telegraph office in Washington, DC. That bit of fraud had fooled no one at the recruiting office, but Alls was determined to wear a uniform—"It was a time," he said, "if you weren't in uniform, you weren't dressed"—so he kept going back with his "boogered up" birth certificate, and finally, to get rid of him, Alls said, the exasperated senior recruiting officer said, "Sign 'im up."

So he was duly sworn in on June 7, 1942, six months to the day after Pearl Harbor and one day after the Battle of Midway, and now, as a sixteen-year-old seasoned veteran a little more than a year and a half later, he was on hand to experience what he termed the "living nightmare" of running aground. He was scared to death, he said, and with good reason—if the boat were to founder, the odds of the men in either of the two engine rooms making good their escape would be slim to none. Among the stratagems Captain Crowley employed to try to elude that fate was ordering his crew to shift in concert from one side of the boat to the other to try to rock it free. Alls and his engine room colleagues complied as best they could, but the two big Winton 16 diesel engines in the room left them only a narrow central aisle in which to maneuver. It was, as Alls aptly described it, a desperate tactic, and one that seems unlikely to have contributed significantly to moving the boat.[11]

But the boat did keep moving. According to Crowley and Lt. James Liddell, his engineering officer, the *Flier* had first run aground inside the channel. By the time it came to something like rest, it was about a hundred yards east of it. A powerful eastward current had dragged it that far along the reef, and even after the sub lodged in one spot at last, the waves continued to rock it, probably a great deal more effectively than the dance routine Crowley choreographed did. Stuck but unsteady, the sub was ill suited to the performance of a delicate medical procedure, but when Daggy climbed back down through the hatch, he had a gash on his right side, another in his lower lip, three broken teeth, three or four loose ones, and what might have been a broken jaw, and he needed immediate medical attention. Assisted by shipmates holding flashlights, Pharmacist's Mate 1/c and registered nurse Peter Gaideczka of Watervliet, New York, treated him on a bunk in the crew's quarter, working a few seconds at a time in the intervals between swells when the sub came briefly upright. According to Alls, when Daggy later went ashore, a doctor or corpsman saw him there, saw what Gaideczka had done for him, and said he couldn't have done a better job himself.[12]

The ranking officer at NOB 1504 that day (in naval parlance, the senior officer present afloat) was Capt. Joseph A. Connolly, USN. Connolly's first indication that something was amiss with the *Flier* apparently came by way of a conversation he overheard that afternoon between the operations officer and the signal tower in which the *Flier* was reported first as two hundred and then five hundred yards from the channel entrance. The sub seemed to be going the wrong way. Then, at about 1430, came worse news: the *Flier* was aground.

A submarine makes a particularly dangerous vessel to be aground in. Avenues of egress are constricted and in short supply. Capsizing can prove fatal for an entire crew, and for all Captain Connolly knew, any one of the huge waves battering the *Flier* as they surged up to break on the reef the sub was trapped on might have sufficed to shove it over.

It may have seemed providential to Connolly at the time that he had the USS *Macaw* (ASR-11) to call on in this crisis. The *Macaw* was a submarine rescue vessel, one of just eleven in commission in the US Navy at the time, and one of just five built as such. The other six were all converted minesweepers more than twenty years old. The *Macaw* and its four sister ships were new and powerful—each ship boasted four diesel electric engines capable of generating a combined 3,000 horsepower—and equipped with the latest in submarine salvage technology. The *Macaw* had arrived from Pearl Harbor just eight days before.

According to his own subsequent testimony, Connolly told the operations officer to order out the *Macaw* and all the tugs on hand, then he proceeded aboard one of those tugs to the *Macaw*. Accounts of the conversation he had with the *Macaw*'s captain, Lt. Cmdr. Paul Willits Burton, USN, upon boarding vary considerably regarding both contents and tone. By Connolly's own brief account to a board of inquiry five weeks later, it would seem to have been entirely civil and matter-of-fact, with two cool-headed commanders quickly concurring in the face of a crisis, the senior officer merely offering a suggestion as to how to address it: "I proceeded to the bridge and asked the Commanding Officer, Lieutenant Commander P. W. Burton, U.S. Navy, if he knew that the FLIER was aground. He said that he had just received word and was getting underway. At this time I suggested to him that messengers be prepared to send wire to the FLIER."[13]

Former Seaman 2/c Robert Gonnoud, who was in the pilothouse with Burton and his guest at the time, described a somewhat less collegial encounter. According to Gonnoud, Burton was not keen on taking the ship out under the circumstances and said as much when Connolly ordered him to, protesting, "My God, there's a terrible storm out there."

Connolly "was an Irishman," Gonnoud said. "His face was blood-red. He was mad as hell. He said, 'I told you to get under way and get to the *Flier*.'"[14]

On another occasion, Gonnoud recalled the meeting in less colorful terms, describing it as merely "kind of argumentative," and Lt. (jg) Worth T. Windle, USN, the *Macaw*'s navigation officer, who spent plenty of time that day with Paul Burton on the bridge, testified later that, to what he termed the best of his knowledge, Burton displayed no apprehension about taking the ship out or back in. But it's not clear how much of the interaction between Burton and Connolly Windle actually witnessed, and Burton, after that initial exchange, may have felt more apprehension than he let on.[15]

He could hardly have failed to feel some. The wind, at about the time Connolly came aboard, was blowing about 30 knots (35 mph) and had gusted within the hour to 54 knots. The squall having passed, visibility was good, but that would have served only to make the view from the lagoon of the huge surf outside it that much more daunting. For all the store it sets by valor, the navy takes a dim view of a captain's putting his ship in danger rashly—Adm. Chester W. Nimitz himself, hardly a shrinking violet, had stressed to his commanders before the Battle of Midway the concept of calculated risk, with its sober balancing of projected costs and benefits—and the potential costs to Burton's ship and crew, not to mention his career, of defying the elements might have weighed heavily in the balance of a calmer analyst than Connolly evidently was that day. Windle, who had enlisted in 1919, would testify, "I'd never seen conditions as bad as they were that day." Quinton Studer, a motor machinist's mate aboard the *Macaw*, shared the sentiments Bob Gonnoud attributed to Paul Burton: "They should never have sent us out there," he said—the sea was too rough, with waves that looked to be twenty to thirty feet high. The *Flier* was in grave danger, but if it could be stabilized for the night, at least, with its bow to the waves, the risk of swamping would be mini-mized. And as Burton may have pointed out to Connolly, as a submarine the *Flier* had a characteristically strong hull, and it was intact. A rational actor might have taken all that into consideration, surveyed the surf and ground-swells, thought, "better one ship on the rocks than two," and counseled for-bearance. If Paul Burton was in fact reluctant to take his ship out that day, subsequent events suggest that he was wise to feel that way. But Captain Con-nolly would have none of it. So, as Bob Gonnoud put it, "out we went."[16]

The *Macaw* had negotiated the channel three times before—on its arrival and twice since, once out and once back, for an exercise at sea, probably tor-pedo practice with a submarine. Each time, and again on January 16, the helmsman was Quartermaster 2/c Herman Ehlers, a small-town bank execu-tive from northeastern Illinois. Worth Windle, the navigation officer, would later vouch for Ehlers as one of the best helmsmen on the ship.[17]

The *Flier* lay pinned backward to the reef amid already tremendous seas mounting even higher as they swelled up to break on it. The *Macaw*'s objec-tive was to tow the *Flier* free. The first order of business was to rig a towing wire, and the first step in that procedure was to pass the sub a messenger. A messenger, in navy parlance, is a light line by means of which one ship hauls in a heavier line from another. Once the messenger is run between the two ships, it is secured at one end to the heavier line and hauled back with it to the other ship. This process can be repeated if necessary, using the heavier line from a previous pass to draw in a still heavier one. The whole process is sim-ple enough in theory, but in practice the first step, passing the messenger from one ship to the other, can be challenging, and under conditions like those at Midway that day, it can be dangerous. The *Macaw* would have to get close enough to the *Flier* to pass it the messenger without running into it or running aground itself. It would mean a very delicate balancing act on a very rough sea.

The *Macaw* got under way at about 1445. Burton; Connolly; the execu-tive officer, Lt. Gerald F. "Bud" Loughman, of New Rochelle, New York; and Windle, the navigator, of Mooresville, North Carolina, were on the bridge, which comprised the pilothouse and chart room and the deck surrounding them and overlooked the forward third or so of the ship. Seamen 1/c Bob Jacobsen and Bert Maas were at their sea detail station on the aft half of the main deck, two decks below, gathering in mooring lines under the super-vision of Bosun's Mate 2/c and St. Louis native Ralph Mennemeyer. Under normal circumstances the mooring lines might have been "flaked"—laid out neatly, probably in coils or figure eights, and left on the deck—but that day Mennemeyer saw to it that Jacobsen and Maas stowed them away. He wanted the deck clear.[18]

Within about twenty minutes the *Macaw* had cleared the channel. Five minutes or so after that it dropped its starboard anchor near buoy No. 2— west of it, according to Captain Connolly; about fifty yards east of it and two hundred yards south of the *Flier,* according to both Windle and 1st Lt. Joseph Albin, the *Macaw*'s damage control officer—and set about trying for the first time in its brief career to do what it had been designed for, to rescue a submarine. By Windle's account, Burton, apparently unaware of the powerful southeastward current at the mouth of the channel, initially suggested working from a spot east of the *Flier* and settled for one more or less due south of the sub instead. Someone aboard the *Macaw* used a .45-caliber line-throwing gun to propel a messenger to a fifty-foot motor launch, the idea being for the launch to haul the messenger, beaded with life preservers as flotation devices, as close as it reasonably could to the *Flier* and try to float it to the sub from there. This strategy failed. The launch got the messenger but struggled to make headway toward the *Flier* and almost capsized trying to. The men aboard the launch played the messenger out onto the waves, but it carried eastward, away from the stranded sub. Their counterparts aboard the *Macaw* tried deploying messengers, likewise buoyed with flotation devices, directly from its fantail, but the rough seas defeated that effort too.

Captain Connolly, having left the bridge for the boat deck aft to oversee the handling of the messengers, called for *YT-188* to deliver one but then thought better of that idea and issued an order instead for that tug and the other smaller craft that had gone out to go back into the lagoon: "I sent word by TBP [a radio transmitter] to the YT-188 to get a line from us and observed her heading up towards the MACAW, but being tossed considerably by the seas. Observation of small craft in the seas led me to believe that further use of them would end in disaster for them. I then noted that the MACAW was underway."[19]

The fact that the *Macaw* was under way at that point was not something Connolly noted with pleasure. Former Seaman 1/c and radar operator Harold Hayes recalled witnessing another conversation on the bridge that day between Paul Burton and a man Hayes mistakenly recalled as a harbor pilot. There was no harbor pilot aboard. The other party to the conversation was

Connolly, and once again a third party's account of it is a good deal livelier than Connolly's own. Here is Connolly's, as presented at the inquest five weeks later:

> I went back to the bridge and asked the Commanding Officer why he was underway, and he told me that he could not remain in that position. I then told him that it was getting late and that we could not get anyplace in these seas with small craft carrying line. I then suggested that the MACAW go back halfway up the channel where the ship could turn around and come back out floating a line so that it would drift eastward to the FLIER. The Commanding Officer said it would only take ten minutes longer to go all the way in, so I said, "All right, let's go all the way in then."[20]

Hayes recalled a more heated exchange. Connolly apparently felt that Burton, whom he far outranked, should have consulted with him before moving the ship. "I'm in command of this ship," Hayes recalled their visitor telling Burton. "I'll say what we're gonna do. Shut your mouth and get off the [bridge], or I'll have you court-martialed." Burton, Hayes said, replied, "Aye aye, sir," and complied. Hayes remarked that Burton had little choice in the matter.[21]

Ens. William "Gunner" Dunn, the *Macaw*'s gunnery officer, meanwhile, was trying to propel a messenger to the sub with a line-throwing gun. According to Hayes, one of Dunn's shots had come "so close" but just fallen short, and it was to angle for a better shot that Burton had weighed anchor. If that was the case, it's unclear whether Connolly understood Burton's motivation. Whether understanding it would have assuaged his anger over the supposed encroachment on his authority is also unclear.

No one but Hayes has Burton being banished from the bridge. Sworn testimony by both Loughman and Windle places him there long after Hayes said he was thrown off it. But if Hayes was wrong sixty-eight years later about some of the details of that exchange, he was probably basically accurate regarding its tone. While attempting to maneuver amid huge seas, with the fates of two vessels, the lives of at least one crew, and his own future as a naval officer hanging in the balance, it appears that Paul Burton was getting bully-ragged on his own ship.[22]

Connolly's subsequent reconstruction of the events of that day mention the *Macaw*'s dropping an anchor during the rescue attempt only once. In fact the ship did so twice, both times its starboard bow anchor. It retrieved that anchor only once. The *Macaw* departed its first anchorage, according to Windle, at about 1535, still connected by a messenger to the motor launch, rounded buoy No. 2 to seaward, and dropped anchor again at about 1545 roughly twenty-five yards north-northwest of that buoy, having lost the messenger en route. The ship's heading approaching this spot was northward, but once it dropped the starboard bow anchor, its stern swung counterclockwise, shoved that way presumably by the current. The *Macaw* swung, according to Windle, to a heading of about 295 degrees, a bearing that gave the men on the fantail a plausible angle from which to try once again to float a messenger to the *Flier,* and they did try again but with no better luck. It cannot have made this delicate task any easier that aboard the ship at the time men were experiencing what Bud Loughman was to describe as "great difficulty remaining on their feet."[23]

The *Macaw* had two bow anchors, or "bowers," each weighing three tons and each on a one-and-a-half-inch-gauge chain 150 fathoms (900 feet) long stored on one of the bower windlass's two independently operable "wildcats" or chainwheels. The windlass, a product of the Struthers Wells-Titusville Corporation of Titusville, Pennsylvania, featured a 40-horsepower electric motor and could under calmer circumstances hoist both bowers and their chain (or "rode") simultaneously from a depth of sixty fathoms at a rate of forty-two feet a minute. It was powerful, like the ship at large, but that day it proved unequal to the task of restraint. The plan at that second anchorage was to run the chain out to thirty fathoms, but with the seas and set both working to drive or drag the ship eastward, the strain was too great, and another forty-five fathoms ran out. Burton ordered the anchor heaved in, and one of that day's many struggles ensued, with the anchor detail apparently more than once reeling in part of the chain only to have it overpower the wildcat and spool out again. During the last such attempt the massive chain snapped. As Bob Gonnoud put it, "The anchor chain just went bing." Seaman 2/c Dave Wallington was in the bow at the time. He said the chain snapped like a rubber band and fell straight down. Had it whipped, he said, "I'd have been a dead goner."[24]

At some point amid all the maneuvering around buoy No. 2, the *Macaw* at the very least came perilously close to it. Quartermaster 3/c John Paul Graaff was in the pilothouse that day. He testified later that someone phoned from the fantail about a buoy (clearly No. 2) within ten feet of the stern.

Dunn, the gunnery officer, wrote, "The Captain maneuvered the ship admirably around #2 buoy."[25]

Chief Commissary Steward Albert Homer Jones was less flattering. Jones was the junior officer of the watch on the flying bridge (atop the pilothouse) that day. He later stated that about four minutes before the anchor chain parted, the ship, in the course of swinging an arc to the southwest on that chain, rode right over the buoy. (The ship might plausibly have swung such an arc, impelled initially by the southeastward current, and then slung southwestward by its momentum.) Of the thirteen men aboard that day who testified before the subsequent board of investigation, only Jones and one other, Seaman 1/c Virgil Anderson, reported this development, but Jones was specific about it—he said the buoy passed directly under the No. 1 three-inch gun mount about fifteen feet forward of the bridge.[26]

According to Worth Windle, the navigation officer, after the chain parted, Burton announced from just outside the pilothouse through a porthole to the men inside that he was taking the ship back into the lagoon. The idea— basically Connolly's, by his own account—was to go back in, turn around, and come back out, and just as the ship was clearing the channel a second time, to try yet again to float the *Flier* a messenger, fortified in its buoyancy with kapok life jackets and cork buoys at twenty-foot intervals and released from a point west of the sub, from which it would be better positioned to ride the current to its mark. Windle would later testify, "You couldn't notice the set that day due to the seas being so high that you couldn't tell whether you were getting a set or getting pushed over by ground swells." But Burton's shifting anchorages, from south and perhaps a little east of the *Flier* to southwest of it, and then Connolly's formulating, or at least embracing, this new plan, with its release point more or less directly west of the sub, suggest that the two of them, at least, had in fact by this time gotten a better idea of the current prevailing at the channel's mouth.[27]

The board of investigation that would convene about two weeks later focused largely on what came next: how Paul Burton initiated his intended return to the lagoon. Worth Windle recalled rounding the No. 2 buoy to seaward, then heading north. Shipfitter 2/c Nord Lester cast the maneuver in terms of turning a circle. By most accounts they started back from within the channel or in line with it. Windle recalled a heading of 356 degrees—which meant, in fact, one of 358 degrees inasmuch as the ship's gyrocompass had an error, one that Burton and his navigation gang had been aware of for two weeks: the actual heading was 2 degrees east of what the device indicated. This error should not have posed a major problem—the man conning, in this case Burton, could simply adjust his instructions to the helmsman by 2 degrees accordingly—but it could not have made his job any easier. Nor could the presence, subsequently testified to by Windle, of a dredge sitting between the range lights and blotting out the rear one. Burton, according to Windle, took a bearing on just the front range light, and Windle confirmed his reading, but with the rear light obscured and the ship lurching violently, both phases of that exercise must have involved a measure of guesswork. The buoys inside the channel offered a more reliable alternative for taking the range, and Windle used them for that purpose, noting that what he took to be buoys Nos. 8 and 10 (probably actually Nos. 6 and 10—no buoy No. 8 appears on a chart drawn three months later) were "open"—that is, from the vantage point of the ship there was open space between them, No. 10, the more distant of the two, standing to the left of its partner, meaning that the ship at that point was west of the north-south line they described, that line being the eastern edge of the channel. In other words, the ship was still inside the channel, or in line with it. It would not stay there long.[28]

Ehlers, the quartermaster who had the wheel that day, would testify that as they entered the channel, the ship was "yawing badly," 3 or 4 degrees to either side of the course Burton was requesting. "I felt, however," Ehlers added, "that we were making good the course that I was expected to make." Windle does not seem to have shared that feeling. "We were getting heavy seas causing the ship to yaw . . . over an arc of 15 or 20 degrees," he would testify, "and things were happening so fast that at one time it would look like we were heading for the opposite side of the channel and the next instant a swell would pick us up and head us the other way."[29]

The wheel Ehlers was trying to steer the ship by was in the pilothouse. On one side of him Bob Gonnoud was on the annunciator, a device that produced chimes—"bells" in naval parlance—to signal orders from the bridge to the "black gang" in the engine room. On the other side, Electrician's Mate 2/c Charles Kumler manned a console that actually controlled the engines and, to Gonnoud's way of thinking, made the annunciator and his role in operating it redundant and obsolete. Six months before, at the *Macaw*'s commissioning ceremony on the Oakland Estuary, Kumler's brother Harry, eleven at the time, in attendance with his parents, had had his doubts about the ship's seaworthiness. "We all laughed" when a tugboat went by, rocking the *Macaw* in its wake, he said. "We all thought, 'How's this thing going to do on the open ocean?'" The ship had since proven up to the task of traversing more than ten thousand miles of it, but now, almost literally within a stone's throw of dry land, it was struggling for its life, wracked by swells that had it yawing badly and rolling, by Bud Loughman's estimate, as much as 35 degrees. Those swells occasionally hoisted its propeller clear of the water, or perhaps sucked the water out from under it, but in either case left it briefly resisted in its revolution by nothing more substantial than spray. The ship was making, or trying to make, its standard speed of 15 knots—one mistake Burton did not make was trying, like Crowley, to ease into the channel at less than full speed—but the sudden fluctuations in the resistance load on the propeller, churning through water one moment and spinning in air the next, wrought havoc on the engines, which Kumler later recalled as having "kicked off line" four or five times that day. While he was doing what he could from the pilothouse to keep the engines on in the face of these fluctuations, the men in the engine room were scrambling to make arrangements with auxiliary generators to handle the load at its heaviest, only to have that load vanish suddenly several times and with it their propulsion. The last time this happened, the engines were "off the line" only momentarily, but under the circumstances even a brief loss of momentum and consequent increase in lateral drift could easily prove fatal.[30]

Some of the men on board seem to have seen what was coming. Worth Windle noted that the gap he had discerned a little earlier between what he thought were buoys Nos. 8 and 10 had closed. As they lurched and yawed at something at least approaching 15 knots toward the surf pounding the reef at the mouth of the channel, an older radioman in the pilothouse, very likely Chief Radioman George Ritchie Gritton, asked Bob Gonnoud whether he'd ever been in a shipwreck. No, Gonnoud said, he hadn't. "Wait a minute," Gritton told him. "It's about to happen."[31]

Gonnoud may have had to wait more than a minute, but not much more. Paul Burton ordered a course correction to 354 degrees, a slight westward adjustment, probably to compensate for the ship's being shoved east, and then another, to 358 degrees, apparently in response to a swing to the left. Windle would testify to what happened next:

The Captain gave the change of course to 358 gyro and walked toward the forward end of the navigation bridge and I started to follow him. And before I could get up to where he was at, the ship took a sudden yaw caused by a swell and swung back over about 20 degrees to the right and I turned around to tell the helmsman to give her left rudder and by the time I had made the pilot house port, I looked around and the ship was swinging to the left again. The Captain came back to look at the gyro repeater in the starboard wing of the bridge. We were both looking at it and about that time a swell hit us and just seemed to pick the ship up and set it over on the reef. The ship hit three distinct times before finally grounding.[32]

Bosun Joseph Albin was supervising the anchor detail when they grounded. "I knew a short time before we grounded, we were going aground— possibly thirty seconds," he said, "because there were three or four big swells the way the sea generally runs, which picked us up and set us over a few feet. The first time we hit was on one of these swells."[33]

Nord Lester was on the flying bridge standing lookout duty, that being a typical assignment for him given his twenty/twenty eyesight. His vision that day penetrated to the floor of the sea and, like Gritton's and Albin's, at least a few moments into the future. "We were in a curved course to the east of [the] marker buoy," he wrote. "The bottom of the ocean was in full view. The Macaw drew about 12' of water. We could see what was going to happen & it did with the help of a large sea."[34]

That sea picked them up and put them down at about 1612. Their excursion that day had lasted about an hour and a half and left them pinned to the reef at the eastern flare of the channel entrance on a heading of 32 degrees true, parallel to, pointing the opposite direction as, and about a hundred yards west of the *Flier*. Aerial photographs of the two of them stuck there suggest a pair of vehicles in neighboring parking spots, one of them, the submarine, having backed in. As Commander Crowley would later observe of the *Macaw*, "She ran aground in almost the identical spot on which *Flier* had originally touched." At about 1615 the base radioed the *Macaw* and asked if it was in trouble. Gritton responded with bad news, but he gave it a hopeful suggestion of impermanence. "I replied," he later wrote, "that we were aground at the moment."[35]

2

On the Rocks

Former Seaman 1/c Clyde Isbell said about sixty years later he figured it was his fault the *Macaw* had run aground. Isbell, of Navasota, Texas, was monitoring the ship's fathometer at the time, a fathometer being an echo-sounding device that gauges depth by measuring the time a sound pulse takes to bounce back from whatever lies under it. As Isbell recalled it, he had given Paul Burton a reading of sixteen feet seconds—"not more than two or three seconds, five or ten"—before the ship struck the reef. In calmer water, sixteen feet should have been enough, if not by much—the ship's draft that day was thirteen feet six inches forward and fifteen feet five inches aft. But the fathometer, Isbell pointed out, was bolted in place thirty or forty feet behind the bow and could take only vertical readings. The sort of sonar familiar to moviegoers from scenes featuring a destroyer seeking out a sub-merged submarine can send its pings in most any direction, but the focus of the *Macaw*'s fathometer was limited to straight down: you couldn't aim it forward at an angle to check the depth at the bow, and as Isbell noted, the depth at the bow and the depth thirty or forty feet aft of the bow could be different. For the *Macaw*, at 1612 that day they were at least two and a half feet different. "'Bout that time," he said, "crash, the bow's up there about forty to fifty feet."[1]

Bob Jacobsen was on the fantail with his second-deck division mates Bert Maas and Ralph Mennemeyer at 1612 that day: "When we piled onto the reef we weren't aware of it until an impact knocked us to our knees. Then several big waves came over the stern. We were in water to our waist—But after about 3 of these waves the stern seemed above the waves and dry. We then forward in time to see [John Robert] Stout SF 1/c come out of the WT [watertight] door to the engine room and say it was flooded and Chunks of coral as big as GI cans on the deck of the engine room."[2]

The engine room, aka the generator room, had indeed flooded—almost instantly, according to former Motor Machinist's Mate 1/c Quinton Studer, who was there at the time. He said the grounding left the ladders there cocked at about 60 degrees and that men were just about hanging from them. "I was scared shitless," he said. "Everyone was." Everyone perhaps but Richard Edwin Mallard, thirty-two, the engine room chief, from Wilmington, North Carolina, by way of San Francisco, among the longer-serving sailors on the ship— he had enlisted in 1929—and surely one of the least perturbable. Studer proceeded, probably in part by way of one of those suddenly skewed ladders, to the deck, and it was apparently there that he encountered Mallard, who, according to Studer, noted that they were going to abandon ship and said: "You know, the kitchen is open. Do you want a ham sandwich?"[3]

Fireman 1/c Dan Weber was in the motor room when the ship hit the reef. The motor room was in the hold, in the bowels of the ship, between the engine room and the shaft alley, the latter a lengthy, normally watertight compartment containing the ship's single propeller shaft. Fifty-eight years later he said, "I can still see when the propeller hit that reef." Upon impact, Weber said, the propeller shaft tore a hole upward through the skin of the ship at the stern. The shaft alley was apparently the first compartment to flood. Weber tried to close the door between it and the motor room to keep the latter from following suit but managed to secure only the lowest of the door's several latches. The door had been warped by the impact. Weber struggled with it briefly, then repaired to the engine room, where, he said, he and one other man waited in water that rose to their chests before someone finally authorized them to leave. "In war an individual is a number," he said. "They thought more of a jeep than of a person. . . . You did what you were told to do. The rule was, you stayed at your post" until you were told you could leave. But he had at least already positioned himself by the exit when they finally got permission to go.[4]

Captain Connolly had gone to the main deck aft to discuss with Joseph Albin, the bosun, the use of buoys on the messenger when the ship struck, pitching Connolly and several other men in a heap against the towing engine. Paul Burton was on the bridge, on its starboard wing, according to Worth Windle, staring with him at the gyro repeater to check whether the ship's rudder was answering to the latest course adjustment Burton had ordered Ehlers, the helmsman, to make. Burton's initial response to running aground, made by Windle's own account at his (Windle's) behest, was exactly what Crowley's had been aboard the *Flier* about two hours before—he ordered full speed ahead.

> He [Burton] gave an order to change course to 354 gyro. We stayed on that, I'd say a minute, possibly a minute and a half, and the next order was "Come right to 358 gyro" which the helmsman tried to do, we were yawing badly, due to heavy seas, swinging I'd say, between 15 and 20 degrees. The next thing that happened, the ship seemed to bounce and the Captain gave the order "Full speed ahead." He and I were both standing on the starboard wing of the bridge watching the gyro repeater. As soon as we hit, I said to the Captain, "Give her full speed ahead, Captain, we might clear." So he gave the order and afterwards I was talking to him about it and he said he'd had the same idea and when I spoke up there was two people with the same opinion and he immediately gave that order. And the ship hit three distinct times before she finally came to rest. And we went ahead about a minute and a half or two minutes at full speed ahead and then he gave the order "All engines astern full speed."[5]

That strategy, pressed on Burton by his navigator, to gun his engines in the hope of propelling the ship over the obstacle it had met may have sealed the fate of the ship and its captain alike. With three thousand horse-power at his disposal, huge breaking waves at his back, and an overbearing superior officer on it, one who had already expressed something less than high regard for his seamanship, the attraction of applying readily accessible brute force to the problem in the hope of resolving it quickly must have been strong indeed. How much thought Burton gave to the potential downside of doing so no one will ever know. Nor is there any way to know just how much more firmly the *Macaw* was stuck on that reef after "a minute and a half or two minutes" of full speed ahead than it already was before—whether, in other words, it could have backed itself off, or another vessel could have pulled it off, if it hadn't first tried so hard to push itself over. Those 90 or 120 seconds of forward thrust, while failing to solve the problem, may not have made it significantly worse, or they may have converted a loose hold into a death grip.

Bob Jacobsen inclined toward the latter view: "One bad order: When the Macaw hit the reef he ordered full speed ahead. Then he ordered full astern — Should never have ordered the full ahead, that drove you further into foul ground."[6]

Burton ordered all astern full at about 1615. About that same time Chief Gritton notified the base of the grounding, and flooding was reported in the shaft alley. Estimates vary as to how long the all-astern-full order remained in effect—Windle suggested about a minute, Charles Kumler about five minutes. About the time Burton rescinded it, flooding was reported in the motor and generator rooms as well, and he went below to inspect the damage.

There was plenty of it. The ship's pumps were initially concentrated on the shaft alley drain. The *Macaw*'s drainage system had five pumps, with a combined capacity of 3,900 gallons per minute. According to the ship's *Damage Control Book*, a one-square-foot hole in the hull at a depth of ten feet would admit water at almost three times that rate. The shaft alley might have rested where it was broached, at a depth of little more than ten feet, but given its length and location, it seems likely that the water flooding it was doing so through a hole or holes totaling much more than one square foot in size. As the *Damage Control Book* states with modest candor, "The entire pumping capacity of the drainage system is sufficient to care for only very minor damage, where the leaks are small," and the leak or leaks into the *Macaw*'s shaft alley were clearly not small. It soon became obvious that pumping it was futile. So the shaft alley was closed off as best it could be, and the pumps in it shifted to the motor and generator rooms, and they proved largely useless there too. The water was just coming in too fast. Apparently either one or both of those rooms had been broached directly too, or no one had any more success in closing the ostensibly watertight door between the shaft alley and the motor room than Dan Weber had had. By about 1630 flooding had knocked out the main engines in the generator room. A few minutes later it did the same to the auxiliary motors in the motor room. By that time Burton had called an order back up to the bridge for William Dunn, the gunnery officer, to inspect the entire ship, and Dunn had begun to do so. He had to finish his tour by flashlight. The ship had no power.[7]

As evening fell, the crews of both vessels prepared for a long, nerve-racking night. The *Flier* succeeded in a second try at dropping a bow anchor and pinning itself into the waves, the task that had cost James Cahl his life. For the *Macaw*, having put itself on the reef more conventionally bow first, the objective was to drop an anchor from the stern, and several sailors on the fantail under the direction of Ensign G. F. J. Crocker were trying to do that—they were rigging the ship's main boom, with its lift capacity of forty-five thousand pounds, sufficient to hoist the ship's massive McCann rescue chamber over the side, with an eye toward doing likewise with an anchor—when the power failed.

Until losing the starboard bower about half an hour before, the *Macaw* had had nine anchors: six weighing four tons each, for use in mooring off-shore in submarine rescue operations; two bowers, anchors deployed from the bow, weighing three tons each; and a five-hundred-pound kedge, used in hauling a vessel along by chain. Now it was down to eight. The kedge was too small to have been of use that night, and the remaining bower was at the wrong end of the ship and would probably not have been possible to dump overboard manually in any case, the others even less so. So in lieu of dropping an anchor they quit pumping altogether, let the broached compartments flood, and let the water itself play the role of anchor in weighing the ship down in place for the night.

> On or about 1630 water had risen so high that main engines went out of commission. Hope was then given up for getting off reef on own power. We then decided to let the ship set heavy and stay on reef as water was coming in faster than could be pumped.
>
> We then secured the ship for the night in order to ride through the storm without too much flooding and damage to personnel and equipment.[8]

With the power failure the ship had lost not just its lights but radio contact with the shore as well. Big seas swept into and over it all night. Burton had taken what precautions he could. He had ordered Dunn to see to it on his inspection tour that any watertight doors, ports, and hatches that could be closed were, and the depth charges secured in their racks; and as disconcerting as the ship's predicament must have been for all aboard, Captain Connolly, for one, seems to have been less concerned about the *Macaw* that evening than he had been about the *Flier* that afternoon. "The ship pounded in the surf all night but maintained her heading of about 032 degrees true as she wore a cradle in the reef," he would testify. "Although seas were breaking over the ship, safety of personnel was at no time considered jeopardized as the ship had negative buoyancy from the flooded shaft alley, motor room and generator room."[9]

The safety of the personnel may not have been jeopardized yet, but the life of the ship itself, not to mention the career of its captain, was very much at risk. Some power would be restored to it through the ingenuity of one of the electrician's mates, who succeeded in generating electricity off a diesel-powered welding machine after what Bob Gonnoud described as "a great big argument" in which Lt. (jg) William H. Smith, the communications officer, who had electrical training, maintained that it couldn't be done. There would be coffee and possibly even at least an occasional hot meal served aboard the vessel yet. But life aboard the *Macaw* would never be the same. The ship sat perched on the reef at an angle, bow up and stern down, so all its surfaces—decks, bunks, tables—sloped, and the slope would shift, in direction and degree, as the ship did. After six months on the water, much of it on the open ocean, the crew suddenly found their ship in an odd sort of stasis, almost but not quite motionless, while the sea outside was all relentless raging motion and the ship itself registered what little freedom of motion it retained with the sound of its gashed hull smashing and grinding against the coral. The deep dark belowdecks might have served to amplify the sounds of that first night, not all of which were coming from outside. Seventy years later Bob Gonnoud recalled how peculiar it was to hear the sea surging and receding within the ship itself.[10]

As disconcerting as things had suddenly gotten aboard the *Macaw,* for the crew of the *Flier* they were worse. Their first war patrol had turned into a deadly debacle of exactly the sort that got submarine captains and their executive officers court-martialed and transferred to desk jobs; they had lost one of their own; and given the few avenues of egress a submarine afforded, they faced the prospect, should the boat founder in spite of the anchor they had managed at last to drop, of dying much as Cahl had, by drowning, except that they were more likely to do so trapped inside the sub than while being swept free of it.

Against the threat of having to abandon ship that night, Commander Crowley put the submarine's rubber boat topside "with all available line," the plan apparently being to secure the line to both boat and sub and, if necessary, get the men ashore in boatloads, with men remaining aboard the sub retrieving the boat as many times as necessary by means of the line before leaving the sub in the rubber boat themselves.[11]

Both ships pounded in place that night. According to Crowley, the *Flier*'s pounding grew worse as the night wore on. The *Flier* having ended up snagged backward, its stern was taking the brunt of that pounding. Shortly before midnight Crowley ordered the forward trim tank (or tanks) flooded and the bow buoyancy vents opened, hoping by weighting the bow down to leverage the stern up and spare the propellers and the rudder some of the terrible beating they were taking. Those measures proving ineffective, he considered flooding the main forward ballast tanks, but thought better of it for fear of compromising the submarine's tenuous stability and making matters worse.[12]

As it happened, the *Flier*'s rubber boat stayed aboard that night. Both ships took a beating throughout the night, but there was no need to abandon either of them. Though conditions abated somewhat the next day, Monday, January 17, they remained too rough by Connolly's reckoning to attempt to bring a boat alongside either ship. But the struggle to connect the two by messenger continued by means of the line-throwing gun, and the line it threw continued to fall short. It occurred at some point to Dave Wallington that the problem might be the weight of the line they were using and that they might do better with the tough but significantly lighter thread the *Macaw* had a supply of for use in sewing canvas capstan covers. Eager to see his idea put into practice, Wallington headed off in great haste toward the ammunition room belowdecks, where the thread was stored, en route to which he encountered Lieutenant Smith, who, according to Wallington, mistook the young sailor's excitement for panic, grabbed him, and shook him as if to restore him to his senses. "Smith thought I was going berserk or something," Wallington said, but "I knew what the hell I was doing." He freed himself from Smith's clutches, ran off, and fetched the thread, and on the way to the ammo room and back, he said, with the ship bearing the strain of sitting on its unsought perch, he could hear metal grinding and rivets popping "like popcorn." The thread, he said, did the trick: the messenger detail secured it to a metal needle and succeeded by about 1100 in shooting the needle to the *Flier*. At the expense of putting itself on the reef, the *Macaw* had taken the first step at last toward pulling the *Flier* off it.[13]

By about 1215 that Monday a seven-eighths-inch steel wire had been hauled from the *Macaw* to the *Flier*, threaded through the sub's bullnose, a sort of steel nostril at its bow, and secured to its port forward cleat. By Tuesday morning hauling lines had been run between the ships and a bosun's chair rigged—a bosun's chair being a seat suspended by a sling from an overhead pulley, spar or line, not unlike a child's swing, though the chair in this case was of the breeches buoy sort, made of canvas and shaped like a pair of trousers, into which the occupant would put his legs—and the first of a batch of twenty-three men from the *Flier* manually hauled by means of it to the *Macaw*. About as they were arriving on the *Macaw*, a larger group, including Captain Connolly, was leaving the ship aboard a forty-foot motor launch handled adroitly by a Bosun Sparks. Connolly later praised Sparks's skill as a boatman. If he had any comparably kind words for his host aboard the *Macaw*, or his host for him, they have gone unrecorded.[14]

From the *Macaw* the *Flier* sailors, too, were ferried ashore, where they were reunited with two of their three missing shipmates. George Banchero had reached Clyde Gerber amid the waves on Sunday, and the two of them had managed after a lengthy struggle to drag themselves onto a sandspit bordering Eastern Island, this despite Banchero's having lost the life ring he had figured on giving Gerber. "It was no picnic," Banchero would note of his swim. "I have never been in such water before. I was rolled over by the surf. I was in the water between two and one half and three hours." They had both been taken to the infirmary, Gerber with a broken arm.[15]

Captain Connolly, anxious to float the *Flier* "before she was thrust sideways to the surf and lost" and "before damage from seas and heavy surf would render her useless for further combatant duty," made that task the first priority of the ensuing salvage operation. The *Macaw*, he felt, was comparatively safe in its coral cradle. It would have to wait.[16]

On Tuesday afternoon Cmdr. Lebbeus Curtis, USNR, the fleet salvage officer, flew in from Pearl Harbor to supervise the operation. The product of an old seafaring family from Maine, son of a sea captain and formerly one himself, Curtis had thirty years of experience in marine salvage, most of it in the Pacific, at sites as far-flung as Alaska and Australia, and probably none of it more intense than at Pearl Harbor, where he had arrived on December 6, 1941, en route to the Red Sea, where he was to have been on loan to the Royal Navy to help clear from the Eritrean port of Massawa several ships the Italians had scuttled there. As it happened, he stayed in Pearl Harbor, where the next day his own navy had a sudden great need of his services. By January 1944, between his civilian and naval careers, Curtis had directed the salvage of more than two hundred vessels.[17]

Curtis conferred upon his arrival with Connolly and concurred in a plan to employ the *Gaylord*, a privately owned derrick barge that happened to be on hand, as soon as sea conditions permitted. Two salvage vessels were on their way—the USS *Florikan* (ASR-9), one of the *Macaw*'s four sister ships, from Pearl Harbor, and the USS *Clamp* (ARS-33) (ARS stands for auxiliary—rescue and salvage) from Apamama, an atoll in the Gilbert Islands—but it would take the *Florikan,* the closer of the two, another day or two to arrive, the *Clamp* almost a week, and it was thought the *Gaylord* might be of use as a towing platform in the meantime.

But in the meantime conditions stayed rough and the *Gaylord* stayed put in the lagoon. On Tuesday morning an anchor detail aboard the *Flier* heaved in by ten fathoms the anchor the sub had dropped at such cost two days before, producing what appeared to be distinct forward progress by the submarine and raising hopes for more of the same at the end of a towline on the next high tide. But that progress was quickly wiped out. By Crowley's reckoning, the waves drove the *Flier* fifty feet back onto the reef on each of the next three nights, a total distance almost half the length of the *Flier*'s hull, this despite his flooding the No. 1 main ballast tank after the second of those nights "to prevent further drift astern."[18]

The *Florikan* arrived that Wednesday. On Thursday, James Francis Peder Cahl's body washed ashore. Cahl was twenty-one, from South Holland, Illinois, just south of Chicago, the son of a postal worker. One of the *Flier*'s few married men, he wrote his wife, the former Violet Van Der Heyden, a letter on January 12, four days before he died, and enclosed a money order when he mailed it from Hawaii.[19]

According to Cahl's shipmate James Alls, a pilot returning to Midway on January 20 radioed in as he made his approach and reported what appeared to be a human body in the water surrounded by fish. "Those fish were porpoises," Alls said. "They knew, believe it or not, that this human was not supposed to be in this environment." Alls recalled that a corpsman at the dispensary said the porpoises, having nudged Cahl's body in toward the shore, waited around until they saw that he was being retrieved, or that he had been, and then swam off. Cahl was brought ashore, sewn into a canvas bag along with a five-inch shell for added weight, and buried at sea the next day from the fantail of a PT boat, offshore from his old boat and its stranded neighbor. A marine honor guard of one sort having conveyed Cahl from the sea, another one consigned him the following day back to it. They would have carried Cahl onto the boat on a burial platform, draped under an American flag. Alls was one of several *Flier* men the chaplain brought along for the ceremony. He said the sight of the men in the burial detail sliding Cahl's body into the ocean was one he would never forget.[20]

3

Troubled Waters

Things had not been going well for Paul Burton for some time even before the *Macaw* ran aground. Burton was thirty-two, from Philadelphia by way of Berkeley, California, and Beijing, China, among other places. He had inherited a strong naval pedigree. His father was a career marine officer. His mother's father was a rear admiral. After a year in school in Beijing (then referred to in the West as Peking), where his father was stationed to protect the American legation, and prep school outside Philadelphia, Paul's own naval career had started promisingly enough with an appointment to the Naval Academy, class of 1933. His time there corresponded almost exactly with the first four years of the Depression, and his class felt its impact. In 1932 the cash-strapped Hoover administration cut the navy's enlisted ranks from one hundred thousand to eighty thousand men, significantly reducing the navy's need for Academy graduates. Along with their diplomas and a commencement address by the newly inaugurated Franklin D. Roosevelt, the graduates of 1933 got the news that only half of them, those ranking in the upper half of the class academically, would be commissioned as ensigns and retained on active duty. Those who were would temporarily get 15 percent less pay than their immediate predecessors at that pay grade (a cut that applied to the entire military) and would be on probation their first two years, during which they were prohibited from getting married.

Paul Burton made the cut. He was commissioned June 1, 1933, and assigned to the USS *Saratoga*, one of the navy's first aircraft carriers. In December 1934 he requested submarine duty, and in 1935, his probationary two years having expired, he married his high school sweetheart, Elizabeth Porter Watson of Asbury Park, New Jersey. By January 1941 he had attended submarine school, completed a Naval War College correspondence course in international law, served aboard two subs, received a commission as a lieutenant junior grade, and been deemed qualified for command of submarines by the Bureau of Navigation.

In February 1941 he began a four-month course at deep-sea diving school in Washington, DC. That April, he became a father with the birth of a daughter, Barbara. In July he began supervising instruction at the submarine escape training tank in New London, Connecticut, where he had been a trainee himself several years before.

In July 1942 Burton was assigned to the USS *Tarpon* (SS-175), a *Shark*-class submarine undergoing an overhaul at Mare Island on San Francisco Bay. The *Tarpon* by then had acquired a reputation as a bad-luck boat—it had gone on four war patrols and sunk nothing. But for its fifth patrol (October 22–December 10, 1942) it would have a new skipper, Lt. Cmdr. Thomas Lincoln Wogan, USN, and a new executive officer, or second in command, in Burton. For a few fleeting moments on November 7, the *Tarpon*'s luck seemed to have changed too. Assigned to patrol north of Bougainville in the Solomon Islands, the *Tarpon* happened that morning upon a ten-ship Japanese convoy. But a Japanese destroyer apparently sighted the *Tarpon*'s periscope about as soon as the *Tarpon* spotted the Japanese. Forced to dive amid the ensuing barrage of depth charges, the sub fired just two torpedoes during the encounter and hit nothing. In fact the only thing it did hit on that patrol was the reef at Midway, where, much as the *Flier* would do thirteen months later, and in about the same spot, it ran aground attempting to enter the channel on the way back to Pearl Harbor. It was able to back itself clear and suffered little damage, but that grounding made for an ignominious end to yet another fruitless patrol.

The review by the high command at Pearl Harbor was scathing: *Tarpon*'s fifth patrol was termed "most disappointing." The attack on the convoy "was not pressed home." Wogan, wrote Admiral Bob English, "failed to take advantage of a golden opportunity."[1]

But another admiral, Charles A. Lockwood Jr., had overall command of submarines in the Pacific, and he decided to give Wogan another chance. The sixth patrol (January 10–February 25, 1943) went much better. During it, the *Tarpon* sank two Japanese ships, a freighter and a seventeen-thousand-ton troop transport. By tonnage, among US subs, the *Tarpon*'s sixth patrol was the second-most productive of the war to that point. For Tom Wogan it was a great success. For Paul Burton it was prelude to a disaster.

Admiral Lockwood is said to have told Wogan after that patrol, "Captain, you can have anything you want." Wogan requested shore leave back in the

States for as many of his men as possible, and the request was granted. About two weeks later he wrote Lockwood with another request—that Paul Burton be barred, not just from commanding a submarine, but from submarine duty altogether.[2]

That request was granted too. Wogan was awarded the Navy Cross for "extraordinary heroism" during the sixth patrol. Burton's reward was to be "blackballed." He was officially detached from the *Tarpon* at Pearl Harbor on March 16, 1943, and as if by way of more thoroughly expunging him, someone crossed out the submarine's log entry detailing his departure.

What soured Wogan on Burton is not entirely clear. In his statement to Lockwood, Wogan charged Burton with "lack of judgment, indecision, inaccuracy, and an unfortunate personal manner which does not inspire confidence in either his superior officers or his subordinates." Wogan faulted Burton in his handling of the enlisted men and "impressionable junior officers," writing "he is wont to condone mistakes and improper performance of duty during the most important operations." He didn't say what mistakes or improper performance Burton condoned, or during what operations he condoned them. He didn't say when, how, or in regard to what Burton displayed bad judgment, indecision, or inaccuracy or just what it was about his personal manner that failed to inspire confidence. He purported to get specific on the subject of navigation, but in fact his allegation in that regard—"Specifically he has failed to navigate this vessel while on war patrol in such a manner as to contribute to the success of the mission"—is conspicuously vague.[3]

Navigational incompetence may have been at the core of Wogan's antipathy to Burton, or it may have been a convenient cover for other grievances. Years later Bud Loughman attributed the falling out between the two to Burton's guiding the *Tarpon* hundreds of miles off course on the way back to Midway at the end of a war patrol. Loughman said Burton told him that on one of his *Tarpon* patrols he had been unable to take sun or star readings the whole trip. Judging from Burton's response to Wogan's damning recommendation letter (which consists of five numbered paragraphs), the war patrol in question was clearly the *Tarpon*'s sixth.[4]

Paragraph 4, pertaining to failure to navigate successfully, astounded me. Two facts I know: (1) that I always did my utmost to navigate according to the planned operations, and (2) that no one on board could have done better. My navigation was not always accurate.

There were times, especially on station during my second patrol (the ship's sixth), when it was poor. . . . If, as was often the case during this period, there are green seas breaking over the bridge, an almost complete overcast and a false horizon due to haze and [the] "mirage effect" of [a] temperature difference of air and water, accurate celestial navigation is impossible.[5]

As much as he might have liked to, Wogan in his letter does not lay to Burton's charge the *Tarpon's* running aground at Midway on its fifth patrol. Burton probably had little or nothing to do with that mishap. In keeping with standard procedure at Midway, a harbor pilot had boarded the boat outside the channel entrance. The pilot was supervising the steering of the boat when the *Tarpon* hit the reef.

According to Bud Loughman, when he would indicate the *Macaw's* position to Burton by pointing to a spot on a map, Burton would likewise point to the spot and tell him, "Bud, don't tell me we're here"—then, putting his open palm to the map and blotting out hundreds or thousands of square miles of ocean—"tell me we're here." Loughman took this as a wry allusion to Burton's own troubled navigational past, but in that construction Loughman himself may have been off the mark. Burton had a sense of humor and may not have been averse to poking fun at himself, but unbeknownst to Loughman, he held his own navigational skills in much higher regard than he did those of his XO (executive officer). So it isn't clear who was the intended butt of the joke—it could have been one or the other of them or both.

If Burton was self-disparaging about his competence as a navigator, at least some of his crew on the *Macaw* would have agreed with him. After the *Macaw* ran into a minelayer at Funafuti in the South Pacific, some of the enlisted men on the ship took to calling him "Crash." "Real nice guy," Robert Gonnoud recalled. "He just didn't seem to have that mathematical ability." Whenever Burton used a sextant, Gonnoud said, he had a "backup man" in the person of Quartermaster 1/c Warden Wingrove of East Bethlehem, Pennsylvania. Wingrove handled much of the navigational work for Burton, Gonnoud said, for the simple reason that he was better at it.[6]

Aside from the issue of navigation, Wogan's complaints about Burton were largely personal in character, and it may have been primarily a personality conflict that inspired them. The two had much in common. Both were Naval Academy graduates (Wogan was class of 1930—they overlapped by one year), both from Philadelphia, both married, both fathers. Both of their fathers had been career military officers, Wogan's in the navy, Burton's in the marines, and both of *their* fathers—Wogan's and Burton's paternal grandfathers—had immigrated from the British Isles, Burton's grandfather from England, Wogan's from Ireland. That may have been part of the problem. Possibly the ancient animosity between the Irish and the English worked to poison the relations between the two men, though the only indication that either of them had any strong feelings in that general connection involves Paul Burton, and the ethnic group he was said to harbor ill will toward was his own, the English.[7]

More plausibly social class may have contributed to their friction. Burton's bloodline, nautical and otherwise, had a strain of blue in it. As noted above, his maternal grandfather, Albert Bower Willits, was a rear admiral. *His* father, Alphonso Albert Willits (1821–1913), was a prominent minister, author, lecturer, and real estate developer, and honorary president of the Lyceum Association, an educational speakers' bureau, active nationwide, founded by Daniel Webster in 1831. The blue on Wogan's side was in the collar. His father appears to have been an orphan. When Albert Willits enrolled at the Naval Academy in 1870, Wogan's father, Michael Wogan, age eleven, was living in a sailors' boardinghouse in New York City, the sole Wogan in residence there, perhaps as a ward of the proprietor. About a year after Willits graduated from Annapolis and received his commission, Michael Wogan, age sixteen, enlisted in New York as a second-class boy (a rating the navy has since dropped) and went to sea on the USS *Minnesota*, a wooden steam frigate that had seen extensive service enforcing the blockade of the Confederacy during the Civil War.[8]

By the time his only son was born in 1909, Michael Wogan had climbed well up in the ranks. He would retire as an officer three years later. The family Thomas Wogan grew up in was not poor, nor was Paul Burton's wealthy, but Wogan's father had clawed his way up from poverty, while Burton's mother's side of his family had a prominent streak of Main Line Philadelphia aristocracy, and Burton himself, an experienced world traveler by age fifteen, went to a prep school and spent at least part of his childhood in a household with a live-in maid.

Or the conflict between the two men may have been one of personality plain and simple. Either of the personalities involved may have been in conflict with itself. Burton, by more than one account, was an odd person. Wogan pretty clearly had his own demons. Probably it was a combination of factors.

Whatever they were, the stress and cramped quarters aboard a submarine on war patrol would have done little to mitigate them. Shipmates at odds on a big surface vessel might have contrived to avoid each other. The commander of a submarine and his executive officer would have had extremely limited scope that way.

A "revocation of qualification" to serve in submarines could itself be revoked, and Paul Burton earnestly hoped his would be, but that prospect was a long shot at best. Wogan's experience after the *Tarpon's* fifth patrol notwithstanding, naval officers did not by and large get lots of second chances during the war. The navy, by its own lights, could not afford to be forgiving of failure. When the war began, after two-plus decades of peace, its officers were largely untested by combat, and inevitably some of them were unsuited for it. The war tended to expose incompetence. In peacetime that might be shrugged off, concealed, or overlooked. In war the consequences were harder to ignore. Ships sank. Men died. The stakes were too high and the contest, against two formidable foes in Germany and Japan, too uncertain for lenience. Officers deemed unequal to their jobs—justly or not—were promptly cashiered. There was little due process and little recourse. When a ship suffered an avoidable calamity such as running aground, there was an inquest, but personnel matters involving individual officers tended to proceed along more summary lines. Wogan's declaration recommending that Burton's submarine privileges be revoked is stamped March 10, 1943. One day later, according to a memo in Burton's personnel file, the matter had been "personally investigated" by the administrative commander of Submarine Division 42. Within a week, Burton was reassigned.

It was standard practice during the war to consign blackballed submarine officers to submarine rescue vessels—Bob Gonnoud said of another ASR, there were so many washed-out submarine officers aboard, "it almost tipped over"—and so it went with Paul Burton.[9]

Submarines have long had a special cachet in the navy. They're the stealthy predators, the wolves of the sea. A submarine rescue vessel is a lot less glamorous—a sort of beast of burden, like an aquatic ox, or at best a sort of oceangoing Saint Bernard. It's an auxiliary vessel, part of the supporting cast. As former Motor Machinist's Mate Quinton Studer said of the *Macaw,* "It was a tugboat, a glorified tugboat." Despite the theoretical step up the ladder, from second in command of one vessel to command of another, Burton's new assignment was in fact a humiliating demotion. He had been banished.[10]

At the end of his statement in response to his revocation, Burton wrote: "After all is said and done I feel toward my submarine duty as the little lad must feel whose ice cream cone slips into the filth of the street on a hot summer day. Nothing was more cherished, and yet spoiled with such finality."[11]

If the ship Paul Burton had been relegated to was unglamorous, it was at least modern. The very concept of a submarine rescue vessel was new. The US Navy had had no ships designated as such as recently as fifteen years before. The first six assigned that title were all converted minesweepers. Minesweepers were in heavy demand after World War I, in the last five months of which the US and Royal navies had laid more than seventy thousand mines in the North Sea alone. But by 1921 the job of clearing those mines had been accomplished about as thoroughly as it ever would be, and the US Navy found itself with more minesweepers than it needed.

What it still needed was a way to reduce the hazards of submarining. That form of navigation had always been dangerous, a fact demonstrated by no single vessel more often than by the *H. L. Hunley*, a Confederate submersible that sank three times (it was retrieved twice) with a combined loss of twenty-one lives, including that of its namesake inventor, Horace Lawson Hunley—but not without becoming, in its third tour of duty, the first craft of its kind to sink an enemy vessel. On February 17, 1864, it planted a bomb in the hull of the USS *Housatonic*, a screw sloop on blockade duty outside Charleston, South Carolina. Five men aboard the *Housatonic* died. So too, within about forty-five minutes, for the second time, did the entire eight-man crew of the *Hunley*.

Submarines grew much more sophisticated over the ensuing fifty years, and still more so during World War I, but even in peacetime, after leaps and bounds of technological progress, submarine duty remained dangerous. In the 1920s the US Navy lost three submarines—the *S-5*, *S-51*, and *S-4*, in that order, all off the northeastern coast—with a combined loss of seventy-three lives. By the time a Coast Guard destroyer chasing rumrunners accidentally rammed *S-4* off Cape Cod in December 1927, dooming its entire forty-man crew, the navy had already begun refitting some of its superfluous minesweepers for submarine rescue and salvage work. After that disaster the refitting process was formalized. On September 12, 1929, five *Lapwing*-class minesweepers were officially reclassified ASR, for "auxiliary, submarine rescue." A sixth was added to the roster in 1936.

In 1939 disaster struck again. On May 23 of that year the USS *Squalus* sank in 243 feet of water off Portsmouth, New Hampshire, after its main induction valve failed. The after torpedo room, both engine rooms, and the crew's quarters flooded, and twenty-six men quickly drowned. But thirty-three others, who had taken refuge in the control and forward torpedo rooms, were brought safely back to the surface in the navy's new McCann rescue chamber, a diving bell designed to fit snugly onto the coaming of either the forward or aft escape hatch of a submarine. The chamber used in the *Squalus* rescue was supplied by the USS *Falcon* (ASR-2), one of the converted mine-sweepers that had participated in the North Sea sweep in 1919, under the command twenty years later of Lt. George A. Sharp, USN, at age thirty-three the youngest CO (commanding officer) in the navy. With its capacity of eight men (nine in a pinch) in addition to two operators, the chamber brought the *Squalus* survivors up from the forward hatch in four dives over a period of thirteen hours. A fifth descent was made in the hope, unrealized, of finding someone alive at the other end of the boat.[12]

The rescue chamber and a specialized vessel from which to deploy it having proven their worth, the federal government announced a contract seventeen months later with the Moore Dry Dock Company of Oakland, California, for five ASRs and two sub tenders. The ASRs were each to be equipped with a McCann chamber and, to lift it, a crane capable of hoisting forty-five thousand pounds. Like their six converted minesweeper counterparts, all would be named for birds. The keel of the *Macaw* was laid down in October 1941. The ship slid from its construction berth at Moore Dry Dock into the Oakland Estuary in quick succession with its sister ship *Greenlet* on July 12, 1942, and was commissioned exactly one year later.

The commissioning party for the *Macaw* took place in the Spanish Ballroom of the Alameda Hotel in Alameda, just across the narrow estuary from Oakland, one evening within a week or so of the commissioning itself. The captain and executive officer gave speeches. The celebrants helped themselves at the buffet table, got drinks at the bar, and danced. Seaman 2/c Edward James Wade, of Jersey City, New Jersey, perhaps acting on a dare, cut in on Bud Loughman, the executive officer, as he was dancing with his wife, Patricia. It was strictly taboo for an enlisted man to cut in on an officer on the dance floor, but Wade was not one to take that sort of thing too seriously, nor was Loughman, who yielded his place graciously and enjoyed recounting the episode years later. His wife was eight and a half months pregnant with the couple's first child at the time. Wade promptly sought to allay any fears she might have had on that account in the arms of an impetuous stranger. "Don't worry," he told her. "I won't bump your belly."[13]

Bob Jacobsen got to the party about four hours late. His seventeen-year-old girlfriend's parents wouldn't let her go to it, so he had spent the earlier part of the evening with her before heading off to the party alone. Wade's bold violation of naval protocol no doubt generated some commentary, but by the time Jacobsen arrived and served himself a ham sandwich and sides of potato and macaroni salad, most of the talk at the table he proceeded to sit at concerned Coxswain Augie Paul Koepke, who had had too much to drink, and whose date, a telephone switchboard operator, had stalked off with some angry parting words—"You drunken son of a bitch I never want to see you again," by one account—after the two of them stumbled against the rim of the circular goldfish pond in the middle of the entrance hall while attempting to dance and almost fell in. On a subsequent visit to the men's room, Jacobsen said, he found Koepke passed out on the tile floor and had to step over him to get to the urinal.[14]

Koepke acquitted himself more honorably four days after the commissioning ceremony when the manila topping lift (in layman's language, a rope) supporting the *Macaw*'s port boat boom (a sideways-projecting spar from which a small boat was suspended) parted during a test at Moore Dry Dock. The test involved using the boom to hoist a large block of concrete. A civilian rigger, Alameda resident Vincent Leonis, twenty-three, the son of immigrants from Spain, was reportedly standing on the concrete block when the topping lift failed, dropping Leonis and his perch into the estuary—Leonis, by one account, entangled in the topping line and minus an arm. Koepke, aided by Radioman 3/c Leo Kelly, leapt in after him and pulled him to safety. Whether Leonis actually lost an arm is unclear, but he seems at the very least to have been bleeding profusely enough for Koepke to apply a tourniquet. Paul Burton that same day commended Koepke on his "prompt and fearless action" in rescuing Leonis, and Kelly for helping him.[15]

Koepke lacked social graces when he had had too much to drink—which, for him, may have been anything at all—but sober, he was a good man to have around in a pinch. He had been in more than one. Koepke had survived two ship sinkings within a span of two weeks the previous fall, and he would survive a third. He was on the transport USS *George F. Elliott* (AP-13) off Guadalcanal on August 8, 1942, when a Mitsubishi G4M "Betty" bomber, in an incident that foreshadowed the desperate kamikaze strategy Japan would employ on a grand scale two and a half years later, crashed into it and set it ablaze. The ship was abandoned and scuttled within about two hours.

Thirteen days later, Koepke was one of twenty-nine men aboard the transport *Lakatoi* en route from New Caledonia to Efate in the New Hebrides when the ship foundered in heavy seas. Once again came the order to abandon ship. The sea having just swept off one of the *Lakatoi*'s two lifeboats, the men (apparently all *George F. Elliott* survivors) climbed into the other and a pair of rubber rafts, and within minutes the *Lakatoi* went down.

By the time they washed ashore twelve days later on the other side of the same island they had set out from, the rafts were abraded, the lifeboat was leaking badly, they had gone through their hard tack, chocolate, and canned tomatoes and were down to two cans of peaches in syrup; and one man, Radioman 3/c Hugh A. Middaugh of Peoria, Illinois, had died, apparently as a result of drinking seawater (something Koepke would caution his daughters against years later). They buried him at sea, an unpleasant task made more so by their assumption that he would become food for the sharks that had been following them.

Koepke could still walk when they got to land—not everyone could at that point—so he set off barefoot in search of sustenance and was soon feeding his crewmates small quantities of coconut milk. Two of his shipmates, likewise seeking food, encountered a Frenchman (New Caledonia was then and remains a French possession), a Monsieur DuBois, who supplied the Americans with water and boots and arranged for his son to escort one of them by pony to a patrol station thirty miles up the coast. US Army soldiers met them en route, and by 1700 that day the *Lakatoi* survivors were receiving care from personnel of the army's 2d Field Hospital.[16]

A month and a half later, Koepke was back in San Diego, and by the following summer he'd been assigned to the *Macaw*. That assignment may have been at least in part his own doing. Motor Machinist's Mate Howard Rechel was on Terminal Island in Los Angeles Harbor circa April or May 1943 when he was assigned to the *Macaw*, and when he saw Koepke in Oakland he recognized him as the guy who had assigned him. Submarine rescue vessels were not designed to be front-line combat ships. Rechel surmised that Koepke, having had enough of combat and sinking ships for the time being, had arranged to have himself assigned to the *Macaw* in the hope of toiling at least temporarily in comparatively untroubled waters. If he did, he was to be disappointed.[17]

For more than one reason, Koepke was never entirely out of danger. In his susceptibility to alcohol he posed a danger to himself. And whether he sought to avoid danger or not, when it appeared, he seems to have rushed to embrace it.

As a bosun's mate on the *Macaw*, Koepke occupied a position on the ship roughly analogous to that of a floor boss in a factory, overseeing, along with Bosun's Mate Ralph Mennemeyer, much of the nuts-and-bolts, day-to-day work of the second deck division, a group of sailors assigned topside care and maintenance on the after half of the ship. Koepke, as Rechel remarked, was "Old Navy." Having enlisted in 1936, he was by general acclamation one of the more knowledgeable sailors aboard the ship, and one of the best liked. "Augie Paul Koepke was a favorite of everyone," Bob Jacobsen wrote. Former Seaman Eugene Van Buskirk recalled Koepke as "an amazing fellow" and a good storyteller: "He was the guy. . . . Seemed like everybody loved him. He loved people." Radar operator Bob Gonnoud echoed Howard Rechel in recalling Koepke as an "Old Navy" man, full of bull and stories, who "talked to anybody all the time." Dave Wallington recalled him as very vocal, a good guy, "just a typical roustabout type guy." For someone that expressive, Wallington said, "you almost have to have the capacity of leadership," and Koepke did. His one problem, Jacobsen wrote, was that he couldn't hold his liquor. It was a problem that would leave him prostrate and helpless in full view of his shipmates more than once during his time aboard the *Macaw*. He emerges in photos, interviews, and written reminiscences as an intriguing compound of affability, courage, expert seamanship, and hapless susceptibility to alcohol, at once a leader and a laughingstock, a lifesaver and a drunk. Trouble seems to have had a way of finding him, or he did of finding it, and when the trouble that destroyed the *Macaw* engulfed the ship and dragged it down, Koepke typically would find himself in the middle of it.[18]

4

Off to War

After a shakedown cruise to Monterey and back, the *Macaw* was assigned to Task Group 116.11, whose task it would be to convey eight of the ten sections of ABSD-1, an enormous prefabricated floating dry dock, and most of its crew from San Francisco Bay to Espiritu Santo in the New Hebrides, 1,300 miles northeast of Brisbane, Australia. By late summer 1943 the main theater of combat had shifted from the Central to the Southwest Pacific, and damaged ships were having to make round trips of thousands of miles—some merely to Pearl Harbor, others all the way to Bremerton, Washington, or Mare Island—for repairs. Having repair facilities closer to the action would save the US Navy vast quantities of time and fuel.

The navy had anticipated this problem and taken steps, even before Pearl Harbor, to address it. Navy planners had foreseen the possibility of war with Japan for decades. Deploying floating repair facilities to the Southwest Pacific had figured in their plans since World War I but had languished in the conceptual stage amid meager interwar military budgets. By 1938, as war clouds loomed, Congress had begun opening the spigots on military spending, and among the programs greenlighted for production was the Advanced Base Sectional Dock, or ABSD.

A wartime ABSD consisted of either seven or ten prefabricated sections. A dry dock is a berth that can be flooded to allow a ship to enter it, then pumped dry or drained to facilitate repairs. Dry docks go back at least as far as the Song Dynasty in eleventh-century China, and the concept of a floating dry dock at least as far back as sixteenth-century Venice. By 1925 the navy had developed plans for a single-unit, self-propelled, closed-bow floating dry dock with a lifting capacity of 3,500 tons—enough to accommodate a destroyer but nothing much bigger than that. In 1938 Vice Admiral Ben Moreell, chief of the Bureau of Yards and Docks, approved the concept of the sectional ABSD. Building a floating dry dock in sections that could be moved independently to the point of assembly offered numerous advantages: the individual sections were small enough that almost any shipyard could build one; any one section could negotiate the Panama Canal or be replaced easily enough if lost; and ABSDs could be lengthened or shortened as needed by the simple expedient of adding sections or removing them.

Seven "large auxiliary floating dry docks," two of ten sections each and five of seven, were constructed for the navy during the war to service its biggest ships. Prior to assembly, each section amounted to a ship in itself (or would have, but for lack of a drive train), 256 feet long and about 93 feet abeam, displacing 15,400 tons, with a crew of fifty to seventy and an independent diesel-driven power plant but no self-propulsion—to move, a section had to be pushed or towed.

Designated an ABS, a section consisted basically of a steel pontoon hull bearing two hinged "wing walls"—four-hundred-ton steel boxes 80 feet long, 55 high, and 20 wide that housed everything from officers' quarters to dental offices and cobblers' shops. Running across the deck of a section, one fore and one aft, the wing walls folded down onto it to reduce wind resistance and lower the vessel's center of gravity in transit and stood upright when deployed to form the side walls of the assembled dry dock. With the sections joined side by side as if to form a pontoon bridge, the connected upright wing walls enclosed a repair bay 135 feet wide, wide enough to accommodate a battleship or an aircraft carrier.

With its wing wall sides and open ends, an assembled ABSD looks a lot like an enormous floating miter box. To receive a vessel for repair, it partly submerges itself by flooding ballast compartments in its pontoons, allowing the ship to pull between the still visible upper reaches of the wing walls, then it pumps itself dry enough to elevate most of itself and all of its cargo above the waterline. The lifting capacity of a ten-section ABSD in the war was about ninety thousand tons.

Fully assembled, ABSD-1 and its twin, ABSD-2, the two ten-section behemoths, would each be 927 feet long and 256 wide, about three football fields by most of one, and displace 154,000 tons. They would be among the biggest man-made floating objects ever devised. They would also be recognizable. Piecemeal, they were considerably less so. The prefabricated sections fit the profile of no familiar category of watercraft. Mystified American aviators who spotted the sections in convoy reported them variously as aircraft carriers, aircraft carriers in tow, and, "Don't know what the hell they are!"[1]

Eight of ABSD-1's ten sections were built on the West Coast, at yards in Washington and California, the remaining two by the Chicago Bridge & Iron Co. in Morgan City, Louisiana. The two Morgan City sections headed out to sea first, on July 14, 1943, and proceeded through the Panama Canal on a voyage of just over ten weeks. During the first six weeks of it, their eight West Coast counterparts congregated off the Tiburon Peninsula in San Francisco Bay with the towing vessels and escorts assigned with them to Task Group 116.11.

That task group was to form a convoy, designated PW 2294, and each dry dock section in it was to be towed by a Liberty ship. Liberty ships were the maritime workhorses of World War II. They were cookie-cutter cargo ships, constructed, like their tows on this trip, in prefabricated sections, welded together and designed to be cheap, serviceable, and quick to build. They were typically constructed under contract with the US Maritime Commission, an agency Congress had created in 1936 to build up and modernize the nation's meager and aging merchant fleet.

The original plan called for five hundred new cargo ships, fifty a year for ten years. That was an ambitious goal at the time, but after war broke out in Europe, production quotas shot up. After Pearl Harbor, they soared. The ensuing frenzy of shipbuilding in the United States had no precedent. The greatest industrial power in history suddenly began building ships as if its survival and that of democracy depended on them, as in fact they did. Shipyards sprang up on mudflats almost overnight. Plants operated around the clock. Workers—including large numbers of women and minorities—poured into those plants and the towns surrounding them. The population of Richmond, on the east shore of San Francisco Bay, home to four wartime shipyards, almost quadrupled from 1940 to 1943. Ten years before the war the workforce at Moore Dry Dock, the Oakland firm that built the *Macaw*, numbered about eight hundred; local press estimates of its wartime peak range up to thirty-nine thousand. US yards had built a grand total of two oceangoing dry cargo ships (as opposed to tankers) from 1922 to 1937. During the war, US production averaged more than two Liberty or Victory ships (somewhat bigger and faster versions of the same thing) every day. The Maritime Commission oversaw the production of 1,896 cargo vessels in 1943 alone.[2]

Early in the war, Allied shipping losses far exceeded production. In 1942 the Allies lost on average more than thirty ships a week (a toll vastly understated in American newspapers for fear of the grim reality's undermining morale), mostly to German submarines, and US shipyards managed to replace fewer than half of them. In 1943, as the Allies got better at antisubmarine warfare and US shipyards went into overdrive, Allied ship losses fell by more than half and US production more than doubled. That year US shipyards turned out more than three merchant vessels for every such Allied ship lost. In 1944 that ratio was more than eight to one.[3]

Overall, from 1941 to 1945, eighteen US shipyards produced 2,710 Liberty ships and another 530 or so Victory ships. No one built more Liberty ships than Oakland-based industrialist Henry J. Kaiser. Son of a German immigrant shoemaker and his wife from tiny Sprout Brook, New York, Kaiser had built or helped build lots of things, including the Hoover, Bonneville, and Grand Coulee Dams and a two-hundred-mile stretch of highway in Cuba, but never a ship as of the time he opened his first yard in Richmond in 1941. By war's end the four Kaiser yards in Richmond had produced 747 Liberty and Victory ships (including four of the eight Liberty ships in Convoy PW 2294), almost a quarter of the total nationwide, at a cost well below the national average, and pioneered the adaptation from the automobile industry of assembly-line techniques that helped drive down the overall average construction time for Liberty ships from about 230 days to 42.[4]

Liberty ships were prone to developing hull fractures, especially those built early in the war, before the problem was diagnosed—three broke in half without warning. But the greater danger to their crews came from operating in combat theaters. The merchant marine being more a concept than an organization, no one kept careful track of its casualties during the war, but by one count, one US merchant mariner in twenty-six who served during the war died in it—more than nine thousand in all. Their fatality rate may have slightly exceeded that of the marines, at 3.7 percent the highest among the uniformed services.[5]

Convoy PW 2294 was supposed to sail on Friday, August 27, but in typical San Francisco summertime fashion, a heavy fog set in at about 0630 that day. So it was not until 0705 on August 28 that the order went out by signal flag to "Proceed with sailing plans." There ensued a sort of lumbering, slow-motion parade headed up initially by a pair of *Auk*-class minesweepers, sister ships USS *Token* (AM-126) and USS *Tumult* (AM-127), whose comparatively sleek lines might have served to make their companions look that much homelier by comparison. There were twenty-five other vessels in the convoy—eight Liberty ships, eight dry dock sections, five barges, two yard tugs, a fleet tug, and the *Macaw*, which was close kin to a tugboat and functioned that day as one—and all of them looked homely enough. Liberty ships were modeled after a British design dating back to 1879. Franklin D. Roosevelt called them ugly ducklings. The *Macaw* and the three tugs were less than rakish, the dry dock sections were big blocky things that had to be towed, and the barges must have borne at least a vague resemblance to garbage scows. These were not the sort of vessels you would see in a recruiting poster. But the procession—its Liberty ships each stretching almost 150 yards, and their tows, about 85 yards long and 31 wide, displacing more than fifteen thousand tons each—might have compensated somewhat in sheer magnitude for what its components lacked in glamour.[6]

The *Token* got under way at 0706, the *Tumult* following twelve minutes later. One by one the Liberty ships weighed anchor, fell in line, and proceeded in single file, dry dock sections in tow, around Angel Island, past Alcatraz, and under the Golden Gate Bridge. The *Macaw*, with two barges temporarily in tow, passed under the bridge at about 1530. The *Navajo*-class fleet tug USS *Lipan* (AT-85) and its three tows brought up the rear. By the time those four vessels passed Alcatraz later that afternoon, they formed the tail of a column that stretched more than thirty miles under the bridge and out to sea.[7]

The sight of this plodding procession may or may not have been stirring to an onlooker, but to Bob Jacobsen at least, the view from it, and his participation in it, were stirring indeed.

> The convoy was gathered together off of Angels Island on San Francisco Bay. After 3 days we sailed down the Bay headed for the Pacific. . . . We were in single file—a long line of ships and tows. I was on the "fan tail" and I was looking at the hills of "Frisco" wondering if I would see them again. I was thinking this may be the great adventure of your life. Wondered how long before I would get back to the states? (was 24 months) We were heading off to war—we heard all the time of ships being bombed, torpedoed, strafed and hit with gun fire. Just heard of a Navy transport, the USS President Coolidge that was sunk by a mine off of the New Hebrides.
>
> Rumors were wild: Were going to Pearl Harbor—to Samoa, to the Fijis, to Guadal Canal, to Nemea, to Australia. Rumor we will stay on

convoy duty—we'll get this convoy to wherever and be back in the states for another convoy.

You looked at your shipmates and wondered if you would all make it back or not.[8]

A little more than two weeks later, as the convoy neared the equator about 750 miles south-southeast of the Big Island of Hawaii, the odds of making it back, or of making it more than a few moments into the future, looked bleak. At 1820 on September 13, the *Tumult*, one of the two mine-sweepers doing picket duty on the flanks, reported an unidentified ship at a distance of eighteen miles. By 1912 the stranger had closed to fifteen miles. Attempts to raise the ship by radio meeting with no response, the *Macaw* loaded its main battery, two three-inch guns, and went off to have a closer look. Just before midnight a large vessel emerged from the gloom six and a half miles away. According to Jacobsen, Paul Burton took the stranger for a Japanese cruiser, which would have vastly outgunned a submarine rescue vessel. Howard Rechel happened to come up on deck about then. "I saw this monster," he said, "guns sticking out everywhere." He thought perhaps it was a troop carrier. Burton, he said, was prepared to take it on, but that proved to be unnecessary, for when they got to within about a mile of the mystery ship and shined a searchlight on it, they found it to be a large merchant vessel fly-ing the Stars and Stripes.

The sight of that flag gracing the ghostly leviathan in the dead of night came as a great relief to Bob Jacobsen inasmuch as it meant that he and his shipmates would not all be promptly blown to bits. "God it was good to see that big American flag," he wrote. The merchant vessel was another Liberty ship, the SS *Philip Kearny*. The *Macaw* escorted it for about three hours, saw it off, and reclaimed the lead spot in the convoy. The whole diversion took about six hours.[9]

For some of the less experienced sailors on the *Macaw*, especially early in the voyage, a more immediate enemy than the Japanese was seasickness. For some of the men this was a fleeting, one-time condition. Seaman Jack Vangets of Elwood, Indiana, had it just once, during a training run on San Francisco Bay. His friend Dave Wallington likewise suffered it just once, on the shake-down cruise to Monterey. It struck him in the same place and about the same time as it did Edward Wade, the brash young sailor who had cut in on Bud Loughman and his wife at the commissioning party. Wade and Wallington were on the flying bridge together, and Wade was vomiting into a bucket when "Gunner" Dunn, the gunnery officer, walked by and told the comparatively hale and hearty–looking Wallington, "Well, Wallington, I see you got yourself sea legs." Moments later Wallington was vomiting too.[10]

For other men seasickness was a more persistent problem. Ship's Fitter Nord Lester of San Diego got sick at the outset of the voyage and stayed sick. Despite his condition, he still had to stand his watches. Finally, he recalled fifty-six years later, after weeks of torment he decided, "To hell with it, I'm not gonna do it," and told the chief warrant officer, "You can keep your damn war. I'm not gonna fight it."

News of his rebellion spread up the chain of command. Bud Loughman visited the invalid, Lester recalled, and told him, "Nord, you're gonna hafta stand your watch or I'll have to write a report on you." Lester, by his own account, replied, "Put me on report. Shoot me." Loughman spoke to Paul Burton, who called on Lester in turn and told him to go to the officers' mess and get something to eat. Steward's Mate Robert Vaughn of Winston-Salem, North Carolina, was on duty at the time, Lester recalled, and served him "a big hunk of mutton, dripping with grease." If that does not sound like a dish to whet the appetite of a nausea victim, the grease did not bother him. He ate the mutton, grease and all, Lester said, and felt better. He and Burton were "great friends" after that.[11]

Newer sailors were prone to more than one sort of seasickness. "Body not used to steady 24 hour a day pitch & roll," Bob Jacobsen wrote. "Seems that new hands who hadn't been to sea suffered real severe constipation. [Pharmacist's Mate 1/c William Roscoe] Funk gave some a black pill called the black bomb that 'blew' them open. Others a shot glass of a black liquid that kept them on the 'throne' all night."[12]

Seasickness aside, the health of the men on the *Macaw* was generally good. "'Doc' had it made," Jacobsen wrote of Funk. "When we left the states, 10 days later all colds and sniffles had cleared up. Out on the ocean the air was pure. No germs, no way to get any contact with germs."[13]

But if the men were healthy, they were not as a rule comfortable. The convoy's path to Espiritu Santo lay largely within the tropics. The air temperature for much of the trip was in the 80s—not blistering, but the air was humid and the steel ship compounded the heat by absorbing and radiating it. In the engine room, where typically two or three and occasionally all four of the ship's four-cycle, six-cylinder, 950-horsepower American Locomotive Company diesel engines were at work, the men got heat rash. They'd go on deck and cool off when they were off duty, former Fireman Donald Srack of Maywood, California, recalled, then they'd go back down and break right out in a rash again. There was nothing they could do about it.[14]

The heat affected the vital issue of hygiene. So did the limited capacity of the ship's distillation system. "A week after we left 'Frisco' it was found that our water distillery could not supply enough fresh water for our big crew," Jacobsen wrote. "So the fresh water was shut off to the showers — a salt water shower was rigged on the fan tail. RHIP — Rank has its priveledges: I don't believe the officers and chief[s'] fresh water showers were cut off."[15]

The other officers may have gone on enjoying their freshwater showers, but according to Srack, Paul Burton, at least, "took salt water showers like the rest of us." Srack worked in the engine room, where his primary task was tending to the evaporators, which produced 35 gallons of fresh water an hour from salt water when they were functioning properly, but they were not always doing that. They kept getting encrusted inside with salt and having to be dismantled, cleaned, and reassembled. "Those were a mess," Srack recalled. The men tending them would "make a whole tank of water and throw it away 'cause it was salty."[16]

The men were quick to take advantage when Mother Nature supplied her own freshwater showers.

In the tropics the sun beat down on that steel ship and heated it up like an oven. The heat and humidity had us a streaming sweat. Once in a while we would hit a tropical rain squall. The rain would come down in a torrent—All hands not on watch would get out on deck, peel to the buff and shower and wash all the salt off. God, it was cold but refreshing. The cold rain would cool that steel ship down and it was bearable for a while.

Lot of guys suffered heat rash in there arm pits and crotches.[17]

Appropriately enough for a small ship on a long, hot voyage with a limited supply of fresh water, sartorial standards aboard the *Macaw* were lax. The *Macaw* was emphatically within what was called the Dungarees Navy. The men often went shirtless. Even Paul Burton did so. This was a practice Capt. Andrew R. Mack, USN, the commander of ABSD-1 and the convoy's OTC (officer in tactical command), apparently took a dim view of. According to former Sonarman Clyde Isbell, word came down from atop the task force's chain of command that sunbathing was to be restricted to certain designated hours, shirts to be worn at all other times. Burton's response, Isbell said, was to post on a bulletin board on the *Macaw* a sign that read: "Sunbathing from sunup to sundown only."[18]

The sheer number of bodies aboard was still another problem. Designed for a "normal complement" of six officers and eighty-five enlisted men, the *Macaw* left San Francisco Bay with a crew of 120—the six officers and 114 enlisted men. The ship was overcrowded.[19]

> When we knocked off ships work at 4:00p (1600) and liberty began at 4:30 PM (1630) it was a mad house in the crews head. 2 urinals, 3 toilets—2 shower stalls and either 6 or 8 wash basins. And 2/3 of the crew all trying to get cleaned up for liberty—
>
> Chow down was a problem with a mess deck that could only handle 40 men. . . .
>
> The crews berthing had all these extra bunks sandwitched in all over the place. One bulkhead had the crews lockers—All your worldly possessions were in a locker—2' × 2' × 16 inches.
>
> God, at nite when you would come down the berthing after being in the fresh, sea air at say midnite or 4AM and the stench an[d] sour odors were like a sewer—Guys a groaning, snoreing, belching and farting. The fresh air blowers were inadequate—you hit your bunk and sweated. You fell asleep from exhaustion.[20]

The "sandwitching" in the crew's berthing made for bunks stacked at least three high (four, by one account) and about six inches apart. Some of the men sought out alternate sleeping accommodations. Motor Machinist's Mate Daniel Weber strung up a hammock in a recess used for storing wire near the stern. Seaman Joseph Throgmorton crawled under the canvas cover of the flag bag, the bag containing the ship's semaphore flags, behind the search and signal lights toward the rear of the flying bridge, and slept there. Weber, found out after a couple of weeks, yielded his spot, but Throgmorton, whose friend Signalman 1/c Frank Zuroweste of Clayton, Missouri, was the flag bag's primary caretaker and, as far as Throgmorton knew, the only man aboard who knew how to use its contents or would have occasion to open it, enjoyed his slumber in it largely undisturbed throughout the voyage.[21]

If sleeping in the crew's quarters was less than idyllic, so was waking up there, as Bob Jacobsen recalled:

> The Torpedoman [Rush Alfred Parks of Mission Beach, California, originally from Texas] was the Ships Master at Arms. He got up the cooks and mess cooks an hour before the crew to prepare breakfast. At about 6:30 AM he turned on the lights in the crews berthing compartments then he came into the berthing yelling at the top of his lung: "Reveille—Reveille—heave out & trice up—Reveille, Reveille." Then he would shout, "Let go your cocks and grab your socks." He would then take about a ten minute break then come back with a big trash can lid and a wooden baton and any guys still in there bunks he would hold the metal lid by the guys head and bang on it shouting "Reveille." Then he would leave and be back in five or ten minutes and take names of anybody still in the bunk. These men would have to put in two hours extra duty after evening chow—like scrubbing paint work or chipping rust spots.[22]

By most accounts the food aboard the *Macaw* was good, but the reviews are mixed. During the war, according to Robert Gonnoud, the submarine service got the best of everything, food included, and the *Macaw*, as a part of that service, shared in the culinary largesse—cream, fresh eggs, all kinds of fruit, big navel oranges, Washington Delicious apples. But out at sea, he said, the fresh stocks were soon exhausted—120 men eating 360 meals a day go through food quickly—leaving them with canned goods, powdered eggs and milk, and frozen meat.

Bob Jacobsen attributed the shortage of fresh food to the mismatch between the size of the crew and the size of the ship's General Electric walk-in refrigerator: "Our reefers was too small for that big a crew. We had a continuous flow of stew—spaghetti, macaroni, noodles, Fish on Fridays. Powdered eggs, powdered potatoes and powdered milk which tastes like chalk."[23]

The regimen of fish dinners on Friday—a courtesy to Catholics, who were required then, under an injunction the church has since lifted, to refrain from eating meat that day—was not universally well received aboard the *Macaw*. "Every Friday at noon chow," Bob Jacobsen wrote, "we had fish—Usually a very unsavory fish that about 90% ended up in the 'slop chute.'" He recounted how Bosun's Mates Augie Koepke and Ralph Mennemeyer devised a way around the problem: "A.P. & Minnie had prepared for this: In our locker back aft...they had the electricians wire in electric service: a lite & a plug in. They had got a hot plate—a frying pan and a stowage locker. AP had me, his 'wood butcher' [Jacobsen was a carpenter's mate], build some shelves—They stocked the locker with ham, bacon, eggs, bread, cheese, salami bologna & potatoes. Come those Friday fish days we had a feast on the fantail. We use to look forward to Fridays."[24]

Compounding all the other aggravations of life aboard the *Macaw* was boredom. War is often said to be 98 percent boredom and 2 percent sheer terror. If anything, for most of its short life, the proportions for the crew of the *Macaw* were skewed even more toward boredom. Amenities were scarce. "The Macaw was a small ship," Jacobsen wrote. "She did not rate a barber, a tailor a shoemaker, a Chaplain, a doctor or dentist, No recreation officer, no educational officer, no physical ed instructor—No bugler and no movie projector." No rec room or lounge, either. "To write a letter you set on a trash can and wrote on a pad on your leg."[25]

Quinton Studer was more concise about the ship's shortcomings: no movies, he said, no radios, "no nothing." Life aboard the *Macaw* "was a boring, boring thing." To Bob Gonnoud it was "almost like being in prison."[26]

But it was not entirely without diversions. There was a poker game most every night. The bills that kept changing hands night after night got so worn out, according to Gonnoud (an observer, not a participant), the players set them aside and took to keeping track of who owed whom what by paper and pencil. Paul Burton, Bud Loughman, and Herman Ehlers played chess. Some of the men played acey-deucey, some cribbage.

There were fishing rods—you could cast a line off the fantail. If you were content merely to observe the sea life, there was plenty of it to see. "Day in and day out while on watch we seen whales, sharks, porpoises, flying fish, schools of tuna," Bob Jacobsen recalled. "Knew when we were close to Islands cause we would see all manner of birds. Albatross followed us for thousands of miles. They use no energy—they rode the air currents. Never flap a wing. Just glide. When we dumped our garbage they would feed."[27]

At least some of the Regular Navy men (meaning, by and large, men who had enlisted before Pearl Harbor, as opposed to the reservists who flooded in afterward) could alleviate their ennui by means of a medicinal cocktail courtesy of William Funk, the pharmacist's mate, who was a reservist during his time aboard the *Macaw* but had been Regular Navy (USN) before mustering out and reenlisting and apparently felt a discriminatory loyalty to the men he shared, or had shared, that distinction with. "Chief Funk had been USN—enlisted in USNR-V6 when the war began," Jacobsen wrote. "Funk had a big stock of medical alcohol, which was to be used to disinfect sick bay, clean medical instruments and in prescriptions. If you were in the USN Clique, association, fraternity or band of brothers you could drop into sick Bay and Funk would fix you a prescription: Of grapefruit juice & alcohol."[28]

Reservists denied this privilege found other means to get a drink. "Some of these guys," Dave Wallington said, "if they wanted a shot of whiskey, they wanted a shot of whiskey, come hell or high water." Alcohol was not, in theory, allowed on board except for medicinal purposes, but enforcement of that rule seems to have been spotty at best. Seaman 1/c William Wantz got three days bread and water in the brig when the ship was still on San Francisco Bay for "introducing intoxicating liquor aboard a US naval vessel." Two or three months later he is said to have paid someone on a merchant ship fifty dollars for a pint of whiskey, "chugalugged it," and spent a considerable stretch of time (estimates range from six hours to a day and a half) passed out on the deck, or, by one account, the floor of the crew's quarters. Quinton Studer thought he was dying. Paul Burton and Bud Loughman are said to have been aware of the incident and chosen to overlook it.[29]

Wantz took the traditional approach to alcohol—he bought it. Other strategies said to have been employed aboard the *Macaw* included drinking the Freon used to check the ship's compressors, and filtering Aqua Velva through slices of bread, squeezing out the trapped liquid, and drinking that.[30]

Conversing with shipmates was probably the most common form of entertainment aboard the *Macaw*. There were two primary venues for the enlisted men's bull sessions—the fantail and the telephone net that connected the men on watch at various stations like a party line. Most of the casual discourse in the latter venue happened at night.

On a watch aboard ship at sea—on the bridge you Had a port and starboard lookout on the flying bridge you had a sky lookout. In the wheelhouse you had a lee helmsman, a radar man, a sonar man—in the radio shack you had a duty radioman, In the engine room you had a MoMM, at the after 3″ gun you had a man—all of these people had a phone and were all tied into a net. On day watches not much chatter on the phones. But especially on the graveyard watch—(midnite to 4:00 AM) Guys were trying to stay awake and alert—so was a lot of talk over the net work. Lot of talk about sports: Baseball & College foot ball (NFL was a very minor deal then) Was no NBA— Golf was a rich mans game—We all thought tennis was a girls game or for wimps and queers.

Lot of talk about the movies. I think we all favored Western or war movies. Favorite movie stars—and it ended up which movie star women they would like to take to bed—Lot of talk about the jobs they had before the war. Guys telling adventures in the 3 C's in jail, riding the rails—following the harvest etc.[31]

The "3 C's" was the Civilian Conservation Corps, a federal relief program that over its nine-year lifespan (1933–42) took in more than 2.5 million unemployed men, most of them young and unmarried, fed, housed, and clothed them, gave them medical care, paid them thirty dollars per month (twenty-two to twenty-five of which had to be sent home to their families), and put them to work on conservation projects, focused mainly on reforestation and erosion control, in every state and territory. CCC crews constructed more than eight hundred parks, stocked rivers and lakes with almost a billion fish, and planted more than three billion trees nationwide.[32]

Among the CCC veterans on the *Macaw* were Gunner's Mate Ralph Enzweiler and Seaman Albert Bolke, both Chicagoans and both slightly atypical of the young men in the program in that they were from a large city—just over half of the participants were from rural areas. But in another respect Bolke, at least, typified them perfectly: like a reported 70 percent of them, he entered the program malnourished. (In 1933, the CCC's first year, the average enrollee gained twelve pounds in his first two months in the program.) Within his family he was atypical in respect of his last name. His was Bolke. For his parents and seven siblings, it was Bolka. Family lore has it that his father was drunk when he filled out the paperwork attendant on Albert's birth and misspelled his own last name.[33]

Albert Bolke was born May 6, 1923, in Chicago, one of eight children of an alcoholic steelworker and the second of his three wives. He grew up poor on Chicago's South Side. The family moved a lot—typically, by Albert's widow's account, the night before the rent was due. They didn't have enough to eat. Albert was scrawny. His classroom attendance was spotty—as his family tells it, he was too busy much of the time stealing coal to keep the family warm to go to school.

His mother died in childbirth at age thirty-three, when Albert was ten, and within two weeks his father had gotten married again, to a woman by the name of Julia he had hired, poverty notwithstanding, to take care of the kids. Albert and Julia did not get along. Albert is said to have hidden out at his aunt's place on the frequent occasions when Julia called the cops on him. The policewoman who handled one such call, reportedly after Albert intervened to keep Julia from beating up one of his sisters, figured out what was going on and encouraged him to join the CCC. He did, and spent a year, from April 2, 1940, to March 31, 1941, at Camp Rusk in tiny Glen Flora, Wisconsin, doing manual labor and driving a tractor on a road crew, fighting at least one fire, and eating well. Back in Chicago he got a job with a phone book publisher that entailed getting lots of ink stains and hated it. When the Japanese attacked Pearl Harbor, he promptly enlisted in the navy. In this too he was atypical of his family—his three brothers all served in the army. And in the navy he was atypical in at least one respect—having grown up within blocks of Lake Michigan, he couldn't swim. He got through boot camp at Great Lakes despite that deficiency. By February 1942 he had been assigned to the Naval Air Station at Kaneohe Bay in Hawaii, and a year and a half later to the *Macaw*.

Where the phone network discourse took on a focus unique to the *Macaw* was on the subject of Lt. (jg) William H. Smith, USN, widely referred to aboard the ship as "Snuffy" Smith after the popular syndicated comic strip character, or something worse.

> God how the talk went on—on those long midwatches. Then some one on the bridge would say—hey Shitty Smitty is getting on the phone—Us white hats name for Lt Smith was: Shitty Smitty—not Snuffey.
>
> Then there would be a lot of falsetto voices telling Smith where he could go and what he could shove up his anatomy. After a hot tirade Smith would get off of the phone network—then we would be back at it—[34]

It was perhaps fitting that Smith, a regular party to and subject of these conversations, was the ship's communications officer. At least initially, however, Smith himself did not think so. In fact, he found his assignment to that role so ill-fitting that when he received it, he complained to the Bureau of

Naval Personnel in Washington, DC, telling them it didn't make sense—he'd been trained as an electrician. They told him that was exactly why he'd gotten the job. The *Macaw*, being the sort of auxiliary vessel it was, had a lot of electric motors. They figured his expertise that way might come in handy aboard it.[35]

To some of the enlisted men on the *Macaw*, Smith's real expertise lay mainly in being an obnoxious martinet. "He was considered 'Chicken S___,'" Jacobsen wrote. "The crew always watched their step around Lt. Smith or he would 'hang' them."[36] "He seemed to think he wasn't doing his duty unless he 'shafted' some enlisted man. I was #1 on his 'shit' list. I had to stay sharp and on the ball to keep his 'knife' out of my back."[37]

Born in 1909 in south Georgia, the sixth of nine children of a sharecropper and his wife, William Herman Smith, too, grew up in poverty. From about age twelve to fourteen he worked in a fruit basket factory in Springvale, Georgia—six days a week for fifty cents a day, all of which went to his parents.

After his father died, he left home to reduce the number of mouths his mother had to feed and ended up with his brother in Florida. After performing badly on a school placement test, Smith, in his midteens, was assigned to the fifth grade. He attended school there about four years with classmates four years his junior (an arrangement he is said never to have complained about) and never made it to high school, but when he took his brother's advice and enlisted in the navy at age nineteen in 1928, he was educated well enough to pass a test to qualify for electrician training.

By December 7, 1941, Smith had become a chief petty officer supervising electricians' mates aboard the USS *Salt Lake City* (CA-25), a heavy cruiser that had the good fortune to be at sea that morning—en route to Pearl Harbor but not yet in it—escorting the USS *Enterprise* (CV-6) on its way back from Wake Island, to whose ill-fated marine garrison the carrier had just delivered a squadron of fighter planes. Four months later, the *Salt Lake City* was part of the task force accompanying the USS *Hornet* (CV-8) when that carrier launched Army Air Force Lt. Col. Jimmy Doolittle and his fleet of sixteen B-25B *Mitchell* medium bombers on the "Thirty Seconds over Tokyo" raid on Japan.

Honorably discharged back at Pearl Harbor after that operation, Smith reenlisted the next day, April 27, 1942, and resumed his place aboard the *Salt Lake City*. He received a commission as an ensign that October. Five days later the *Salt Lake City* was hit by enemy gunfire in a night engagement off

Guadalcanal. The ship was forced to put in for repairs, and Smith was reassigned, first to Boston for training and then to the *Macaw*, on which he won the respect and admiration of some of his shipmates, including the two highest in rank, Paul Burton and Bud Loughman, and seems to have alienated a lot of others. Not everyone on the *Macaw* who took a less than entirely favorable view of Smith felt as strongly about him as Bob Jacobsen did. To Robert Gonnoud he was merely a "jerk"—"a nice enough guy but kind of a ding-a-ling." He recalled that Smith descended to the crew's quarters once at 0600, blew a whistle, had someone write down the names of men who didn't get right out of their bunks, and submitted the list to Paul Burton, who "kind of told him where to put it."[38]

Joseph Throgmorton felt about Smith much as Jacobsen did. Smith was crabby, Throgmorton said. "He had a terrible attitude, and mine wasn't much better, so me and him just didn't get along."[39]

Neither, apparently, did Smith and Anthony Tomkovicz. Throughout its brief span of active duty the *Macaw* conducted periodic general quarters drills in preparation for a battle that never came, and gunnery practice to sharpen its aim at an enemy that never appeared. According to Bob Gonnoud, during one such exercise, Tomkovicz, originally of Charleroi, Pennsylvania, a fireman 1/c and later a cook 3/c aboard the *Macaw*, was taking a turn at one of the ship's eight 20mm antiaircraft guns when Lieutenant Smith wandered by, almost within his firing arc, characteristically hassling enlisted men. Gonnoud said Tomkovicz, knowing his gun was equipped with swivel stops to keep its firing range clear of the ship itself, swung the barrel as far as it would go toward Smith, who "just about jumped overboard."[40]

Tomkovicz, twenty-seven in 1943, had taken a curious route to the *Macaw*. He dropped out of high school, got a job setting pins manually in a bowling alley for fifty cents a night, seventy-five on a good night, then went to work in a coal mine, in which he and his partner, in their haste to fill their cart, neglected to adequately shore up the ceiling of the tunnel they were working in one day. The ceiling collapsed and a massive piece of slate clipped the visor of Tomkovicz's helmet and partly crushed the safety toe of his boot. Neither he nor his colleague was seriously injured, but had they been a few feet farther into the tunnel, he said, they would have been crushed "to goo."

That experience having soured him on coal mining, Tomkovicz enlisted in the navy in Pittsburgh in September 1937 and served for three and a half years aboard his state's namesake battleship, much of that time as a fireman

2/c. He mustered out in September 1941 at San Pedro, California, and got a job through a friend as a stage hand at Paramount Studios in Hollywood, in which capacity he perched atop scaffolding above a set for *Holiday Inn,* the 1942 musical release starring Bing Crosby and Fred Astaire, and pushed white-tinted cornflakes onto the set below in simulation of falling snow.

Tomkovicz's career in show business was short-lived. As of that December 7, there was a war on, after all. His former ship was in it from the outset. The *Pennsylvania* was in dry dock at Pearl Harbor the morning of the attack there. It had been scheduled for refloating the day before, but a delay in completing its repairs may have saved it from the fate that befell some of its more exposed sister ships. As it was, the ship sustained only modest damage. If Tomkovicz nevertheless felt guilty about not having shared the danger of that day with his former shipmates, perhaps it assuaged his conscience that, after reenlisting that March, he was assigned to the USS *Kankakee* (AO-39), an oiler. Six of the ten and a half months he served aboard it the *Kankakee* spent making the rounds between Pearl Harbor and the South Pacific, refueling ships engaged in the Guadalcanal campaign. With a capacity of more than a half million gallons of fuel, the *Kankakee* was an inviting target and a dangerous assignment in a war zone. Tomkovicz recalled being on deck one day when the ship was carrying a full cargo of gasoline, seeing two torpedoes approaching, and thinking there wasn't a lot you could do in a situation like that, just hope for the best. His hopes were realized. One torpedo passed about fifty yards in front of the ship, he said, the other about fifty yards behind. By the summer of 1943 he had been reassigned to the *Macaw.*

Conversation was not the attraction for one fixture at the bull sessions on the fantail. Seaman 1/c Lyle Millard Webb did the laundry on the *Macaw.* He was the third-oldest man on the ship, arguably the most industrious, and far and away the most zealously entrepreneurial. He seems to have been out to make all the money he could, and neither squeamish nor, by various accounts, unduly ethical about how he made it.

Webb was one of three men aboard the *Macaw* who predated the twentieth century. Born August 31, 1899, the eldest of five children of a farmer and his Swedish immigrant wife, he spent much of his childhood in tiny WaKeeney, Kansas. The family moved by 1915 to even tinier Onaga, Kansas, and then to Topeka, where Webb attended Kansas State Agricultural College (now Kansas State University) for a year, then took a job in the advertising department of the *Topeka Daily Capital.*

From 1929 to 1934 he was the advertising manager of the *Hope (AK) Star* and prominent in civic affairs: president of the Hope Kiwanis Club, post adjutant of the Hope area branch of the American Legion, member of the Young Businessmen's Association, canvasser in a 1931 Red Cross fundraising drive. On June 19, 1931, he married Hope resident Dessa Oretha McIntosh. In 1934 he took a job, briefly, as general manager of the *Arkansawyer,* a daily in Stuttgart, Arkansas, then moved with his wife to Southern California and joined the advertising staff of the *Burbank Daily Review.* By 1940 Webb and Dessa had parted ways. She stayed in North Hollywood and worked as a sales clerk in a hardware store. He worked briefly at papers in Valdosta, Georgia, and Suffolk, Virginia, in advertising and circulation.

On October 19, 1942, an Associated Press story about the Battles of Stalingrad and Guadalcanal shared the front page of the *Star,* Webb's old paper back in Hope, with news of his impending enlistment. This was to take place three days later in Los Angeles. By that October the ranks of the US armed forces were rapidly approaching four million. It was not always front-page news in a town when someone who had moved away enlisted in another state. No mention was made in the story of his age, one element that might arguably have made his enlisting newsworthy. He was forty-three. He turned forty-four three days after the *Macaw* and its convoy passed under the Golden Gate Bridge. By civilian standards he was middle-aged. By naval enlisted men's standards, he was old if not ancient—ten years older than the captain, twice the age of many of his shipmates, almost three times that of the youngest. By the time World War I ended, most of the men on the *Macaw* had not been born. Webb had already registered for the draft (but had not been drafted). "I couldn't understand how he got in the navy," Bob Gonnoud said. Webb didn't fit the profile of a sailor. "He was just too old."[41]

But Webb was clearly not one to let age keep him from either serving his country or exploiting a business opportunity. Or several of them. The *Macaw* often docked between preconvoy training runs at the naval base at Treasure Island in San Francisco Bay. Webb supplemented his seaman's pay there, Bob Jacobsen wrote, by shining shoes and taking in laundry—blues (a sailor's dark-blue uniform worn on special occasions) washed and pressed, seventy-five cents. Don Srack recalled that Webb would buy candy bars in bulk at the commissary on Treasure Island and sell them to men in line at one of the three movie theaters on the base for twice what he'd paid for them.[42]

Going to sea did not slow Webb down. If anything, it gave him a captive market. When Webb went to the gab sessions at the stern of the *Macaw*, he wasn't there to talk—he was there to sell. "At sea . . . after evening chow a lot of the crew gathered on the fantail in their cliques," Bob Jacobsen recalled. "Webb would come out and announce that he was open for sales. He would note he had Mrs Saylors delicious Coffeettes for sale—These looked like toot-sey rolls—But if you bought one you probably never bought another. I think Webb lost money on that deal. He also had combs, fingernail clippers, nail files, shoe laces and chap stick."[43]

Another of Webb's shipboard enterprises was money lending, or argu-ably loan sharking. It was standard practice in the navy during the war to loan money at what in another context would be considered a usurious rate of interest. According to Bob Jacobsen, the standard (and, by implication, Webb's) rate was 100 percent: "In the Navy, the deal on loaning money is 2 for 1—I.E. If I loan you $5, on payday you have to pay back $10. Webb loaned money—every pay day he was waiting as the guys came out of the pay line with his little black book."[44]

Whether Webb actually charged that much interest is unclear. Don Srack recalled a more modest rate of 25 percent and had a correspondingly innocu-ous epithet for Webb himself. "He was a money maker," Srack said.[45]

Bob Gonnoud described him in somewhat harsher terms: "He was just a hustler. He was always selling everything. He would have sold the ship if he could have found a buyer for it."[46] "He ran the laundry and he always had deals," Gonnoud said. "He always had diamond rings and things he was auc-tioning off. He was a real con artist."[47]

Webb's artistry on the *Macaw* extended to haircuts (apparently he com-peted as a barber with Seaman 1/c Albert Muti) and special fee-based laun-dry services like those he had offered at Treasure Island. He seems to have seized any opportunity for making money, no matter how strenuous. He did the laundry in the tropics in a cramped room with no porthole and limited ventilation amid temperatures Bob Jacobsen estimated at up to 150 degrees—an exaggeration, obviously, but perhaps not one of more than 50 degrees or so. Even at a mere 100 degrees, operating a laundry press in his little metal sweat box cannot have been pleasant.

During the war, at least, Webb seems to have been abstemious. Aboard the *Macaw*, he was not known to drink or smoke. Bob Gonnoud remarked of Webb that he was not the sort of guy you'd go out and get a beer with. Harold

Hayes said of him, "He was a little on the weird side," then corrected himself—he wasn't weird, really, it was more a matter of "an ethnic peculiarity." (He did not elaborate.) When Webb went ashore, Jacobsen wrote, it was not to patronize bars or brothels "but for economic reasons. He bought stuff he figured he could make a profit on." Gonnoud likened him to Luther Billis, the Seabee wheeler-dealer in *South Pacific*—the sort of guy who "can walk through a warehouse and they have a photographic memory, they can catalog everything in it." Radioman Stanley Libera and Webb were shipmates, strictly speaking, for only a matter of weeks (in theory, for about three months), Libera having transferred onto the *Macaw* late in its career, but even a brief exposure was enough for Webb to make a lasting impression on him. "I remember him," Libera said more than seventy years later. "Anything to make a buck."[48]

5

Perilous Passage

It was not until Saturday, January 22, 1944, the seventh day of captivity for both the *Flier* and the *Macaw,* that sea conditions were deemed mild enough to attempt a tow. At about 0900 the *Macaw* sent the *Flier* a towing bridle for linking the submarine to the towline. Just after noon, with the *Florikan* standing by, the massive, machinery-laden barge *Gaylord* emerged from the channel towed by a pair of tugboats and took up its station about two hundred yards south of the *Flier*. Its crew was pinning it in place with a four-point mooring at 1245 when Captain Connolly got a call from Lt. (jg) J. C. Appleby, the NOB aerological officer (the base weatherman). Appleby had worrisome news: a storm was coming in. Black clouds were looming in the southwest, but with the *Gaylord* already in place, Connolly decided it was "too late to stop now," as he wrote later, "so went ahead with job." Inspired, perhaps, by those ominous clouds, the salvage crews made quick work of it. By 1332 they had shackled a two-inch wire from the *Gaylord* to the submarine and within another hour had pulled the sub free. By 1600 it had been taken in tow by a yard tug, tested for seaworthiness, handed off to the *Florikan,* and deemed safe for towing to Pearl Harbor.[1]

That judgment by Commander Crowley, that the *Flier* could be safely towed 1,100 miles, was based largely on the fact that its inner hull was basically intact. But part of its seaworthiness exam involved testing its propulsion, and there the results were not entirely reassuring. The *Flier* had two propeller shafts. The port shaft was found to be inoperative. The starboard shaft was tested at one-third speed, forward and back, and deemed "usable in case of emergency."[2]

An emergency would not be long in coming. With the *Flier* in tow five hundred yards back and the sub chaser USS *PC-602* on hand as an escort, the *Florikan* set out for Pearl Harbor just before 1700 that same day, Saturday,

January 22, on a heading of 147 degrees true and began working up to a speed of 8 knots. Three hours later, the little fleet was not much more than twenty nautical miles southeast of Midway, while the *Clamp,* the salvage and rescue vessel summoned from the Gilbert Islands, had drawn to within about three hundred nautical miles southwest of it. Above the *Clamp* the sky was overcast. The seas about the *Clamp* were moderate, from the southwest. A gentle breeze was blowing from the same quarter. The barometric pressure was 30.02 and falling. By midnight it was 29.96 and still falling, a strong breeze was blowing out of the west, and the sea was running rough, with swells. The storm Appleby had forecast was coming in, somewhat later than expected, and what it lacked in punctuality it would compensate for in ferocity. By 0300 on Sunday the wind had grown stronger and started "hauling around" from west-southwest to west-northwest. The barometric pressure bottomed out that morning at 29.92 about 0545 amid what the *Clamp*'s diarist recorded as a fresh west gale, meaning one from that direction with winds of 39 to 46 mph, a "very high westerly sea and heavy swell."

It was just about that same time—0542 according to Crowley, 0613 according to the *Florikan* diarist—that the towline between the *Florikan* and the *Flier* parted. The line had been threaded through the sub's bullnose, and chafing there had worn through it. The *Flier,* a 312-foot steel tube with very little propulsive capacity, suddenly found itself adrift on a very angry sea. The threat of broaching had been grave enough on the reef. Now it was worse. "The wind had by now increased to about forty knots with gusts of greater intensity, and the seas had become very rough," Crowley would write. "Flier was wallowing in the trough, rolling about 35 degrees on a side because of her light condition, so at 0550 an attempt was made to gain steerageway by use of the starboard screw. Although 130 rpm was made without excessive vibration, steerageway could not be attained and the Pit Log showed zero speed."[3]

The *Flier* was light because Crowley had blown out its ballast tanks to maximize its buoyancy in preparation for the successful attempt to pull it off the reef. Now that shedding of pounds worked against the sub, giving it a higher center of gravity and less stability. It might have stood up to the seas better if it had sat a little deeper in them. The *Flier* was bobbing on them now, enfeebled by the coral that had clawed it, all but powerless to propel itself, and in grave danger of rolling over.

The captain of the *Florikan* was Cmdr. George A. Sharp, the man who had commanded the *Falcon* during the *Squalus* rescue five years before.

Sharp, like Paul Burton, had meanwhile been in submarines and blackballed out of them. The challenge facing him was now essentially the same one Burton had faced one week earlier, to get a messenger to the *Flier* amid extremely rough seas, only the *Flier* now was a free-moving target. There was no danger now of either ship's running aground, but for the crew of the submarine in particular, an even greater one of broaching and death. Sharp's initial response to this challenge was basically what Burton's had been, and so were the results—he tried to float the *Flier* a messenger and failed, this while or just after laying down an oil slick about two hundred yards windward of the submarine in the hope of suppressing somewhat the seas rolling into it. Those seas were rolling into the *Florikan* too, of course, and given the fact that it had to get close enough to the submarine to pass it a messenger, and stay there long enough for the *Flier* to haul in the towline and hook it up to its bridle, the *Flier*'s inability to generate its own steerageway forced the *Florikan* to relinquish its and left the rescue vessel wallowing too, heeling at comparable angles—according to former Torpedoman 3/c Al Dobbins, the *Florikan*'s inclinometer produced a reading of 57 degrees portside that morning, indicating a leftward tilt of 33 degrees off vertical—and at only marginally less risk than the submarine of capsizing.[4]

Just before 0700 Crowley asked *PC-602* to stand by on lifeguard duty in case any *Flier* sailors needed to be plucked from the water, and he positioned men on deck to prepare to receive a reconstituted towline. The barometer by then had started back up, but the storm kept growing worse. Meanwhile the *Clamp*, now about 280 nautical miles to the southwest, was struggling in it too, even without the burden of a 1,500-ton dead weight in tow or, worse, wallowing free and threatening to sink. Having found itself on its northward heading broadside to seas sweeping its fantail, the *Clamp* embarked just before 0600 on a series of course and speed changes—left 70 degrees, right 60, left 60, right 140, heading into the seas, then more or less broadside to them, back into them and finally running due east before them, at 8, 12, 3, and again 8 knots—in a disjointed sort of detour taken in the interest of staying afloat.[5]

At 0719 the *Florikan* made a close pass parallel to the *Flier* and twice tried shooting a line to the sub by line-throwing gun. Both shots failed, but another about twenty minutes later found its mark, and one strenuous hour after that the men Crowley had assigned the task of receiving the rehabilitated towline drew it in at the *Flier*'s bow, only to find they couldn't thread it through the bullnose. According to subsequent testimony by Crowley, it was too big. But there's no indication that it was any bigger than the two-inch wire it replaced. If size was a factor, it was likely the size not of the wire itself but of the thimble, or eye, at the end of it that posed the problem. According to Al Dobbins, the problem was not the size of the line per se but its flexibility (or lack thereof, either way a function of size) and the angle of its approach. Under normal circumstances, a towing wire describes a gentle parabola, most of it underwater, but with the two ships at close quarters there was no tension on the massive line, so it hung slack more or less vertically from the stern of the *Florikan* and rose back out of the sea at about the same angle to the men struggling with it at the bow of the *Flier,* and they simply weren't able to bend it far enough toward the horizontal to thread it through the vertically framed "nostril" of the bullnose.

They encountered this problem, according to Crowley, at 0838. About nine minutes later, by the *Clamp* diarist's reckoning, the storm peaked in the form of a "whole westerly gale," one from the west with winds of 48 to 55 knots, or about 55 to 63 mph, and very high seas. While the *Florikan* and *Flier* surged and plunged probably twenty to thirty vertical feet and rolled through arcs in the range of 50 to 70 degrees, men aboard the *Florikan* hauled the line back in and attached a shot, or ninety-foot length, of anchor chain to it, rendering moot the question of flexibility, and men aboard the *Flier* hauled it back again, threaded it through the bullnose at last, and secured it to the forward capstan for reeling in, all under what Crowley termed "the most adverse circumstances." Dobbins corroborated that assessment. During the morning's struggles, he said, "We had guys with twenty years of sea duty getting seasick."[6]

Once the towline was reconnected, all that remained was for the *Flier* to haul it in to the desired length—when they left Midway it was set around five hundred yards—and get back under way. But the combination of the manpower of what was probably a rather numerous anchor detail and the mechanical power of the forward capstan proved unequal to the task. Just as the *Macaw*'s anchor detail had strained in concert with their forward capstan and its 25-horsepower electric motor to draw in their starboard bower just before its chain had parted by buoy No. 2 at Midway one week before, so now their counterparts aboard the *Flier* struggled with the towline like an overmatched team in a tug-of-war. "Despite having all hands and the capstan on the line every bit that was gained would immediately be taken away," Crowley wrote. By Dobbins's account, the strain took a toll on the machinery. He said the *Flier* signaled that its forward capstan was burning out and that Sharp replied with a suggestion (one Dobbins attributed to himself) that the *Flier* apply both of its capstans, fore and aft, to the task, running them in series. That did the trick, but still there was trouble to come. At 1028 the *Flier*'s chief gunner's mate, North Carolinian Charles D. Pope, was washed overboard. But in the wake of James Cahl's death, stricter safety standards seem to have prevailed aboard the sub. Pope had been tethered to the boat and was promptly hauled back aboard. By noon, the storm was abating, the *Clamp* in the process, or about to be, of gradually adjusting its course back toward Midway "as weather would allow," and the *Florikan* and *Flier*, the latter crippled but improbably still afloat, on their way once again toward Pearl Harbor. They would arrive there almost exactly one week later.[7]

The narrative Captain Crowley submitted to the naval panel that convened another week or so after that to inquire into the grounding of the *Flier* covers a fifteen-day period, from January 16 through 30, 1944, and runs to nine pages. In it, the six days from January 24 through 29, representing most of the rest of that passage to Pearl Harbor, get short shrift. Crowley devotes to them a grand total of one word, and though a submarine in tow on the open ocean can never be said to be entirely free of danger, and though he faced the prospect of an investigation that might have gotten him and his executive officer, Lt. Cmdr. Benjamin Adams Jr., thrown out of submarines, just as Paul Burton and George Sharp had been, that one word—"Uneventful"—speaks volumes about the relief he must have felt after all the excitement of the preceding eight days.[8]

6

South Pacific

On September 15, 1943, their nineteenth day at sea, the crew of the *Macaw* celebrated crossing the equator, something they would not actually do until 1339 the next day. (Why they would celebrate early is unclear. Maybe they were so bored, they couldn't wait.) The festivities were presided over by Neptunus Rex in the person of Augie Paul Koepke, whose court included a Royal Princess, a Royal Baby, a Royal Judge, a Royal Barber, a Royal Doctor, and a Royal Executioner, all of whom were "shellbacks" or "walruses"—they had already crossed the equator, a fact that entitled them, in keeping with ancient nautical custom, to rain blows and inflict all manner of indignities on the "polliwogs," who hadn't, under the pretense of punishment for a variety of crimes not found in *Black's Law Dictionary.*

Seaman 1/c Albert Muti, who was in fact a professional barber and practiced that trade aboard the *Macaw,* faced an implied charge of fraud (the wording is a bit vague) for passing himself off as a "barbar" despite that he was "never called a barbar before." Seaman 2/c Jack Vangets was charged with threatening to steal the line of the equator for a kite string. Subpoenas were issued and hapless polliwogs hauled in droves before Royal Judge John Lightner, the engineering officer. Justice was swift and summary. There were no acquittals. There was no mollycoddling. Offenders were forced to run a gantlet, bound and pilloried at the gunwale, shorn crudely by the Royal Barber (Anthony Tomkovicz), made to kiss the Royal Baby's ointment-smeared belly, and compelled to undergo medical treatment at the hands of the Royal Doctor (reportedly Warrant Bosun M. C. Cottrell), who instructed his patients to say "Aahhh" and gave them a shot in the mouth from an oil can or grease gun containing a potion said to consist of diesel oil, alcohol, vinegar, chili powder, pepper, and Tabasco sauce.

The polliwogs had to bathe in the Royal Bathtub, fashioned from a tarp fitted over a wooden frame and filled with brine and galley slop, and as they crawled naked across it, the Royal Executioner, Seaman 1/c William Hale Wantz of Goldsboro, North Carolina, swatted them with a flat-faced wooden club. Other shellbacks stood by the tub and made sure the men in it stayed immersed. You'd lift your head up, Dave Wallington recalled, and someone would shove it back down. Seaman 2/c Stephen Miller made the mistake of crying during these ablutions, Jacobsen recalled, and Wantz just hit him that much harder.[1]

The gantlet, as Quinton Studer recalled it, ran the length of the ship. Having entered it in a T-shirt and pants, he said, he emerged from it stark naked. He didn't recall losing his clothes—they were just gone. "They beat the hell out of you," he said.[2]

They may have beaten it out of no one more thoroughly than they did out of Bud Loughman, the executive officer, almost certainly the only polliwog officer aboard, and in any case the only such officer to participate in the ceremony. Loughman was generally well liked by the enlisted men, but the opportunity to assault and batter an officer—any officer—with impunity does not come along every day and is not to be squandered when it does. Loughman underwent a stay in the pillory, kissed the Royal Baby's belly, and endured a passage through the gantlet. He said years later that he had had to walk the gantlet, and if in fact he did walk it, he may have done so because he thought it would be unseemly of an officer to run. In any case, he said the men swung as if to cripple. "The trip across the equator would have done your heart good to see me were you a spectator," he wrote his Sea Bee friend Jack McCarthy about six weeks later. "The boys really lit in on me and beat the arse off me." Afterward, the Royal Princess presented him with her brassiere, and a delegation of his tormenters with a Jolly Roger, for his pains.[3]

One of the more striking images in the photos of the *Macaw*'s equatorial rites is that of Robert Vaughn, the young African American steward's mate from Winston-Salem, North Carolina, on his knees, eyes closed, head more or less shaved, at once grimacing and smiling, awaiting some form of perhaps only partly mock brutality amid half a dozen white sailors, most of them standing, one, probably Wantz (his face is out of the frame) in a sort of gown emblazoned on the front with a skull and crossbones, another brandishing by Vaughn's chest a wooden lath or paddle. The imagery almost reeks of Ku Klux Klan–style racist barbarity—except that Vaughn seems to be enjoying himself. In other photos he is seen in line at the Royal Barbershop and then getting slathered with some foul sort of marinade by paintbrush even as the Royal Barber makes a hash of his hair—exactly the sort of ritualized mistreatment the other greenhorn sailors received. He looks right at home amid the festivities. At first glance, the photo of Vaughn on his knees looks damning. But upon closer examination of that and other photos, he seems to have been just another polliwog enduring and even enjoying the abuse.

Nor were the equator festivities the only multiracial recreational activities, or the Royal Court and Barbershop the only such facilities, aboard the *Macaw*. Black and white sailors played poker together and hung out together during liberty on the fantail. They bunked in the same fetid crew's quarters. In matters of race, by the standards of the day, Paul Burton seems to have run a fairly enlightened ship. Given the ship's spatial constraints, in one sense it might have been all but impossible not to. "There was no segregation on that ship," Bob Gonnoud said. "There wasn't room for it."[4]

There was obviously systematic segregation with regard to ratings and work roles (as Gonnoud himself subsequently acknowledged), but with regard to mere physical proximity, the ship may in fact have been simply too crowded to enforce racial barriers whether anyone wanted them or not. And if some of the men did, most of them seem not to have much cared. By most accounts (all of them from Caucasians), race relations aboard the *Macaw* were good. According to former Seaman Jack Vangets, they were not a problem—no one even thought about them.[5]

The four African American men aboard may have thought about them. Three of those men were steward's mates, one was a cook. A steward's mate was basically a servant who waited on the officers. Black sailors typically filled that role during the war. Some, like St. Louis resident Hughey Lindsey on the *Macaw*, achieved the comparatively lofty rating of cook—one they would typically share, as Lindsey did, with white shipmates—but in the navy of that era, that was about as far up the ratings ladder as most of them could hope to go. Still, it does seem true—despite the crude jokes lampooning various minorities that were a staple of the nightly "party-line" telephonic gab sessions Bob Jacobsen describes—that there was little in the way of overt racial animosity aboard the ship, except, no doubt, for that expressed for the Japanese. What conflict there was, racial or otherwise, seems to have been the exception rather than the rule. By almost all accounts, the great majority of the men on the ship got along well together.

Word got out aboard the ship that Robert Vaughn had a fear of getting his penis shot off, and his shipmates, or at least some of the white ones, kidded him about it, assuring him that indeed he would. But this appears to have been benign, just some crude lighthearted raillery. "They were friendly," former Fireman 2/c Dan Weber recalled of his African American shipmates. "We were all friendly to one another." Former Seaman Eugene Van Buskirk echoed Weber's sentiments. No one had any problems with anyone else on the ship, he said. He likened the *Macaw* to a small town.[6]

Bob Jacobsen painted a less uniformly rosy picture. "The crew was very well mixed up," he wrote, "Men from all over the country. . . . Were some great guys and then some not so great. Some who would give you the shirt off of there backs—others you had to watch—they'd steal the shirt off of your back."[7]

Jacobsen had issues himself with certain of his shipmates, and he notes other shipboard quarrels he was not a party to. But even in his extensive recollections of life aboard the *Macaw*, there is more of camaraderie than of conflict.

Radioman Stanley Libera survived the attack on Pearl Harbor aboard the battleship *Tennessee* (BB-43), did two war patrols aboard the submarine *Sargo* (SS-188), and served, briefly but memorably, aboard the *Macaw*, boarding it late in its brief career. Perhaps if he had had more time to experience the ship's shortcomings, he would have felt differently about it. But its shortcomings, as big and abundant as they were, seem to have made only a small impression on him, if any at all. "Between the battleships, submarine, and *Macaw*," he said seventy years later, "I loved the *Macaw*." Submarines during the war were legendary for the harmony they had to have, given the crowding within them, and generally did. Libera had experienced that harmony firsthand and appreciated it. But the *Macaw*, he said, was better—like a submarine, one big happy family, but preferable in that it was not underwater.[8]

The day before the equator ceremony, Convoy PW 2294 had assumed Disposition No. 2. Beginning with the *Ganymede* on the right flank, every other Liberty ship slipped into place about a mile behind the one previously abeam of it to port, transforming a single row of eight ships into two rows of four, plus tows. The escorts—the *Macaw* in the lead, minesweepers *Tumult* and *Token* on the flanks, and fleet tug *Lipan* at the rear—maintained their positions. The move seems to have addressed a gradual shift in the balance between competing dangers. The earlier formation had minimized the likelihood of collisions but stretched thin the escort protection fore and aft and extended communication lines. The reconfiguration, while perhaps increasing somewhat the risk of friendly entanglement, consolidated the formation, reducing by about one-third the length of its perimeter and cutting by more than two miles the distance a message as by semaphore would have to travel across it.

As the risk of encountering the enemy grew, so did the volume of friendly traffic the convoy encountered and with it the frequency of scares. Within eight days of crossing the equator, the crew of the *Macaw* went to battle stations six times. Once the threat turned out to be a pair of *Dauntless* dive bombers, another time another Liberty ship, the SS *Glenn Curtiss*. Never did the Japanese appear.

As the convoy passed Samoa and began threading its way into the fringes of an active war zone, it was also entering an active volcano zone. On September 24 the *Macaw* passed the entrance to the harbor at Pago Pago. At 2001 hours on September 25 a red glow appeared on the horizon. Battle stations again. Within a half hour the source of the ominous glow was found to be the volcanic island of Niuafo'ou, erupting fifty miles away.

The danger Japanese submarines and airplanes posed in the South Pacific in 1943 was real enough, but when the *Macaw* went to general quarters, the source of the alarm typically turned out to be either a friendly craft of one sort or another or, as in the case of the volcano, Mother Nature. The *Macaw* had two three-inch .50-caliber guns and eight 20mm antiaircraft guns and never fired a shot in anger. It dropped at least thirteen depth charges, including twelve practice rounds, two off San Francisco and ten outside Pearl Harbor, but none on a Japanese submarine. No such thing ever appeared to drop one on. In what may have been the only time the depth charge detail actually took aim at anything in particular, the target was, by several accounts, a school of tuna, for which Paul Burton is said to have had a hankering, and the ensuing blast almost did to the ship and the men aboard it what a number of them said it did, or was intended to do, to the fish. Apparently, given the ship's modest speed at the time, the device was set to explode at too shallow a depth. "That 300 lb depth charge exploded very close to our stern," Bob Jacobsen recalled, "damn near lifted our stern out of the water."

Robert Gonnoud was in his bunk taking a nap at the time. A veteran sailor doing likewise nearby jumped up, Gonnoud said, and exclaimed, "We caught a fish!"—sailor slang for getting hit by a torpedo. They may in fact have caught a whole school of fish—"Was a school of Bonita and there seemed to be a hundred fish belly up," Jacobsen recalled—but apparently none were actually brought aboard.[9]

The *Macaw* entered Pallikulo Bay at the southeastern tip of Espiritu Santo on the morning of October 2, 1943, and set about escorting various dry dock sections to their anchorages. Espiritu Santo is a tropical island of volcanic origin, at 1,420 square miles the largest and westernmost of the New Hebrides chain about 1,300 miles off the northeast shoulder of Australia. Its name, meaning Holy Ghost, stems from its discovery in 1606 by a Portuguese navigator working in the service of Spain. Home to a population of Melanesian subsistence farmers, Espiritu Santo suddenly became a very active place in the spring of 1942 when the Americans arrived and began construction at Luganville on the island's southeast corner of a base that was to support the invasion of Guadalcanal, in the Solomon Islands about six hundred miles to the northwest.

The *Macaw* arrived at Espiritu Santo about eight months after the fighting on and around Guadalcanal came to an end. It had lasted about six months, from August 1942 to February 1943. The images Americans have of the fighting there tend to feature haggard marines, and the marines did handle much of the ground and aerial combat at Guadalcanal under extremely difficult circumstances. Ammunition, food, planes, and parts were all in short supply much of the time, supply lines tenuous, naval support spotty. Planes were cobbled together with parts cannibalized from wrecks. Guadalcanal was hot, humid, fetid, and thick with mosquitoes. Men on both sides fell prey in droves to malaria and dysentery, the latter with its attendant diarrhea. The 1st Marine Division, which bore the brunt of the ground fighting in the early months, suffered almost four times as many casualties from malaria as from gunshot wounds. As the fighting wore on, unburied Japanese bodies putrefied and attracted clouds of flies. There was little fresh water for bathing. Men who resorted to bathing in streams frequently contracted fungal infections. The dense vegetation provided cover to Japanese snipers, and from it emerged waves of suicidally determined Japanese soldiers in some of the first banzai attacks of the war.[10]

But as bad as the marines and the army infantry who reinforced and replaced them had it on the ground at Guadalcanal, in sheer grim statistical terms the sailors offshore had it worse. About five thousand Americans died in naval battles off the coast of Guadalcanal, almost three times as many as died there on land. The Japanese for their part lost fewer men in the sea battles, about four thousand, but overall suffered even worse than the Americans did. The material losses were remarkably even. Each side lost two dozen ships. The Americans lost 436 planes, the Japanese 440. But on land, in what would prove to be a consistent pattern throughout the war, the toll of Japanese fatalities vastly outnumbered that of Americans, about 20,000 to 1,800, a ratio of more than eleven to one.

Six agonizing months after the Americans landed on Guadalcanal, the Japanese withdrew the last of their troops from it and began a long, grueling retreat northwest. The die at that point was cast. Most of the fighting in the Pacific was yet to be fought, but the momentum had swung, and between their losses in planes, ships, men, and expertise in the battles of the Coral Sea, Midway, and Guadalcanal, the Japanese found themselves in a hole from which they would never emerge.

Guadalcanal had special meaning for at least four of the men on the *Macaw*. Three of them, Augie Paul Koepke, William Smith, and Ship's Fitter Lloyd George Fox of Watford City, North Dakota, had all been in the thick of the fighting, each in a separate engagement and aboard a different ship— Koepke aboard a transport, Smith a cruiser, and Fox a destroyer. Koepke's ship was struck kamikaze-style on August 8, 1942, by a Japanese bomber and scuttled. Smith's ship and Fox's were both hit by shell fire, Smith's on the night of October 11–12, Fox's a month later. Smith's ship was damaged, Fox's sunk. Koepke and Fox both had to abandon ship, Fox at about 0230 on the morning of November 13. There were thirty-nine ships between the two sides in the area that night, Fox recalled, and so much light from bursting star shells (designed to burst in midair and shed light), "you could sit there and read a newspaper." He jumped overboard and floated all night with several shipmates. They were wearing life vests. The water wasn't too cold, he said, but his teeth chattered nevertheless. He wasn't worried about sharks. "After all the goddamn banging and shelling and everything that went on that night," he said, "I don't think there were too many sharks around."

When it started getting light, they saw an empty life raft and climbed aboard. In it they found cigarettes and matches sealed in tin cans, and Fox had what he recalled sixty-four years later as the best smoke he'd ever had. Marines came out in the morning in PT boats and landing craft. The boat that picked Fox up had gallon cans of peaches and pears. No knives or forks. They ate with their hands. "Tasted damn good," he said. "They didn't have to beg us to eat it."

There were about seven hundred survivors from US ships in the water that night, Fox said. There were Japanese in the water too, he added, but none of them survived. The Americans shot them. "War is war," he said. They were not far from Japanese-held territory at the time. If the Japanese had survived, he said, they might have returned to combat. His ship, the USS *Cushing* (DD-376), exploded that afternoon.[11]

Among the many other American casualties off Guadalcanal that night were the USS *San Francisco* (CA-38), a *New Orleans*–class heavy cruiser, and the USS *Atlanta* (CL-51), a light cruiser. Amid the chaos and confusion, the *San Francisco* mistook the *Atlanta* for an enemy ship and fired on it. Pounded by friend and foe alike, the *Atlanta* was scuttled later that day. The *San Francisco* took forty-five hits that night and survived—none of them was below the waterline—but 77 of its crew, including its captain and a rear admiral, were killed and 105 wounded. Among the wounded was Coxswain Hoyt Hannah of Fort Smith, Arkansas. Two days later he was transferred to the USS *Solace*, a hospital ship, and two days after that his younger brother, Claude Winford "Toby" Hannah, followed him into the navy. Toby was probably still in boot camp on December 20 when Hoyt died at the Naval Hospital in Oakland, where the *Macaw*, launched five months before, was being fitted out. Seven months later Toby was in Oakland, a seaman 2/c assigned to the *Macaw*. Toby Hannah had a good sense of humor, according to his friend Bob Jacobsen, but a bitter hatred of the Japanese.[12]

From Espiritu Santo the *Macaw* was directed to Wallis Island, the site of a marine base about 1,200 miles to the east-northeast. If anyone on the *Macaw* harbored any illusion about the South Pacific being one big tropical paradise, Wallis Island must have thoroughly disabused him of it. Various diseases, tropical and otherwise, including tuberculosis, yaws, and filariasis (also known as elephantiasis) were endemic there. A nearby islet housed a sanatorium for lepers. Bob Jacobsen described graphically the party that greeted the ship upon its arrival.[13]

Wallis Island. Never foreget it. Steaming up the chanel you would see off to Port the rusty remains of a ship which had piled up on the reef. Ahead you would see a huge rocky clif with a huge white cross painted on it. When we anchored we were soon surrounded with a host of outrigger canoes. They came out with loads of fruit and vegeatables to trade—but no one could think of eating what they brought. These people were the most ghastly sights we had ever seen: People with leprosy—Flesh rotting away—could see hand bones—leg bones, arm bones—half faces rotted away—Others with elephantitus: Women with breasts as huge as big watermelons—Men with testicles as big as cantaloupes—Fingers like sausages arms big as legs—ears big as a head of lettuce—captain had us rig fire hoses and blast them off if they tried to come on board.[14]

Former Motor Machinist's Mate Quinton Studer had similar recollections —women with huge breasts and one man with something like a little wheel-barrow to support his testicles.[15] The welcome the marines on Wallis Island gave the *Macaw* was reportedly not much warmer than the one the *Macaw* gave those unfortunate produce vendors (none of whom, apparently, did try to board the ship—there is no record of the *Macaw*'s actually turning its fire hoses on them). The marines, by one account, did not expect the *Macaw* or seem especially happy to see it, greeting the ship with a chilly "Who are you and what are you doing?" According to Robert Gonnoud, when they learned that the *Macaw* was there to retrieve a barge that had sunk, they replied, "No barge ever sunk here."[16]

The *Macaw* left Wallis Island twice—within about five hours of its first arrival, and again three or four days later, having returned in the meantime apparently to report, without risk of sharing the news with the Japanese via intercepted radio transmission, its discovery of a previously unknown coral reef. On one of those departures, Bob Jacobsen recalled, the *Macaw* almost collided in the entrance channel with an incoming army transport. Having narrowly avoided it, the *Macaw* set its course for the US base at Funafuti, another atoll about 450 miles north-northwest, where an even closer encoun-ter awaited it.

As the *Macaw* neared the entrance channel at Funafuti early on the morn-ing of October 16, it transmitted a recognition signal to the base. The reply that transmission provoked, as Bob Gonnoud recalled it, made the greeting the *Macaw* had gotten at Wallis Island seem cordial. It was: "You've got five minutes to send the right signal." Quartermaster 1/c Warden Wingrove of East Bethle-hem, Pennsylvania, was summoned. Wingrove had dropped out of school after eighth grade, but, according to Gonnoud, he was smart and highly skilled in the art of navigation and did a lot of it for Paul Burton. He sized things up quickly, Gonnoud recalled, and said, "My God, you've given yesterday's signal." Two PT boats were dispatched to inspect the mysterious visitor. Wingrove helped straighten things out with them, and the *Macaw* was allowed to proceed into the lagoon.[17]

For Bud Loughman, once the *Macaw* found its mooring at Funafuti, things seem to have stayed problematic. Funafuti, one of what were known at the time as the Ellice Islands (now the nation of Tuvalu), shares with Midway and about a hundred other small islands and atolls scattered about the globe the distinction of having been claimed as US territory under the Guano Islands Act of 1856. That law authorized the president to deem as "appertaining to the United States" any island—"not within the lawful jurisdiction of any other Government, and not occupied by the citizens of any other Government"—on which an American citizen had discovered a deposit of guano, which consists mainly of bird droppings and was highly valued in the nineteenth century as fertilizer. The Ellice Islands had been inhabited for several thousand years, but apparently whatever indigenous civic structures may have evolved there over the millennia did not qualify in Washington's eyes as a "Government," which meant Funafuti was up for grabs, and the United States at least nominally grabbed it.

Britain, not to be outdone, laid claim to the entire island chain, along with the neighboring Gilbert Islands, proclaiming the two of them a protectorate in 1892 and a colony in 1916. By the time the *Macaw* came calling in 1943, the United States had a long-standing claim to Funafuti based on bird excrement, and the newly constructed Allied base there was manned by thousands of US Marines, but the local flag featured a Union Jack, and the official anthem was "God Save the Queen." It was part of a British colony, and that fact posed a ticklish diplomatic problem inasmuch as protocol required the commander of a visiting ship of foreign nationality to pay a courtesy call upon arrival to the chief local representative of government, and, according to his executive officer, Paul Burton, both of whose paternal grandparents were from England, for some reason took an exceedingly dim view of the English:

> When we came into this island, I think it was Funafuti, there was one British . . . Britisher who was the representative of . . . Britain, and the captain . . . he hated the Japanese, and just a little below that he hated

the English, and he couldn't bring himself to go and visit the . . . Englishman, who was the only Englishman, too, on the island. . . . So Paul Burton told me, he said, "I want you to go in and represent me." And I forget what his reason was. And at that time . . . I never was much for drinking anything, and one thing in particular I didn't like was beer, and when I got in to meet this Englishman, very pleasant guy, he apologized profusely for having nothing to offer me but a warm beer. I drank it and I almost threw it up.[18]

The *Macaw* remained at Funafuti or in its immediate vicinity for almost a month, from October 16 to November 13, putting its powerful crane to use unloading cargo, much of it in the form of amphibious landing vessels called LCTs (LCT stands for landing craft, tank), and frequently shifting about among mooring sites, reportedly as a precaution against the Japanese mapping out ship positions for bombing runs. That was not an idle threat. Funafuti lay within range of Japanese bombers based on Nauru and Tarawa, the latter a heavily fortified atoll in the Gilbert Islands about 730 miles to the northwest, soon to become the site of one of the bloodiest engagements of the Pacific war. When the *Macaw* arrived at Funafuti, American forces were preparing to invade Tarawa. The Japanese commander there had boasted it would take a million men a hundred years to take the atoll. In fact, it took thirty-five thousand Americans about a week (the heavy fighting lasted just over three days) beginning November 20, 1943, and about 1,700 lives. But during the *Macaw*'s stay at Funafuti, both Nauru and Tarawa were still in Japanese hands, and Funafuti was still subject to bombing raids. There were nine altogether from March 27 through November 17, 1943, and at least one while the *Macaw* was on hand.

Funafuti was probably as close as the *Macaw* ever came to combat. Japanese bombs fell near the ship there but did it no harm. In fact, the *Macaw* itself did more harm to US assets at Funafuti than the Japanese ever did to it. On November 8 the USS *Terror* (CM-5), a fleet minelayer, arrived at Funafuti. Appropriately enough, given its name, the *Terror* was an imposing warship, 454 feet long and 60 wide, with a battery of four five-inch guns, four 40mm guns and fourteen 20mm guns, and the flagship at that time of a vice admiral, John Hoover. It arrived early that morning and moored in anchorage C-12, and it was there that the *Macaw*, assigned to help offload the *Terror*'s cargo of pontoon barges, drew alongside it at 1430 that afternoon. It was an awkward encounter. Bob Jacobsen described it vividly sixty-six years later: "Capt. Burton had too much speed on the Macaw as we came alongside the Terror, he backed down but not soon enough. Our forward movement raked the side of the Terror—the overhang of our bridge ripped into some of their superstructure. A screeching, ripping, tearing of metal. The Captain of the Terror came onto his bridge and yelled into a bull horn: 'Get that damn metal scrap heap away from my ship or I will have my gunners sink you as a navigational hazard.'"[19]

If Cmdr. Howard Wesley Fitch of the Terror really did issue such a threat, Paul Burton failed to heed it, and Fitch, to make good on it. The Macaw remained right where it was for another six hours or so, doing what it had gone there to do, unloading barges. It was after that day's misadventure that some of Burton's men took to calling him Crash.

The Macaw stayed at Funafuti four weeks, and ten days of that time it stayed put and went nowhere. There was work to do even when the ship was at rest, of course, on and sometimes off the ship—some of the men helped the Seabees build a landing strip there—but the men did have some time at Funafuti for R&R and a place well suited to it. They were in a lagoon in the South Pacific with a beautiful beach. Men dove off the first and second decks and swam, vied like kids for possession of a homemade raft, fished off the fantail, and went to the outdoor movie theater onshore. The prime attraction at the theater, regardless of what movie was showing, was a tightrope-walking rodent, by most accounts a rat, that would run across a cable strung above the stage every evening before the movie began. As the big moment neared, a spotlight would be trained on the cable. "A lot of those guys, they'd sit there an' just stare at that cable," Gunner's Mate Ralph "Shorty" Enzweiler recalled. Then promptly at 2000, by one account, the rat would appear and dash across the cable, left to right, and the audience would erupt in thunderous applause. The place was always packed ahead of time, Bob Gonnoud said, but "After that you could get all the seats you wanted because half the men would get up and leave."[20]

The swimming, by all accounts, was lovely at Funafuti, but not entirely carefree. Nervous about sharks, swimmers generally stayed close to the ship. Typically, whenever anyone from the Macaw went swimming, a shipmate with a rifle would stand guard and watch for sharks. At Funafuti they put air pipes overboard to scare them off. "Nobody was eaten," Dave Wallington noted, but "if a shark had wanted to go through a few bubbles to get to someone, he probably would have."[21]

Lucky Lager fell from the sky at Funafuti like manna from heaven. An estimated twenty-five or thirty cases of one-quart bottles of it, intended for the officers' club, fell into the lagoon during the *Macaw*'s stay there when the sling in which it was being unloaded from a merchant ship broke. The *Macaw*, having eight deep-sea divers aboard, was uniquely qualified to respond to this disaster. After a day or so underwater the beer was retrieved, and in keeping with the law of maritime salvage, or at least with that of finders keepers, it became the property of the *Macaw* and fueled what Bob Jacobsen recalled years later as some great parties on the fantail. But it was not squandered. It's not clear who on the ship had custody of the beer, but it was husbanded with enough restraint—the limit was one bottle per man per authorized occasion—that the men were still drinking it at a picnic at Pearl Harbor about a month later.[22]

It seems unlikely that Paul Burton participated in that salvage operation—he and his peers in rank might have regarded scavenging beer off the sea floor as conduct unbecoming a ship's captain. But he was not above indulging himself at a world-class swimming hole. Quinton Studer recalled Burton diving from high on the ship. Burton was athletic. He had run track in high school and cross-country at the Naval Academy, and he had astounding lung capacity, a fact he demonstrated at Funafuti by descending the anchor chain without benefit of breathing gear and returning, as was the custom, with a fistful of muck to prove he'd gotten to the bottom. Just how far down the bottom was is unknown—Bud Loughman spoke of Burton's descending at least a hundred feet, but in fact the depth at the mooring sites the ship occupied at Funafuti varied from 10 to 21 fathoms, or about 60 to 126 feet. But more than sixty years later former Seaman Eugene Van Buskirk, one of a group of sailors who timed Burton one day, recalled him being underwater an astonishing two minutes and fifty-six seconds.[23]

Burton apparently made something of a habit of this kind of diving. Bud Loughman saw his diving as symptomatic of Burton's character, and saw other behavior as possibly symptomatic of what the diving was doing to his ears.

Burton was a person who believed in punishing himself. I remember when we went into . . . this island, and . . . he used to dive in the harbor down to the anchor to fetch something up from the bottom, and this would be at least a hundred feet of water. And when we were in the ward room, I . . . remember, he . . . always had trouble with his ears.

And of course to dive any depth, if you go down a hundred feet, you have to stop numerous times to clear your ears. Well, I don't know that he had a malfunction in his ears or if he had wax or what, but he would sit in the ward room and he was always picking at his ears with a paper clip that was open, and . . . trying to clear the wax or whatever it was . . . and I often wondered, if pictures had ever been taken of the condition of his eardrums and the like, they must have been terribly perforated by his probing with these metallic paper clips.

He was a very strange man. I liked him, though.[24]

The fact that Burton would engage in the diving-for-muck game (even if not in diving for beer) points to one of the things about him that Loughman and others on the ship liked: he did not put on airs. He didn't lord it over his men. If a job needed doing, even a rather arduous one, he was not above doing it himself. Former Motor Machinist's Mate Howard Rechel recalled an instance when a line got wrapped around the propeller. A couple of men having tried and failed to disentangle it, Rechel said, Burton dove in himself and worked it free.[25]

Before the convoy sailed, Burton and Loughman got a flat tire while crossing the Bay Bridge from Oakland to San Francisco in Loughman's Oldsmobile sedan. "And I remember he hopped out—he had on his blues, I think, at that time—he hopped out of the car, he took his jacket off and just turned right to, changing the tire, and we had it done in short order," Loughman recalled. "So he was really a very down-to-earth individual. He wasn't at all stuffy."[26]

Almost certainly among the divers who did participate in the Lucky Lager retrieval was the aptly named John Robert Stout, a ship's fitter 2/c from Inglewood, California. In Bob Jacobsen's estimation, Stout was probably in the best physical shape of anyone on the crew. His intestinal lining may have matched or even exceeded the rest of him in that regard, or it may have been in tatters, for Stout was known to eat glass, in light bulb form at least, and reportedly that of at least one whiskey glass as well. Dave Wallington and Howard Rechel both spoke of seeing him unscrew a bulb from a ceiling fixture in the crew's mess and eat at least part of it. He was not gluttonous about it—he took small bites, Wallington said, and left some of the bulb uneaten. Rechel said Stout would engage in this activity while waiting in the chow line. He emphasized that Stout actually swallowed the glass. He said he saw him do this once or twice.[27]

Bob Jacobsen, who was of a skeptical bent, never witnessed this phenom-enon, but he did not discount his shipmates' accounts of it. "Stout was a very good man," he wrote. "Was always ready to take a dare or a gamble—but he had a good IQ. I never heard of the lite bulb incident—but heard he ate a wine glass in a bar in Oakland on a big bet." Bob Gonnoud also heard stories of a diver, one he didn't know by name, eating a whiskey glass. Presumably this too was Stout.[28]

Seaman 2/c Jack Vangets of Elwood, Indiana, ran afoul of the navy's criminal justice system one morning at Funafuti when he failed to respond promptly to the call to get out of bed. The man who issued that call (probably Chief Torpedoman Rush Alfred Parks, the master-at-arms) underscored it, Vangets recalled, by smacking the chains that supported his bunk with a billy club. Vangets took exception to this battery. As he explained about sixty years later, "I didn't wake up too good."

"At that time I didn't take too much offa anybody. . . . I was half asleep . . . I jumped up and grabbed him. . . . We scuffled around a little bit."

At a captain's mast on November 1, Burton sentenced Vangets to two days in the anchor chain storeroom that passed on the *Macaw* for a brig. That was letting him off easy. Per naval law, striking a superior officer was potentially a capital offense. The master-at-arms was an enlisted man, not an officer, but he served much in the capacity of a police officer, so given the awful response the navy allowed itself to that general sort of transgression, Vangets might have expected punishment harsher than two days in the brig. But the capacity to inflict harsh punishment—something of which Paul Burton had had firsthand experience—was not in Burton's nature. Vangets said he was supposed to be on the prisoner's traditional diet of bread and water, but Ship's Cook 1/c Dean Fred-erick Jewell of Eugene, Oregon, sliced the heel off a loaf of bread destined for the miscreant and stuffed it full of meat, and sympathizers scrubbing down the deck outside supplied him with orange juice through a port hole. William Funk, the pharmacist's mate, weighed him before and after his incarceration, Vangets said, compared the two figures, and said, "I can't believe you gained weight!"[29]

On November 12, the day before the *Macaw* left Funafuti, Vangets's life-long friend and fellow Elwood resident Eugene Van Buskirk got into trouble of another sort when he, Vangets, and Seaman 1/c Joseph Verkennes of Flint, Michigan, were playing king of the raft, struggling for dominion over a homemade raft just off the beach. (Dave Wallington may also have been a participant.) Van Buskirk had just staked his claim to the little floating king-dom, planting his left foot, or inadvertently dangling it, in one of the gaps between the two-by-fours that comprised its upper surface when one or more of his rivals mounted a challenge in the form of a charge that broke his leg. "My foot slipped down between two two-by-fours," he said. "About that time Verkennes took a flying tackle at me. . . . I went one way, he went the other, and my foot stayed put. . . . He wanted to be king."[30]

Vangets recalled that he and Wallington made the assault. Whoever did the deed, it fractured Van Buskirk's left fibula. It snapped, he recalled, like a board. He had the leg set on a larger ship with better medical facilities, probably the USS *Sumner* (AG-32), a survey ship, then reboarded the *Macaw* before it sailed the next day, his leg in a cast, which many of his crewmates, of course, proceeded to sign.

By the time the *Macaw* left Funafuti, it had probably received word that on November 2, one of the prefabricated sections of ABSD-1, the floating dry dock it had escorted eight sections of to Espiritu Santo, had sunk there. Thirteen members of its crew had drowned.

The *Macaw* got a lively sendoff from Funafuti courtesy of the Japanese, six of whose bombers arrived over the island just after midnight the day the *Macaw* headed out, and proceeded to drop about thirty bombs in the course of two high-altitude bombing runs. Bob Gonnoud's battle station was one of the two searchlight platforms, where his job was to operate the light, but in the interest of keeping ships from making visible targets of themselves, the harbormaster had prohibited the use of either guns or lights that night, so there was little either Gonnoud or anyone else on the ship could do but watch the attack and hope not to get hit in it. According to Gonnoud, the *Macaw* almost did get hit. He said bombs fell about two hundred feet to either side of the ship, maybe three per side. Eugene Van Buskirk recalled seeing a Japanese bomb hit an ammunition depot at Funafuti. "It looked like fifteen Fourth of Julys," he said. Two Americans were wounded in the raid. The *Macaw* was unscathed.[31]

There was talk at Funafuti of the *Macaw* towing an ammunition barge to Tarawa. About a dozen of its crew, including Motor Machinist's Mate Richard Blaine Williamson, originally of Beaver, Oklahoma, reportedly volunteered to go ashore at Tarawa. Issued rifles and helmets, they conducted bayonet practice on a sea bag strung up toward the stern, to the amusement of cheering shipmates, according to Howard Rechel. But the order to go to Tarawa either never came or got rescinded. Tarawa lies northwest of Funafuti. When the *Macaw* left Funafuti one week before the invasion of Tarawa, it set a course northeast, for Pearl Harbor.[32]

7

The Loneliness of the Long-Distance Runner

The Battle of Tarawa, in which 1,700 Americans and more than 4,000 Japanese soldiers and Korean forced laborers died in three days of fighting on an islet about the size of fifty city blocks, took place during the *Macaw*'s ten-day passage from Funafuti to Pearl Harbor, not far, by Pacific Ocean standards, from the path the ship followed on that trip. Life aboard the *Macaw*, meanwhile, proceeded peacefully enough. A submarine scare may have provided the only excitement en route. During it, Paul Burton reportedly strapped on a .45-caliber automatic, climbed to the crow's nest with a pair of binoculars, and spent what Bob Gonnoud recalled as a whole day hunting the Japanese sub whose destruction he hoped would pave his way back into an American one.[1]

The Japanese sub, if there was one, eluded him. In seeking it, the *Macaw* apparently deviated somewhat from its prescribed course. The Navy frowned on unauthorized detours—the more so, it seems safe to say, the less a commander had to show for one afterward. Having nothing to show for his, Burton, according to Gonnoud, ordered fudging of the ship's records to conceal it. This, Gonnoud said, occasioned an argument with Bud Loughman, the executive officer—"kind of straight-laced," in Gonnoud's words, "a good Catholic boy"—who was largely responsible for the ship's record keeping and apparently more squeamish than Burton himself about falsifying it. The argument, Gonnoud said, did not last long. Burton won it. As Gonnoud noted, he was the captain.[2]

The *Macaw* was even more crowded than usual on the way to Hawaii due to a complement of thirteen passengers from the survey ship USS *Sumner* (AG-32), and no doubt just as boring as ever. But if boredom remained a problem on the *Macaw,* one sailor did his part not just to alleviate it but to uplift the cultural tone aboard the ship in the process. Radarman Stephen Miller, son of a prominent attorney in Norman, Oklahoma, stood watches, like Bob Gonnoud, on one of the two searchlight platforms, in Miller's case the forward one, a steel disk about six feet across that hung on the fore side of the foremast about ten feet above the flying bridge (i.e., the roof of the pilot-house), overlooking the forward third or so of the ship. Encircled to about waist level by a steel shield, the forward searchlight platform might have stood in nicely for Juliet's balcony or the rampart at Elsinore but for the searchlight itself with its twenty-four-inch lens standing six feet tall in the middle of it; and Miller, who seems to have had a theatrical streak and an irrepressible devotion to the work of a certain Elizabethan playwright, made it his stage, strutting and fretting parts of his four-hour stretches upon it and reciting Shakespeare. If his goal in these declamations was to raise the literary consciousness of his shipmates, he apparently did not achieve it. According to Gonnoud, the other men were not greatly appreciative. Miller "was just a screwball," he said. "They just figured he was nuts."[3]

In the evenings off-duty enlisted men continued to congregate on the fantail and shoot the breeze. "What did the guys talk about in the B.S. sessions, scuttle butt and 'social time': Women, girls, sex," Bob Jacobsen recalled. "Sexual exploits and hopes & dreams. Sports, sports, sports, food, brands of beer, bars, hookers, hunting & Fishing. Jobs, travel. When the wars over: All knew we would go back into the depression—The consensus was to get a job with a utility: Water, gas, electric big oil company, Post office or a State, County or City job. Maybe go to College if Congress passed the new GI Bill they were talking about."[4]

Another staple of conversation there was the state of Paul Burton's marriage. Rumor had it where his ship was soon to be, on the rocks, and rumor, it seems, was right. The source of the rumor might have been Shipfitter Lloyd George Fox. Fox handled the mail aboard the *Macaw* and took at some point to opening Paul Burton's mail and reading it. Among the letters he read was one from Burton's wife requesting a divorce. Burton, according to Bud Loughman, had struck up an acquaintance with a navy nurse, and word of the affair had somehow gotten back to his wife, Betty, in New Jersey.[5]

The captain of any ship is apt to be the subject of shipboard gossip. Paul Burton, given his personality, his recent history, and perhaps the violation of his privacy, offered plenty of grist for the mill. Bob Jacobsen heard the rumors. If they cast Burton in a less than favorable light, so did Jacobsen in his recollections long after the war. (An AKA was an armed cargo vessel designed to carry troops and heavy equipment and provide gunfire in support of amphibious assaults.)

> Scuttlebutt—Rumor? Burtons marriage was on the rocks. Burton a qualified submarine officer had been kicked out of submarines for psychological reasons?
>
> Most ships every friday you had "field day" Clean the ship. Saturday the capt tours the ship and inspects it. In all my time on the Macaw we never had one personnel or lower deck Inspection— Other ships I was on the Captain would informally roam around the ship. The AKA I was on he would come in the shop set on the work bench and have a cup of coffee and shoot the breeze.
>
> Burton never left the bridge—Seemed to be there 24 hours a day. When on watch we talked on our phones—The bridge talker would say the Captain is napping in the chart room or is in his chair on the wing of the bridge. Your Dad [Bud Loughman], Lt. Smith and I don't recall the other officer stood all the watches 4 on 8 off while at sea. The Captain did not stand a watch but was always on the bridge. Never roamed the ship. Never came down to eat in the crews mess— not once.
>
> Rumors? Didn't trust his officers? A Captain Queeg?[6]

Lt. Cmdr. Philip Francis Queeg was the captain of the USS *Caine*, the destroyer featured in Herman Wouk's 1951 novel *The Caine Mutiny*, and the movie, starring Humphrey Bogart, based on it and released three years later. The comparison is not flattering. Nor is it entirely fair. Queeg is petty, pompous, abusive, overbearing, racist, and petulant. Burton was none of those things. Burton had his faults and may have even shared a few with the fictitious or not-so-fictitious neurotic forcibly relieved of his command by his executive officer in Wouk's novel, but if he did share any unlovely traits with Queeg, Burton was a lot less egregious about them. Queeg is sneeringly disdainful of pretty much everyone. Burton could be condescending. He did not repose a great deal of confidence in Bud Loughman in particular, but he apparently had the decency to confine his disparaging remarks about him to an audience of one, his wife. He was not the hale-fellow-well-met type, but he was not as aloof as Jacobsen makes him out to have been. It's not true that he never left the bridge or interacted with the enlisted men. There are at least two photographs of Burton on the main deck, one a group shot with officers and enlisted men, in both of which he looks very much like just another very casually attired sailor. The fact that his casual attire, consisting entirely of a pair of shorts, is the same in both photos suggests they were taken on the same occasion, so all they prove is that he left the bridge at least once. In fact, it may have been the very rarity of the event that inspired someone to record it with a camera. But the man they show emphatically does not fit the profile of a sneering elitist.

Paul Burton was almost certainly depressed the whole time he was aboard the *Macaw*. His career and his marriage had both foundered. The closest thing to friendship he experienced aboard the *Macaw* may have been the rapport he established over a chessboard with Herman Ehlers, an enlisted man, the quartermaster and bank manager from Illinois; and as much as they may both have relished their games, it seems unlikely, given Burton's personality, that they would have managed in the course of them to bridge the gulf between officer and enlisted status—a yawning divide at the time—sufficiently to afford Burton much in the way of emotional support.

Burton, as noted before, had run cross-country and track, and he seems to have embodied perfectly the loneliness of the long-distance runner. It may be a measure of his loneliness during his time aboard the *Macaw* that the one person to whom he seems to have vented his frustrations then was his wife—this at about the time, maybe after it, that she wrote to him demanding a divorce. He had a light, lenient touch with authority, and most of his men (Bob Jacobsen being a notable exception) seem to have liked him—to have seen him as a basically good-hearted, troubled loner, at once distant and down-to-earth, firm enough when he had to be but never overbearing, less than masterful in his seamanship, usually mild-mannered, occasionally humorous, and pretty much always sad.

To Robert Gonnoud, Burton was "kind of screwy but very nice." Howard Rechel said of Burton, "From his actions and everything, he was very low-key. Nothing seemed to bother him." Nor, he added, did Burton ever bother his crew.[7]

Seaman Joseph Throgmorton spent a good deal of time with Burton during night watches on the bridge, drinking strong coffee and talking, and for all their talking, he said, Burton "was sort of hard to know, a little bit distant."[8]

But there was no mistaking certain things about Paul Burton. If (as Bob Jacobsen noted) he was no Captain Cook, neither was he a Captain Bligh. While the *Macaw* was being "fitted out," before the commissioning, some of the crew spent about two months living in barracks in Alameda, just across the Oakland Estuary from Moore Dry Dock. Gunner's Mate 3/c Ralph Enzweiler was among them. One night he came back from liberty drunk and took a swing at a marine guard. "He laid his billy alongside o' my head," Enzweiler recalled, "an' I woke up in a brig." The matter was referred to Burton. A conversation between captain and offender ensued. Burton noted that Enzweiler had gotten pretty drunk the night before and told him, as Enzweiler recalled it sixty-six years later, "I gotta restrict you to the ship—you're restricted until 12 noon." That was when Enzweiler's next liberty was already scheduled to begin. He couldn't have gotten off the ship before that anyway.[9]

In *The Caine Mutiny,* in response to the theft aboard the ship of about a quart of strawberries, Captain Queeg conducts a preposterously elaborate criminal investigation, including strip searches, in pursuit of a duplicate key he's convinced someone used to break into the wardroom icebox. According to Eugene Van Buskirk, somewhere in the South Pacific Paul Burton hung "a big ol' stalk of bananas" in one of the ship's storerooms in a manner calculated to discourage theft. "You could see 'em," Van Buskirk said, "but you couldn't get to 'em." Not with great ease, anyhow. But Van Buskirk and one or more partners in crime found a way. "We hadn't seen a banana in so long," he said. "We was kind of leery" about pilfering them, but their hunger overcame their qualms. They ate them all, he said, and Paul Burton never said a word about it.[10]

The *Macaw* docked at the submarine base at Pearl Harbor, at berth S-15 portside to Pier No. 5 at the northeast end of Magazine Loch, about 0945 on Monday, November 22, 1943. Arrival there meant news from home, among lots of other things, and as much as sailors and soldiers have always relished getting mail, the news for a group of more than a hundred men could not all be good. Some of the bad news came in the form of Dear John letters. Bob Jacobsen would get one from Colleen, his girlfriend in Oakland, the young woman whose parents had not let her go to the commissioning party. Dave Wallington got one from his girlfriend back in Michigan. Motor Machinist's Mate Donald Whitmarsh of upstate New York got one from his fiancée. Seaman Myron Froehlich got one, or got the oral equivalent of one, by way of a third party, from his wife. Radio technician Harold Hayes of Decatur, Illinois, might have gotten one from his wife if she was thoughtful enough to send him one when she left with their baby daughter for Portland, Oregon, and a new life with another man, with whom she had, as Hayes put it almost seventy years later, gotten "acquainted."[11]

The news of his fiancée's reconsidering came as a terrible blow to Whitmarsh, a quiet, competent man, well liked by his shipmates and somewhat straitlaced. He and fellow Motor Machinist's Mate Quinton Studer used to hang out on the fantail in their free time and talk. According to Studer, Whitmarsh was not one to discuss personal matters but made an exception for his Dear John letter. "Definitely, definitely," Studer said, "he was really despondent over that letter."[12]

Not every Dear John took his rejection that hard. Lots of guys would get Dear John letters and be distraught, Dave Wallington said, but, happily married more than sixty-five years later, he couldn't remember whether he'd been one of them when he got the news from his girlfriend, Irene, back in Flint that she'd married a 4-F and moved to California. "I was probably all broken up," he said, "but life goes on."[13]

Myron Froehlich emphatically did not take his news hard. One of about a dozen sailors who joined the *Macaw* at Pearl Harbor, Froehlich was summoned there to a chaplain, who informed him, no doubt as delicately as he could, that his wife and former high school sweetheart, Mary Lou, had met a soldier and wanted a divorce. If the chaplain was worried about having to console a sobbing wretch, he was probably relieved to find that Froehlich took the news entirely in stride. He had suspected all along, he said sixty years later, that his wife's mother, only fifteen years older than her daughter, had been the real driving force behind their marriage, that she had taken more of a shine to him than her daughter had, and that she had pushed the two pliable teenagers into matrimony thinking, regarding the groom, something like better son-in-law than stranger. The demise of his marriage left him unfazed. "I figured," he said, "if she don't want me, I sure as hell don't want her."[14]

Radioman 2/c Stanley Libera of Russell, New York, was another newcomer to the *Macaw* at Pearl Harbor, and for Libera the *Macaw's* appearance there meant a different and happier if even shorter-lived sort of romance. For Libera, it was love at first sight. Two war patrols amid the fetid confines of the submarine USS *Sargo* had left him with a condition that required him to sit for what he recalled as an hour a day in a tub containing a blue solution in the hospital at Pearl Harbor. Sidelined by this malady, he missed the boat, literally, and his friends aboard it, when the *Sargo* went on patrol again that October.

Libera loved submarining despite its dangers and hardships. A World War II sub, he said, was like "a bottle with a cork plugged in it." After a war patrol, "you're white as a ghost in all your pores. It's like being in a dungeon." The air got foul. You got "all kind of sicknesses." Or you might get killed—submariners had one of the military's highest casualty rates in the war. But you got friends too. Submarines were noted as much for camaraderie as for danger and stale air. There were personality conflicts, of course (as Paul Burton could have attested), but former submariners frequently invoke the word "family" in reference to their crewmates, and for most of them, the bonds of fraternity and the prestige of being in the "secret service" outweighed the drawbacks. The *Sargo*'s departure without him left Libera as blue as the solution he had to sit in at the hospital. But the sight of the *Macaw* dispelled his disappointment entirely. He thought she was beautiful. "When I saw that ship in the harbor," he said, "that ship hit me. I said, 'I gotta get on that goddamn ship.'"[15]

That did not prove hard to do. Ten enlisted men transferred permanently off the *Macaw* at Pearl Harbor, to the hospital or other assignments, leaving it in need of a radio operator. Libera approached the ship at dockside and asked to see the officer in charge. He was directed to Burton. "He looked at me," Libera recalled, "and said, 'You look okay.'" There was more to it than that, but not much more. Libera's service records looked okay too. Burton shook his hand and welcomed him aboard. "Beautiful ship," Libera was still saying seventy-two years later. "Wonderful captain."[16]

That fall was not Libera's first time at Pearl Harbor. Like his *Macaw* shipmate Ralph Mennemeyer, he had been aboard a battleship there on the morning of December 7, 1941. Mennemeyer had been on the USS *California* (BB-44). Libera was on the USS *Tennessee* (BB-43). The night before, Libera had been on the fantail taking in a different sort of battle, one between the bands of the *Tennessee,* the USS *West Virginia* (BB-48), moored abreast of the *Tennessee,* and the USS *Arizona* (BB-39), moored just aft of it. The *Arizona*'s band had set up on its bow, the others on their fantails, all within a short stone's throw of one another, and they were taking turns playing mainly what Libera recalled as standard, patriotic naval fare while the other enlisted men on hand boisterously cheered on their shipmates and disparaged the competition. That evening's benign raillery might have constituted the last conversation some of the men on the bow of the *Arizona* ever had. The next morning's raid claimed the lives of almost 1,200 of the *Arizona*'s crew.[17]

When the Japanese planes arrived just before 0800 that Sunday morning, Libera reported to his battle station on the *Tennessee* and began loading powder for the No. 2 gun turret two or three decks above. That task was promptly rendered moot when a bomb from a plane in the first wave hit the turret and knocked out its guns. According to Libera, it was a piece of the steel plating protecting that turret, shattered in the bomb blast, that flew across to the bridge of the *West Virginia* and struck its commander, Capt. Mervyn S. Bennion of Vernon, Utah, in the abdomen. Bennion, using one hand to hold his intestines in place, kept giving orders and resisted efforts by crewmen to remove him to a first-aid station. He died soon after they finally got him to one. He was posthumously awarded the Medal of Honor.

Libera spent much of the rest of that morning amid the smoke and confusion on the afterdeck untangling the fire hoses used in the largely successful struggle to keep the flames ravaging the *Arizona* from spreading to the *Tennessee*. After the attack, bodies kept bobbing up from the *Arizona*. Four or five days later, while walking to chow by the chain railing along the edge of the *Tennessee*'s deck, he saw a white, cooked corpse bobbing in the water with its guts spilling out. It was not an appetizing sight. "Pearl Harbor," he said, "that was a hellhole."[18]

In the fall of 1943, Pearl Harbor cannot have been a very pleasant place for Paul Burton either. The *Macaw*, being a part of the submarine service, was instructed upon its arrival there to dock at the sub base and temporarily assigned to Submarine Squadron 4. That was the *Tarpon*'s squadron. The *Tarpon* was there. It was one of a number of subs undergoing refits there at the time. The sight of any submarine had to be painful for Burton. At Pearl Harbor he was surrounded by about two dozen, his former boat among them.[19]

But as bad as things must have been for Burton at Pearl Harbor, they probably could have been worse. After five war patrols aboard the *Tarpon*, Tom Wogan was detached from it three days before the *Macaw* arrived and assigned to command a new boat, the USS *Besugo* (SS-321), under construction at Electric Boat in Connecticut. Things moving as fast for naval officers as they did during the war, it seems unlikely that, by the time the *Macaw* got to Pearl Harbor, Tom Wogan would still have been there. So Burton was probably spared an encounter with him and probably did not find himself compelled to congratulate him on the *Tarpon*'s successful, just-concluded ninth patrol.[20]

Another of the *Macaw*'s neighbors at Pearl Harbor, docked next door in berth S-16, was its sister ship USS *Florikan* (ASR-9). While the *Macaw* was making its way to and about the South Pacific, the *Florikan* had gone to Alaska and sent seven divers into what remained of Imperial Japanese submarine *I-7*, scuttled but only half-demolished after a fatal encounter with the destroyer USS *Monaghan* (DD-354) off Kiska Island in the Aleutians in June 1943.

That was under the *Florikan*'s first captain, Lt. Cmdr. Neill K. Banks, USNR. Having set out on that assignment from Midway, the *Florikan* returned to it on October 9, 1943, and two days later had a new CO, Cmdr. George A. Sharp. It was Sharp who had commanded the ASR USS *Falcon* during the *Squalus* rescue four years before, and he was soon to command the *Florikan* through its troubled passage from Midway back to Pearl Harbor with the stricken *Flier* in tow (and, briefly, at large). Being captains of sister ships and temporary next-door neighbors, George Sharp and Paul Burton probably conversed at least once during the five weeks they were both at Pearl Harbor. There was a lot they might have talked about and a lot they might both have preferred not to talk about. As noted previously, they had both been black-balled out of submarines.

Sharp, a native of East Hartford, Connecticut, had descended a little farther in his fall from grace, having started it a notch higher. After the *Falcon*, he was given command of the submarine *Spearfish* (SS-190). He presided over that boat's seventh war patrol, during which it crossed paths with a Japanese convoy of about a dozen ships including, by Sharp's count, no fewer than three aircraft carriers and what appeared to be a battleship. To see that many capital targets through a periscope at one time was to behold a vision of which most sub skippers could only dream. For Sharp and his men, the dream turned abruptly sour. They botched their approach, fired four torpedoes, and hit nothing.

Vice Admiral Lockwood was harsh in his assessment of the *Spearfish*'s performance. "An opportunity to inflict irreparable damage upon the enemy was missed when the ship's fire control party failed to function properly," he wrote. "Steps will be taken to correct the deficiencies shown in this and other attacks." Among the steps taken was the replacement of the commanding officer. Sharp was reassigned to the *Florikan*. Like fellow Naval Academy graduate Paul Burton, he had been tried in submarine warfare and found wanting. They had both been downgraded by their naval fraternity and retained in a sort of janitorial role. They were rejects.[21]

The *Macaw* spent six weeks at Pearl Harbor, the *Florikan* on that visit about eight, much of it in both cases in submarine target practice, in which they stood in for Japanese ships and then retrieved the dummy torpedoes that subs would fire under them in an exercise zone just out to sea. In lieu of explosives, the head of a practice torpedo contained ballast in the form of water. At the end of its run, the water was expelled by means of compressed air, rendering the weapon buoyant and causing it to bob up to the surface amid a stain of dye released along with the ballast water to facilitate retrieval. At that point the *Macaw* would work its way to within twenty yards or so of a floating "fish" that had, in theory, just destroyed it, someone (probably Curtis Wainscott or Edward Wade, or perhaps both of them) would jump in, swim to it, and pass a line through an eye on the head of the device, and the ship would reel it in with its boom.[22]

If someone had wanted to devise an exercise to impress upon the crews of auxiliary vessels the subservient nature of the role they played in the submarine service, it would have been hard to come up with anything more effective than torpedo practice. A support craft—typically a submarine rescue vessel, minesweeper, tugboat, or Coast Guard vessel—was targeted for near misses, not unlike an assistant in a knife-throwing act, then tasked with retrieving the spent, unarmed weapon like a hunting dog retrieving an arrow. Paul Burton—perhaps by chance, perhaps through the merciful intervention of someone (possibly Tom Wogan himself) who knew of his history with the *Tarpon*—was spared the indignity of rendering these services to his old boat at Pearl Harbor. The *Macaw* rendered them there to other subs, and the *Tarpon* drew on them there from other auxiliaries, but they did not conduct this practice together. The *Tarpon,* under the command of Wogan's successor, Thomas Benjamin Oakley, left Pearl Harbor on its tenth war patrol on December 4.

The *Macaw* continued its career of navigational misadventures at Pearl Harbor. By various accounts, it collided with a fishing boat, almost ran down a seaplane off Ford Island, and managed to wedge itself sideways inside a slip it was trying to back out of, like a car turned 90 degrees to a narrow driveway—this last reportedly under the supervision of Bud Loughman and to the great amusement of onlookers onshore. Evidently Paul Burton did not share their amusement. "Poor old Burton was just about ready to jump overboard," Bob Gonnoud said. "People on the dock were busting their sides laughing."[23]

A major factor in the ship's troubles that way may have been the departure on November 29 of Warden Wingrove, the quartermaster and skilled navigator from East Bethlehem, Pennsylvania. About twenty men left the *Macaw* at Pearl Harbor, some only briefly, some for good, and a like number joined or rejoined the ship there. Most of the permanent departures were reposted within the submarine service. Wingrove went to the *Sargo*, Stanley Libera's old boat. Eugene Van Buskirk, having a broken leg, went to the hospital. So did three other enlisted men and Melvin Cottrell, a widely esteemed warrant bosun—"a nice pleasant guy," Bob Jacobsen recalled. "Always a good word." Cottrell had been diagnosed with a bleeding ulcer.[24]

One of the new arrivals came conspicuously battle-ready. "When we got to Pearl we lost several of our crew—guys to Sub duty—others to the hospital," Jacobsen wrote. "So we got replacements. One new guy I can't remember his name. He use to go down the deck a bobbing & weaving and shadow boxing. He claimed he was a professional boxer. We all felt he was a little punchy—a ding bat."[25]

He wasn't the only boxer aboard. Seaman 1/c Albert Bolke, the formerly malnourished Chicagoan, got enough calories from navy chow to burn some in the ring—there was organized boxing in the navy—but he was apparently less ostentatious about it.

Among the many attractions of Honolulu were the bars. Getting into them was a problem for the younger men, but not an insurmountable one. The drinking age in Hawaii was twenty-one. Sonarman Clyde Isbell, seventeen at the time, had a phony ID and never had any trouble using it there. Bob Jacobsen enjoyed rum-and-Cokes at the Black Cat Café, a popular wartime watering hole, but the real draws for him in Hawaii were movie theaters, ice cream counters, and the branch library at Waikiki. For others of a less literary bent the primary attraction of Waikiki was the beach and the presence on it of women in bathing suits. In town you could get a tattoo. Seaman Bert Maas got one—almost sixty years later his friend Dave Wallington recalled seeing it "bleeding like crazy" through Maas's white uniform.[26]

The *Macaw*'s stay at Pearl Harbor neatly bracketed the holidays—the ship arrived a few days before Thanksgiving and left a few days after New Year's Day. Perhaps in lieu of a traditional Thanksgiving dinner, the enlisted men had a picnic there at a beachside recreation area (or two picnics, one for each of two halves of the crew). They ate barbecued beef, baked beans, and garlic bread and drank from quart bottles of Lucky Lager—"The residue of our Funa Futi salvage"—and Augie Paul Koepke, typically, drank more of it than he could handle. There was a tub of ice water on hand for chilling the beer, and Koepke ended up in it. Apparently his shipmates placed him there to revive him after he passed out lying on his side on a picnic table bench with his left hand still clutching the top of one of those bottles.[27]

Probably no one on the *Macaw* had less interest in the typical sailor's traditional Hawaiian pursuits than Seaman 1/c Lyle Webb. What Pearl Harbor and Honolulu seem to have represented for Webb were lucrative business opportunities, and he seems to have been typically zealous in exploiting them. Pearl Harbor gave him access not only to whatever merchandise he needed to replenish his depleted stocks of retail goods, but wide scope for dubious business practices better suited to a shore facility with a large and transient population than to a little ship at sea. Bob Jacobsen describes an enterprise Webb may have dabbled in aboard the *Macaw*, but one the rewards of which would have been too modest in a small floating theater of operations, and the risks too great. It needed a large and credulous client pool constantly refreshed by turnover. It was a series of sham raffles, as Jacobsen describes it, and Pearl Harbor was perfect for it. "Webb claimed his diamond ring was worth a $1000 bucks — He sold a thousand chances at a buck a piece," Jacobsen wrote. "Webb had it rigged, the winner was always some seaman on the Sub base. Webb would pay the 'Winner' $150 or $200 dollars— then sell chances on the ring again. He had all the Sub Base, Navy yard, receiving station, Marine Barracks & all the ships coming & going."[28]

Having survived its friendly-fire scare off Panama, the USS *Flier* arrived at Pearl Harbor on December 20, 1943, and spent a little more than three weeks there preparing for what was supposed to be its first war patrol. For all but the final four days of that stay the *Flier* and the *Macaw* were docked in close proximity at the sub basin. They would soon be near neighbors again.

Paul Burton wrote his wife a letter dated December 22, 1943. Given the troubled state of Burton's marriage, the letter is as remarkable for what it does not say as for what it does. Much of what it does say, after some grousing about striking workers and other noncombatants back in the States, concerns his executive officer. ("Windy" was Lt. [jg] Worth Windle of Mooresville, North Carolina, the navigation officer.)

> I said I'd tell you about Bud. Poor feller is so utterly out of his element in the Navy that it's pitiful. He spends so much time on things

that should only take a few minutes. On our long slow trip in September I let him mostly alone, as our job was naturally to stay with those we were protecting. And as *they* had to know where *they* were, he had over a month to iron out navigation. Well, when we got on our own and he couldn't get the picture I *had* to do my own on the side and would often get pretty exasperated with him. He just doesn't realise we play for keeps now. On our easy days operating here he can handle everything reasonably well, but when the operations are the slightest bit complicated he *can't think on his own.* He can't apply little thumb rules such as the hypotenuse being twice the small side of a 30, 60, 90 triangle; and the fact that for every 3 knots of speed you cover 100 yards per minute. Little things I (and all those I've been with) can do in my head he can't even *start* to do on paper. It's just lack of training—not being geared to *think* at sea. But now the navigation is on Windy's shoulders, and Bud can do a good job with personnel—when he concentrates on it. He's remarked several times in wonderment (unless it's just bluff for sake of flattery) that he doesn't see how I can stay up on my feet for 36 hours. Well, there again I've never been with anyone who couldn't. It's just that civilian idea that you quit after working hours.

After expanding his critique to various other officers and mixing in some praise, even a little for Bud Loughman, he closes on a note of resolve and affection. ("Mel" was Warrant Bosun Melvin Cottrell.)

I'm trying my damnedest not to have a sour disposition—I know it's not as sunny as it used to be. But the best I can do the minute the bawling out is over (for giving full right rudder instead of left, or for forgetting one important step in a maneuver which is based on several details in exact and well-timed sequence) is to pat the guilty one on the back, laugh it off, and tell him he'll get there yet. You see it's not like it used to be—teaching young squirts; it's a case now of beating older dogs into entirely new (to them) tricks. My one principle is that the MACAW will never "request instructions" nor fail to do an assigned task *and on time.* Often it has been something none of us had ever done. All during October and up until your birthday it was Mel's perseverance which kept our flag flying. Since then it has become more and more *my* efforts. I was the only one on board who had the vaguest idea of what our job was and how to do it. Now all hands are pretty well broken in (or down!). But at times I've been a whirling dervish and a furious one at that. But we've kept our "honor" and have *never failed.* Sometimes the lads have been fit to kill me— but I know there are no grudges. They'll get the idea someday: I'll punish *ourselves* to the limit, but our heads will always be high. I love you so—and know my crankiness is a great deal due to my hungry yearning to be home again. Lots and lots of love from Paul.

Lt. Comdr P.W. Burton, USN,
USS MACAW
c/o Flt. P.O., 'Frisco

December, of course, brought Christmas. Christmas dinner was served on the ship: cream of turkey soup with "crisp crackers," stuffed tom turkey, spiced ham, cranberry sauce, stuffed olives, mashed potatoes and gravy, candied sweet potatoes, green peas, buttered asparagus, pumpkin pie, fruitcake, ice cream, and coffee. On the way out of the mess the men were handed bags of nuts and candy. After dinner Bob Jacobsen, Seamen Toby Hannah and Jack Cunniff, and Sonarman Nathan Turner went to the Block Recreation Center, drank beer, and bowled. It may not have been all that merry a Christmas for Jacobsen. The day before, his friend Seaman 1/c Charles "Chuck" Pierson of Pasadena, California, had been reassigned to Submarine Division 45.[29]

Within a week and a half the *Macaw* had been reassigned too, to Midway. Eugene Van Buskirk was still in the hospital recuperating from the leg fracture he had suffered at Funafuti when he heard of the ship's impending departure. He was still on the ship's roster as of that December 31. So were his friends Dave Wallington and Jack Vangets. Van Buskirk's leg had not fully mended, but he did not want his friends or his ship to leave him behind. "I told 'em in the hospital, 'I believe I can make it how it is.'" And, he said, to prove the point, "I walked on it like it wasn't hurting, but it was about to kill me." His sham nonchalance worked—he got discharged, only to find that the sailing date he'd been told of was a day off. The *Macaw* had sailed the day before.[30]

Midway Atoll, ca. 1942–1943. View is from the southwest. Sand Island is in the foreground, Eastern Island in the background. Brooks Channel runs due north and south between them. (USN photo courtesy NARA)

The *Macaw* and *Flier* on the reef, January 16, 1944. View is from the west, from a vessel at the entrance to Brooks Channel. The vessel in the distance on the right is unidentified. (USN photo courtesy NARA)

The *Macaw* and *Flier,* January 17, 1944. View is from the east. John Crowley managed, after first hitting the reef, to swing the *Flier* about to head into the waves. The *Macaw* came to rest more conventionally bow first. Sand Island is visible in the background. (USN photo courtesy NARA)

Paul Burton. (USN photo
courtesy Bud Loughman)

Paul Burton (*right*), age two and a half, with his mother; brother, Thomas; and an
unidentified companion in Manila, 1914. Virginia Willits Burton and her sons traveled
at least twice to the Far East to live with or visit her husband, a career Marine Corps
officer posted overseas nine times from 1899 to 1928. Paul attended the Peking American School in the Chinese capital ca. 1923–1925. (Photo courtesy Traci Burton)

Paul Burton (*right*), with his brother and father, Norman G. Burton, on the Great Wall of China, October 7, 1923. (Photo courtesy Traci Burton)

Paul Burton and his future wife, Elizabeth Porter Watson, ca. 1929. Burton lettered in track at the Haverford School, a prep school outside Philadelphia. (Photo courtesy Traci Burton)

The *Macaw* "in the ways" at Moore Dry Dock in Oakland, California, July 12, 1942. Behind the *Macaw* is its sister ship *Greenlet*. Both were launched that day. (USN photo courtesy NARA)

Jack Vangets with his sister Jeannie and niece Nancy, Elwood, Indiana, ca. 1944. (Photo courtesy Tami Paddock)

Paul Burton (*front row, right*) and company (including Joseph Verkennes, directly behind him) in front of the McCann rescue chamber. Sartorial standards aboard the *Macaw* were less than rigid. (USN photo courtesy Bud Loughman)

Bud Loughman (*front row, center*) with the Navigation Gang, or part of it. *Front row, left to right:* [Nathan Turner], Bud Loughman, Warden Wingrove; *back row:* [Dwight Harvey], Robert Gonnoud, Frank Zuroweste, Herman Ehlers, Clyde Isbell. (Brackets indicate uncertain ID.) (USN photo courtesy Bud Loughman)

Albert Bolke. (Photo courtesy the Bolke family)

Bud Loughman kissing the Royal Baby's belly, September 15, 1943. (USN photo courtesy Bud Loughman)

Robert Vaughn at the equator-crossing festivities. (USN photo courtesy Bud Loughman)

Herman Ehlers appears twice in this double exposure featuring fellow "Nav Gangers" displaying what purports to be a captured Japanese battle flag in the pilothouse. The war is said to have sparked a brisk trade in fake souvenirs. The doorway in the background is the one through which the men trapped in the pilothouse departed it on the morning of February 13, 1944. (USN photo courtesy Bud Loughman)

Left to right: Jack Vangets, Eugene Van Buskirk, and Dave Wallington. Vangets and Van Buskirk grew up together in Elwood, Indiana. They met Wallington after the bus delivering him to the destroyer he'd been assigned to arrived late at Mare Island. The destroyer left without him, and Wallington was reassigned to the *Macaw*. The three remained friends for life. (Photo courtesy the Vangets family)

A picnic—or two picnics, half of the crew invited to each—may have stood in for Thanksgiving dinner at Pearl Harbor. *Sitting (or leaning on the table), left to right:* John Paul Graaff (*facing away*), Frank Zuroweste, Herman Ehlers, Claude "Toby" Hannah, Ralph Mennemeyer, John Cunniff, [Floyd Harvey], Charles Scott; *standing:* Edward Wade, Donald Whitmarsh, Clyde Isbell, Bob Jacobsen, unidentified, Ralph Enzweiler (*facing away*), [Charles Pierson], unidentified, Bud Loughman, unidentified. (Brackets indicate uncertain ID.) (USN photo courtesy Bud Loughman)

Pearl Harbor picnicker Augie Koepke before his shipmates deposited him in a tub of ice water. "He was a real 'Salt Horse,' a sailor's sailor," Bob Jacobsen wrote of Koepke. "One fault: He could not hold his liquor." But he could hold his beer in his sleep. The bottle he's gripping contained Lucky Lager salvaged at Funafuti. (USN photo courtesy Bud Loughman)

Joseph A. Connolly. (USN photo courtesy NARA)

The seaplane basin at the eastern end of Sand Island, January 29, 1944. The Contractors Tower, a converted water tank from which Captain Connolly and his colleagues would monitor the sinking of the *Macaw* two weeks later, appears at the lower edge of this photograph, Eastern Island toward the top. Brooks Channel runs between them, just beyond little Swan Isle. The *Macaw* lay pinned to the reef at the mouth of the channel at the time, just out of view to the right. (USN photo courtesy of NARA)

The *Macaw*, February 12, 1944. At least two men, one in an officer's hat, appear to be standing on the flying bridge, the uppermost deck, which lay atop the pilothouse and chart room. The 9,500-pound McCann rescue chamber is missing from the stern, having been swept off it on January 25. (USN photo courtesy NARA)

LeRoy Lehmbecker (*center*) and friends, probably at Pearl Harbor, ca. 1943. (Photo courtesy the Lehmbecker family)

Lehmbecker (*center*) and friends, probably at Hopkins, Minnesota, ca. 1937. His nickname was Pee Wee. (Photo courtesy the Lehmbecker family)

Edward Anthony Pitta. (Photo courtesy James Pitta and Chelsea Parker)

The *Macaw*, February 13, 1944. (USN photo courtesy Bud Loughman)

Robert Vaughn en route to his burial at sea, Midway, February 18, 1944. (USN photo courtesy Bud Loughman)

The surviving crew of the *Macaw*, plus a few guests and minus some absentees, posed for a group shot at a beer party on Midway on March 12, 1944. Most of the men cruised past their sunken ship aboard the submarine *Nautilus* en route to Pearl Harbor four days later. (For a roster of the men in the photo, see appendix A.) (USN photo courtesy Bud Loughman)

Twelve of the seventeen sinking survivors. *In front*: Edward Wade; *first row, from left*: Curtis Wainscott, Joseph Verkennes, Stanley Libera, Bud Loughman, Herman Ehlers, Lawrence Mathers, Charles Kumler; *back row*: Richard Williamson, Albert Bolke, Erwin Knecht (or, possibly, Nord Lester), George Manning. *Absent*: Tom Brown, Lewill Horsman, Augie Koepke, Charles Scott, and (apparently) Nord Lester. (USN photo courtesy Bud Loughman)

Paul Burton on the fantail of the *Macaw*. The cans against the gunwale behind him are depth charges. (USN photo courtesy Bud Loughman)

8

Midway

Geologically one of the Hawaiian Islands, Midway began as a volcano that popped up from the Pacific tectonic plate over a plume, or "hot spot," beneath the Earth's crust near the present site of the Big Island of Hawaii about twenty-seven million years ago. As the Pacific plate drifts northwestward, new volcanoes keep forming over the plume, and the old ones glide off toward the summer sunset at the stately pace of about three inches a year. Eighty-two million years or so of slow-motion tectonic sliding has brought Meiji Seamount (a seamount is an underwater mountain), the oldest and northernmost volcano in the chain, to the brink of the Kuril-Kamchatka Trench, just off the coast of Siberia's Kamchatka Peninsula. The northern flank of Meiji has slipped into that trench and is undergoing subduction there. If there were older peaks in the chain, they have already met that fate. Meanwhile more than eighty other volcanoes, including the one Midway sits atop, most of them entirely submerged, are slowly gliding to their doom behind Meiji in a broadly V-shaped line 3,600 miles long that describes the wings of a bird in flight, Meiji representing one wing tip, and the Big Island of Hawaii the other.[1]

Often referred to as Midway Island, Midway is in fact, as noted previously, an atoll containing two main islands, Eastern and Sand, and a smattering of tiny islets. An atoll is a coral reef, usually more or less ring-shaped, and the lagoon it encircles. The coral that forms a reef consists of the aggregated calcium carbonate exoskeletons of stationary little sea creatures called polyps. Some polyps eat hapless passersby, often plankton or fish larvae, effectively harpooning them, but most derive the bulk of their nutrition from colorful algae called photosynthetic dinoflagellates, single-celled organisms that live by the billions within the translucent polyps and give them their bright hues. The polyps feed on by-products of the photosynthesis their resident dinoflagellates engage in. Dinoflagellate-dependent polyps grow only underwater, but not too far under. Because the parasitic algae they rely on require sunlight, such polyps do too—live ones are seldom found at depths of more than two hundred feet. And being stationary, they need a surface on which to grow. Undersea surfaces less than two hundred feet deep are most often found just offshore, which is typically where coral reefs form—just off tropical and subtropical shores. There are exceptions, but most polyps don't do well in colder water. Midway's near neighbor Kure Atoll is the northernmost atoll in the world.

As a volcano grows, its added weight causes it to settle into the crustal matter underlying it. Once tectonic plate movement shifts a marine volcano off its plume, the volcano stops growing, and the elements start nibbling away at it. If at its peak a marine volcano projects above sea level, given enough time, settling, and erosion, the ocean will swallow it back up. As a volcano sinks below the surface, the coral polyps occupying the upper reaches of the reef encircling it must keep building that structure higher, with new generations setting up shop atop the skeletal remains of their predecessors so as to stay within a photosynthesis-enabling range of sunlight. An atoll's perimeter reef may look from above like a coral necklace, but in fact it's more like a coral wall, often hundreds of feet high, enclosing a generally shallow bowl the rim of which sketches a rough outline of the submerged volcanic stump it rests on, like a contour line on a topographic map. In Midway's case, that wall stands five feet above sea level in some places—uneven settling can elevate parts of a reef above the surface—and dips well below it in others, notably on the western side. Stretches of the reef are more or less flat on top and six to fifteen feet wide, and the lagoon inside it varies in depth from a few feet to about sixty.

The two wings of the volcanic chain of which the Hawaiian Islands are a part—the Emperor Chain to the north, the Hawaiian Ridge to the southeast—form an angle of about 60 degrees. Midway sits on the shoulder of the southeastern wing, about 450 miles southeast of the bend. First named Brooks Islands and Shore (or, by another account, Middlebrook Islands) after N. C. Brooks, the ship's captain who discovered it in 1859, Midway took on the name merchant sailors applied to it because of its location about halfway between San Francisco and Tokyo. On August 28, 1867, Capt. William Reynolds of the USS *Lackawanna* took formal possession of the atoll for the United States on the strength of the Guano Act of 1856, the same legislation the United States would later use to justify its claim to Funafuti, making Midway's islands the first offshore Pacific islands annexed by the United States.

Perhaps not entirely coincidentally, it was also in 1867 that the Pacific Mail Steamship Company began the first regularly scheduled steamship service between the United States and the Far East, with ships departing San Francisco weekly for Hong Kong and Yokohama. Pacific Mail wanted a mid-Pacific coaling station somewhere outside what was then the Kingdom of Hawaii, to which the company did not wish to pay taxes, and Congress obligingly appropriated fifty thousand dollars to dredge a channel so that steamships could access the lagoon. The sidewheel sloop-of-war USS *Saginaw*—the first ship ever built at the Mare Island Navy Yard, a San Francisco Bay facility that was to play a vital role in World War II—was assigned the task of supporting the project. The project itself went badly enough—the dredging crew, in exhausting its funding over seven months, from March to October 1870, succeeded in blasting out a passage only fifteen feet wide, less than a tenth of what was deemed the minimum required width. But it was on the way home that things went completely awry. The *Saginaw*'s captain, Lt. Cmdr. Montgomery Sicard of New York, decided to detour around nearby Kure Atoll to survey it and check it for castaways. Two whalers, one British and one American, having run aground and broken up there about thirty years before, Sicard figured a third crew might since have met that fate and needed saving, and his reward for undertaking this speculative mission of mercy was to run aground himself and repopulate barren little Ocean Island with just such a third crew, his own.[2]

Among the items the crew of the *Saginaw* managed to salvage from it was the twenty-two-foot captain's gig. Five men, led by the executive officer, twenty-six-year-old Lt. John G. Talbot of Danville, Kentucky, set off in it on November 18, 1870, for Hawaii. Thirty-one days, three storms, and 1,500 miles later, they drifted, wracked by hunger, exposure, and diarrhea, up to the north shore of the island of Kauai, only to overturn there in the surf. Talbot and three other men died. The lone survivor, Coxswain William Halford, a native of Gloucestershire, England, got a ride to Honolulu from a sympathetic mariner and alerted the authorities there to the plight of his shipmates on Kure. The royal steamship *Kilauea*, dispatched courtesy of King Kamehameha, found them there on January 3, 1871, malnourished but all still alive, and delivered them safely to Honolulu.

Fifteen years later, ships began running aground at Midway itself, two within the space of fourteen months in the late 1880s. Both ships were fishing vessels on sharking expeditions. The crew of the second, the *Wandering*

Minstrel, was greeted by the lone remaining survivor of the first, the *General Seigel,* frantically waving a shirt at them from Sand Island. This was Adolph Jorgensen, a Dane, three of whose shipmates, suspecting him of murdering two of their other shipmates, had abandoned him when they left the atoll in a boat that had washed ashore.

Between the two stranded crews, three parties totaling about a dozen men sought to escape Midway in small boats. Two of those groups succeeded—the three men from the *General Seigel* in one boat, and Jorgensen, Scotsman John Cameron (the *Minstrel's* mate), and a young Chinese sailor they called Moses in the other. The third group, comprising five or six men from the *Minstrel,* was never heard from again. Of the three dozen or so castaways marooned at Midway in those years, about half made it back to civilization, most of them courtesy of a passing schooner after about a year of subsisting on a diet of seabirds, eggs, fish, sea cucumbers, and salvaged rice.[3]

Homicide (assuming there had in fact been some involving Jorgensen and his shipmates) would eventually undergo a truly epic resurgence at Midway and in the waters surrounding it, but most of the violence perpetrated there over the ensuing half century or so was directed at the wildlife on Sand and Eastern Islands and at the coral that rings them. Among the most notable species of that wildlife are Laysan albatrosses, aka gooney birds. They were also among the main targets of that violence. Midway is home to the world's largest colony of Laysans, about a million strong. Noted for their grace in flight and comically awkward takeoffs and landings, Laysans range widely over the North Pacific, from California to Japan and the Gulf of Alaska, on wings spanning up to six and a half feet. The apparent ease with which they fly, negotiating hundreds of miles while seldom if ever flapping their wings, is no illusion. Two remarkable adaptations— a shoulder-locking mechanism that eliminates the strain of holding their wings up, and a vaguely roller-coasterlike flight pattern of long leeward swoops and sharp windward climbs that exploits the vertical gradient between lower-velocity winds at sea level and faster winds above it—enable them to fly tremendous distances at no net expense of mechanical energy. Their heart rate in flight is about the same as it is at rest. They do come to rest occasionally, on land or sea, but aside from taking off, landing, courting, or diving for food (or squabbling over it), they experience little exertion to rest from. A gooney in flight is about as close as the animal kingdom comes to a perpetual motion machine.[4]

Midway's birds and the atoll itself have perhaps never been more vividly described than by the author of *Treasure Island.* Robert Louis Stevenson met

John Cameron at Tarawa shortly after Cameron's Midway sojourn, and the accounts Cameron gave his countryman of the *General Seigel* and the *Wandering Minstrel* and their crews may have inspired *The Wrecker* (1892), an adventure novel set in part at Midway and cowritten by Stevenson and his stepson Lloyd Osbourne. In the book the authors have their hero and narrator, Michigan native Loudon Dodd, describe his first view of Midway, to which Dodd and a business associate have sailed to retrieve a mysteriously abandoned merchant vessel they have purchased. (The names that Dodd's "Directory" assigns the "two islets" in the following passage subsequently changed to Eastern and Sand.)

> I climbed into the rigging, stood on the board, and eagerly scanned that ring of coral reef and bursting breaker, and the blue lagoon which they enclosed. The two islets within began to show plainly— Middle Brooks and Lower Brooks Island, the Directory named them: two low, bush-covered, rolling strips of sand, each with glittering beaches, each perhaps a mile or a mile and a half in length, running east and west, and divided by a narrow channel. Over these, innumerable as maggots, there hovered, chattered, screamed and clanged, millions of twinkling sea-birds: white and black; the black by far the largest. With singular scintillations, this vortex of winged life swayed to and fro in the strong sunshine, whirled continually through itself, and would now and again burst asunder and scatter as wide as the lagoon.[5]

Around the turn of the twentieth century the American tugboat *Iroquois* arrived at Midway to take soundings and found Japanese sailors harvesting gooney eggs and feathers there. The eggs presumably were for eating. Most of the feathers probably found their way into women's hats, ladies' feathered headgear being fashionable in Europe and the United States at the time. Word of the Japanese sailors' depredations reached President Theodore Roosevelt, a great lover, and killer, of wildlife and a vigorous imperialist, who issued an executive order in January 1903 placing Midway under the jurisdiction of the US Navy—whether primarily to benefit the birds or his imperial ambitions, perhaps only he could say.

Three months later, the Commercial Pacific Cable Company set up shop on Midway, and Sand Island became a relay station for the firm's transpacific cable, which ran in sections from San Francisco to Manila via Honolulu, Midway, and Guam. The company began laying the cable from Ocean Beach in San Francisco in 1902. On July 4, 1903, President Roosevelt used it to send the first globe-girdling cable message, which made the round trip in nine minutes.

The Washington Naval Treaty of 1922 prohibited the erection of fortifications on Midway, but that did not keep the navy from studying the atoll in 1924 for use as a seaplane base, or later from conducting fleet maneuvers nearby. In 1935, Pan American Airways moved in, and Midway became a refueling stop, complete with a forty-five-room hotel on Sand Island, for Pan Am's Flying Clipper service to Asia. In 1938 work resumed on gouging out a shipping channel, expanding on a trough in which the telegraph cable had been laid through the middle of the south wall of the reef. By 1940, Japan having long since repudiated the Washington Naval Treaty and made clear its own imperial ambitions by invading China, construction had begun on a naval air base at Midway. It was commissioned August 1, 1941. Four months and six days later, as six Japanese aircraft carriers north of Oahu were welcoming back the second of two waves of planes that had just reduced Pearl Harbor to a shambles, two Japanese destroyers, the *Ushio* and the *Sazanami*, spent the better part of an hour shelling Sand Island. A power plant, hospital, and hangar were hit, a PBY Catalina seaplane destroyed, and four men—two sailors and two marines—killed.

Midway was a sideshow that day, but six months later the Japanese were back, and this time Midway and the waters around it were the main stage.

Japan's Midway operation was basically an attempt to deal with business left unfinished the previous December. The Japanese had hoped in attacking Pearl Harbor to destroy enough of the US Pacific fleet to bring the Americans to terms. But by chance none of the Pacific fleet's three aircraft carriers was in Pearl Harbor on December 7, 1941. It was in the hope of destroying those carriers and with them the Americans' willingness to fight that in May 1942 the Japanese assembled a fleet of more than a hundred ships, including four aircraft carriers with 248 planes, eleven battleships, forty-six destroyers, and sixteen submarines.

As powerful as it was, this fleet wasn't quite as powerful—nor the US fleet that engaged it quite as weak—as it might have been. In the Battle of the Coral Sea, May 6–8, 1942, both sides had lost one carrier—the Japanese the *Shoho*, the Americans the *Lexington*—and sustained severe damage to another. Two

Japanese carriers, the *Zuikaku* and the *Shokaku,* survived that battle, but the *Shokaku,* hit by three bombs, required months of repair in dry dock, and the Japanese were slow in replacing the pilots the *Zuikaku* had lost. Neither ship was available for the Midway operation. The crippled American carrier *Yorktown* was made available through a herculean effort by repair crews at the Pearl Harbor Naval Shipyard. Its presence at Midway came as a rude surprise to the Japanese, who thought it had gone to the bottom of the Coral Sea along with the *Lexington.* If the battle there hadn't happened, the Japanese advantage in carriers at Midway might have been six or seven to four instead of four to three.

But perhaps the most decisive factor at Midway involved intelligence. By early 1942 US naval cryptanalysts, aided by their Dutch and British counterparts, had cracked JN-25, the main Japanese naval code. Japanese radio messages intercepted after the Battle of the Coral Sea pointed toward an impending attack on an objective the designation of which translated as AF. Joseph Rochefort, a crossword puzzle and auction bridge aficionado who headed up Station Hypo, the navy's cryptanalysis office at Pearl Harbor, suspected that AF was Midway. To confirm that hunch, one of his assistants, Lt. Cmdr. Jasper Holmes, suggested a ruse. Having done research at Midway before the war, Holmes knew that the residents there relied for their fresh water on a desalinization plant. On May 19 he suggested having the base at Midway send an uncoded message to Pearl Harbor reporting that the desal plant was broken. Adm. Chester W. Nimitz of Fredericksburg, Texas, commander in chief of US Naval forces in the Pacific and devoted horseshoes tosser, approved the plan, the message was sent, and two days later the Japanese duly forwarded the news via JN-25 that AF was facing a water emergency. AF, clearly, was Midway. Some US officials still had their doubts, thinking the Japanese may have been deliberately feeding the Americans misleading clues. But by late May, Nimitz had decided to take the Japanese at their intercepted word and was planning accordingly.

On May 27, the day the *Kido Butai,* the Japanese carrier group, sortied from an anchorage off the island of Hashirajima, south of Hiroshima, the Japanese changed their codebook. The Americans could no longer read their messages. But by then the cat was out of the bag. The Japanese, planning to lure the American carriers into rushing to Midway's defense, then to pounce on and annihilate them, were themselves cruising into an ambush.[6]

The ensuing battle could still have gone badly for the Americans. It was fought mainly by airplanes. The Americans had about a hundred more of them on hand, but the Japanese planes were by and large faster and more maneuverable, their pilots more experienced, and their armaments, or at least their torpedoes, more reliable than their American counterparts. The Japanese struck first, with 108 planes, equally divided among dive bombers, torpedo planes, and fighter escorts, descending on Midway at about 0620 on June 4, 1942. The Americans sent nine waves of planes against the Japanese carriers that morning. The first seven of them did little or no direct damage to their targets, instead becoming targets themselves for the nimble Zero fighters flying combat air patrol (CAP) over the Japanese fleet. The lumbering American torpedo planes made especially easy targets. Of the three squadrons of carrier-based torpedo planes the Americans launched that morning, only the *Yorktown*'s had fighter cover. Even with it, only two of its twelve planes made it back to their ship. Four of the fourteen from the *Enterprise* did. The *Hornet*'s fifteen torpedo planes were wiped out.

But those planes and their crews did not go to the slaughter in vain. Nor did the Midway-based fliers that preceded them. For much of that morning, the American aerial assault on the *Kido Butai* reflected more grim determination than aeronautical or tactical brilliance. Piecemeal, uncoordinated, and, for many of its participants, effectively suicidal, it featured undertrained pilots, obsolete planes, flawed flight planning, mechanical breakdowns, launch delays, defective torpedoes, premature bomb drops, and a mutiny (this last by Lt. Cmdr. John Waldron, the *Hornet*'s torpedo plane squadron leader, who broke formation in a navigational dispute), but it was unrelenting. For more than three hours it kept the Japanese carriers on the defensive, too busy doing evasive maneuvers to launch their own assault on the American fleet, and ultimately, at great cost, it distracted the Japanese carriers from the threat that would destroy them.

That threat materialized over the *Kido Butai* at about 1020 that day in the form of dive bombers from the *Enterprise* and *Yorktown*, the *Enterprise* planes, under the command of Lt. Cmdr. C. Wade McClusky, having been guided to it just as they were nearing or exceeding the round-trip limits of their gas tanks by a directional arrow in the form of a wake made by a Japanese ship. Emerging from clouds that concealed their approach about the time the last of the US torpedo planes were getting shot down or driven off three or four miles below, McClusky's planes found three carriers, the *Kaga*, *Akagi*, and *Soryu*, still unscathed, and the sky at their elevation blessedly devoid of Zeros. Their torpedo plane brethren, most of them by then dead, had largely drawn the forty-two or so Zeros flying CAP over the Japanese fleet at the time down closer to sea level.

The *Enterprise* planes proceeded to dive about three to four vertical miles at about 275 miles per hour and at angles in the range of 45 to 70 degrees. Toward the nadirs of those dives some of those planes released five-hundred- and others one-thousand-pound bombs. There was confusion as to which of the two nearest carriers, the *Kaga* and the *Akagi*, to attack. One of McClusky's two squadrons was supposed to have gone after each. As it happened, one entire squadron and most of the other attacked the *Kaga;* only three planes, led by New Jersey native Lt. Cmdr. Richard Halsey Best, dove on the *Akagi*. Those three were enough. Within minutes both ships were flaming wrecks. So was the *Soryu,* hit by dive bombers from the *Yorktown.* The *Yorktown* planes had taken off about an hour and a half after McClusky's group, but the two carrier fleets having gotten a better idea of each other's whereabouts and con- verged in the meantime, the *Yorktown* planes flew a shorter and far more direct path to their target than the *Enterprise* planes did and arrived at it at almost exactly the same time.

The fourth Japanese carrier, the *Hiryu,* extracted a measure of revenge with a pair of midday attacks that crippled the *Yorktown,* but by that after- noon planes from the *Yorktown* and *Enterprise* had fatally damaged the *Hiryu* too. By the time the smoke cleared three days later, the Americans had lost a carrier, a destroyer and about 150 planes. The Japanese had lost four carriers, a heavy cruiser, 248 planes, about three thousand men, including some of their finest pilots and support crews, and much of their momentum in the conflict at large. For Japan, it was the beginning of the end.[7]

The day the *Macaw* ran aground at Midway, there were 120 men assigned to it, 8 officers and 112 enlisted men. Thirteen enlisted men who had gone ashore stayed there that day. More than 50 of their shipmates joined them over the ensuing week. There was no point in keeping anything like a full complement aboard, and there were good reasons not to. "After the ship piled up on the reef—after a couple days it was decided, due to only so much pota- ble water in the peak tanks, Only so much food—loss of all electric power all food in the freezers would go bad—It was determined to send a lot of mouths over to Midway," Bob Jacobsen wrote. "They kept engine room gang, electri- cians, ship fitters, metal smiths, carpenters, signalmen, cooks, some seamen & firemen. Sent ashore Radarmen, Sonarmen . . . and others."[8]

Radar and sonar operators were not in great demand aboard the stranded ship. The primary function of both ratings was to detect the enemy, and as of about 1612 on January 16, 1944, the Japanese were the least of the *Macaw's* concerns. The enemy was the reef, or the ocean, or the two of them together, and no one needed electronic equipment to locate either of them.

For those who remained aboard, there was not always much to do. Dave Wallington was assigned that most mundane of all nautical tasks, swabbing the deck. "Believe it or not," he said, he and another man were given that duty, one to which he saw little point under the circumstances. "You could call it housecleaning," he said. "We were trying to keep the ship shipshape."[9]

Fireman 1/c Don Srack stayed aboard the first week or so, and he didn't have much to do either aside from eating ham sandwiches. "We had ham sandwiches and ham sandwiches and ham sandwiches," he said. "All the ham you wanted." They ran a generator, he said, but apparently either it generated too little power to keep the refrigerator working or its power was deemed better applied elsewhere, because the refrigerator by multiple accounts remained a casualty of the initial flooding, and it became a matter of urgency to get rid of the food inside it.[10]

During that week, Srack recalled, the ship was moving, and depth charges would roll around loose on the deck astern. (They may have come loose after "Gunner" Dunn's inspection tour just after the grounding.) They were unarmed, Srack noted, but the sight was apparently disconcerting nonetheless. After running aground, he said, the *Macaw* was not a good place to be. Nor was it a pleasant one. Bud Loughman would write afterward of steak and eggs for breakfast on the reef, but by most accounts the food was mostly cold there, and so were the men. It never gets very cold at Midway. February and March are the coldest months, but even then the air temperature is generally in the 60s, seldom much lower than 59 degrees or much higher than 72, with surface water temperatures ranging from 66 to 72 degrees. But if those figures sound temperate enough, they can be much less than pleasant in combination when you're wet, and the men working on the stranded *Macaw* were wet much of the time. In the words of former Seaman Myron Froehlich, who contracted what may have been pneumonia while manning a pump aboard the stricken ship, it was "colder than hell out there."[11]

Deprived of their usual sleeping quarters, the men found others where they could. Dave Wallington slept in the armory on the second deck, rolled up in a blanket on the floor of the clipping room, a narrow compartment about six feet wide and ten deep, its bulkheads lined with shelves loaded with sixty-round magazines for the 20mm guns. He figured, what with the rocking of the ship, that if any of that ammunition were to fall on him in his sleep he'd be crushed, but none ever did. Aside from the danger of sudden maiming or death, he said, it was not a bad place to sleep. He was warm enough.[12]

The ship listed on the reef, sometimes one way, sometimes the other, and sometimes it stood more or less erect. Sometimes, Wallington said, you could look over the side and see the keel, a sight he took to indicate a tilt of at least 30 degrees. It listed 5 degrees to port its third day on the reef and 21 degrees the day after that. This complicated the delicate matter of human waste disposal. The ship's sewage pipe drained to starboard. When the ship listed beyond a certain degree to port, the pipe didn't drain. When that happened, Bob Gonnoud said, "You did what you had to do in a bucket and threw it over the side."[13]

The full force of the storm that almost brought the *Flier* and *Florikan* to grief on their way to Pearl Harbor struck on the morning of Sunday, January 23. The *Clamp*, the salvage and rescue ship that had struggled amid that storm en route from Apamama, arrived the following day. The weather remained bad enough to preclude salvage work that Monday. On Tuesday it was worse. By early that morning another heavy gale had arrived from the southwest, with winds of 40 knots and gusts to 69. The *Macaw*'s McCann rescue chamber was torn loose that day and tossed overboard. A 9,500-pound pear-shaped steel diving bell about ten feet tall and seven in diameter at the top, it had been bolted in place near the stern and strapped down for good measure with four one-inch turnbuckles. A wave "just swept it clean offa there," former Seaman 1/c Clyde Isbell said. In departing, the chamber gouged a five-inch hole in the deck, further flooding the crew's quarters, but as Quinton Studer noted, it left the bulwarks, which projected about two and a half feet above the deck, undented. The wave, he said, lifted it right over them.[14]

The *Macaw* was still stuck a week later, Tuesday, February 1, and another fresh gale was blowing at Midway when a board of investigation into the grounding of the *Flier* convened aboard the USS *Bushnell* (AS-15), a *Fulton*-class submarine tender, at the submarine base at Pearl Harbor. Commander Crowley was the first to testify. With his future as a naval officer on the line, he declined legal counsel. The *Flier* itself was probably in dry dock by then, undergoing repairs sufficient to enable it to make its own way back to Mare Island, where it would be thoroughly rehabilitated and put back into service.

Meanwhile, back at Midway, the *Clamp*, the main salvage vessel, stayed in the lagoon that Tuesday. In its absence, the hauling wires were secured to buoys, and by Wednesday those buoys had carried away, dropping the wires to the bottom. On Thursday, rough seas frustrated an attempt to float drums half filled with drinking water from a tug to the *Macaw*.

That Saturday, conditions having calmed, Paul Burton and a group of enlisted men went ashore. Upon arrival, they all received medical exams. A freshly relieved "section" of twenty or so *Macaw* sailors had gotten checkups two weeks before and were all found to be in good health. A round of check-ups aboard the ship on January 31 yielded similar results excepting only some fatigue and "a few colds." But as the struggle aboard the ship wore on, it began taking a more visible toll. Electrician's Mate 1/c and Muskegon, Michigan, native Ernst Luders slipped aboard ship one day around the beginning of February and fractured his jaw. Chief Gunner's Mate Edward Frey of Santa Cruz, California, fell about the same time and hurt his back. Lt. Ivan "Frank" Duff, the base medical officer, wrote of the enlisted men who accompanied Burton ashore on February 5: "All showed evidence of fatigue and some weight loss and exposure." So did Burton himself, though judging from what Duff wrote about him, he probably showed a lot less strain than he felt. "Other than for fatigue and some weight loss," Duff would testify, "his general physical condition was satisfactory. A twenty-four hour stay ashore was recommended."[15]

Burton remained ashore more than twenty-four hours. How much more is not entirely clear. According to the personnel transfer records, only two officers returned to the *Macaw* after that Saturday, one early Monday, one that Thursday. Those records do not list names, but it was almost certainly Burton on Monday. Any hope of salvaging his already compromised naval career hinged on salvaging his ship, and as much as he presumably did need rest, it seems inconceivable that short of a nervous breakdown he would have exiled himself from it for anything longer than a brief respite. Forgoing three days aboard in the thick of the struggle, when any one day might have proven critical, would have been tantamount to throwing in the towel, and he clearly had not done that.

It was probably that Sunday, February 6, that Burton assembled some or all of the eighty-six or so *Macaw* men onshore and addressed them. Bob Jacobsen wrote twice about the gathering, and as he recalled it, Burton looked haggard but hopeful—hopeful to the point of delusion.

They assembled all us people "on the beach" together one day—Captain Burton came ashore. He asked us how we were doing? He said that in a few days he thought they would get the ship off of the reef—Was a big extra high tide predicted. His big worry: I don't want to be towed to Pearl, he was hoping he could rig sails so we could go under our own power. Captain Burton looked like hell. Looked old, care worn and like he had lost weight.[16]

Burton came ashore once from the Macaw. He looked like hell—He had lost a lot of pounds and he looked hagard. Yes he seemed upbeat—he thought with all the pumps, air compressors and with all the pulling wires squared away that the next time the weather was good they would float her off and into the lagoon.[17]

That Burton would contemplate fitting his mangled ship out with jury-rigged sails and literally sailing back to Pearl Harbor—if he actually did—speaks eloquently to the stress he was under and the toll it was taking on him. Jacobsen, not generally disposed to go soft on the subject of Paul Burton, was understated in his comments on the idea. "I think Burton was just doing some wishful thinking that he would sail the vessel to Pearl," he wrote.

Sure sails could have been rigged — but it was not feasible. Would have taken all the canvas on the Macaw and probably on Midway to have sewn all the sails needed. You have to have spare sails in case a squal or storm rips out a set.

With all the leaks in her bottom I think they would have had a hard time keeping her afloat at the dock. I think they would have needed to bring an ARD (drydock) out from Pearl Harbor, so they could get under her bottom to make temporary repairs. And the powers that be would have said a tug will tow her to Pearl or the States.[18]

That Sunday marked three weeks of captivity for the *Macaw*. They had not gone well. Salvage efforts the first week focused, successfully, on the *Flier*. Freeing the *Macaw* proved to be more difficult. Sea conditions were generally awful. "The salvage was hampered and frequently halted altogether by heavy seas and a 10 knot current in the channel, which perforce closed the harbor of MIDWAY for about a week," NOB 1504's war diary explained. Towing lines, when they could be rigged, kept snagging on coral heads. When they were freed and all the horsepower the salvors could muster applied to them, the *Macaw* wouldn't budge.[19]

Weight may have been a factor. Bob Jacobsen thought it was. He cited legendary eighteenth-century British mariner James Cook, who confronted much the same problem when his ship, the HMS *Endeavour*, ran aground on a coral reef off the coast of Australia in 1770. Cook, by his own account, wasted little time in throwing overboard "40 or 50 Tuns" of stores, ballast, and equipment, including his cannons, and then, finding himself still stuck, tossed some more and freed his ship within a day. Jacobsen compared Cook's response to that of Paul Burton and salvage officer Lebbeus Curtis and company. He felt that Cook had done the better job.

> I can't believe they didn't strip the ship and get all the weight possible off of her—stuff like 40 or 50–300 lb depth charges, 4–5 ton anchors on the stern deck. The diving bell—Two 26 or 27 foot whale boats that were still "griped" down when the Macaw went down . . . tons of ammunition . . . Blocks, Chain falls, lots of Cable. . . . Jetison it—Hey your gonna lose it all if the ship goes down—Most of this could have been found and recovered.
>
> Last, you had a diesel oil storage that ran from bow to stern— Between the outer hull plating and the lowest deck were nothing but tanks of diesel. Get oil barge from shore or pump it over board into the sea where it went when the Macaw was lost.[20]

In another letter, Jacobsen wrote, "Oh God for a Captain Cook."[21]

Jacobsen's shipmate Nord Lester seems to have shared his general sentiments about the salvage effort, if not the historical perspective. Lester and his friend, fellow deep-sea diver and Shipfitter 2/c Lewill Horsman, had been assigned the task of capping vents and securing hatches to make the ship as airtight as possible, the plan being to pump water out and compressed air in, the latter much in the way of inflating a balloon, and have the ship ride as high and as nearly free of the coral as possible. As Lester put it, the idea was to put the ship "on a bubble." Having toiled to make that bubble possible, Lester was chagrined when a hole was cut in the deck aft with an acetylene torch. The purpose (of which Lester was not aware) for cutting that hole was to allow the use of a pump on various compartments below. To Lester, it undid all the work he and Horsman had done—it burst their bubble, or the chance of making one—and undermined his faith in the whole campaign. Fifty-five years later he wrote: "(Damm) all our efforts were wasted, now it was junk, more storms, more days, now the Sea was winning."[22]

Events on Tuesday, February 8, might have confirmed that belief. A strong current ran in the channel that morning. The *Macaw* listed 7 degrees to starboard, its stern half underwater or, when waves swept past, submerged altogether. Between the use of compressed air to expel water from the shaft alley and standard pumping elsewhere, the list diminished and the stern came afloat, but when the *Clamp* tried to retrieve a pair of fallen hauling wires, one was found to be irretrievably fouled on the coral, the other lacking the eye at its end. Commander Curtis concluded that a submarine propeller had sliced the cable in two six days before. By about 1130 the planned towing was put on hold again on account of deteriorating sea conditions, the *Macaw* was told once again to brace for heavy weather, and two tugs undertook to tow the barge *Gaylord* back into the lagoon, only to find themselves unable to make headway against the current in the channel. The *Clamp* relieved them of their burden and towed the *Gaylord* in itself.[23]

Work resumed on Thursday, February 10, and this time, despite a four-hour delay to allow other vessels the use of the channel, it seemed for a while as though the humans and their equipment were winning at last. The *Clamp*, armed with almost half a mile of new hauling wire, laid new moorings, and aboard the *Macaw* dewatering proceeded in rare compliance with the salvors' plans. "At 1700, the MACAW's stern was fully afloat, list 2 degrees to starboard and the entire vessel was light and lively, apparently aground only in the midship section," Commander Curtis wrote. "All compartments except the generator room were pumped down to a satisfactory level."[24]

But there was a problem with the pump suction in the generator room—the water there remained five feet deep—and the *Clamp*'s two hauling wires fouled yet again on the coral. According to Captain Connolly, at some point that evening the east wire was cleared and a strain put on it, but the west wire remained snagged, and tension on the east wire alone was unequal to the task of pulling the ship free. By midnight the wind was picking up and the pulling put in abeyance until daylight, when the west wire was to be cleared. Meanwhile, pumping continued on the *Macaw*, keeping it comparatively light, and probably as a result the stricken ship pounded badly that night.

At about 0630 that Friday the *Clamp* made what proved to be its final attempt to free the *Macaw*. It failed. The hauling wires, as usual, had snagged on the coral. The weather had deteriorated overnight. By midmorning a strong wind was blowing out of the south, and seas were rough and building. At about 0900 Connolly and Curtis conferred and decided to put things on hold once again.

> 0900 (about)—The Salvage Officer and Captain Connolly decided to wait until the weather cleared but to keep everything in readiness for pull as soon as it did. The forecast was for wind averaging 18–20 knots with gust to 30 knots from the south shifting to west, tonight and tomorrow, surface wind northwest 18 knots with gusts to 26 knots. Started to flood the ship to hold her in position. Conferred with Commander Curtis and Commanding Officer, MACAW, in regard to the shipkeepers. The Commanding Officer wanted to keep two sections on board but finally agreed one sufficient to maintain the gear and get the ship ready for the next pull.[25]

The weather forecast Captain Connolly cites in that passage makes no mention of sea state, and there may have been no accurate way to forecast it. Over the following two days, that would prove to be a critical factor. Winds can greatly increase the size of waves, but waves can propagate far beyond the range of the winds that build them. The two are not always evenly matched in magnitude at a given time and place. If they were, and the worst seas the *Macaw* had to contend with over those next two days were proportionate to 30-knot gusts of wind, the ship should have been fine. As Connolly would note a few paragraphs later in the narrative he presented to the subsequent board of investigation, it had already, in its stay on the reef, endured worse.[26]

At about 1030 that Friday Captain Connolly, Commander Curtis, the salvage crew from the *Clamp*, and about two dozen *Macaw* sailors, all but one of them enlisted men, made the trip to shore. Despite being fouled, the hauling wires from the *Clamp* to the *Macaw* apparently remained in place at both ends for several hours, and taut enough, at least one of them, to serve an anchoring function, for the *Clamp* was able to hold the *Macaw*'s stern in place about that long while the stranded ship was once again allowed to flood by way of hunkering down. Yet another fresh gale was blowing by 1600, about when the *Clamp*, pitching on the seas and unable to hold its position any longer, secured its ends of the hauling wires to spring buoys, slipped its mooring, and made its way back into the lagoon, leaving the *Macaw* to weather the seas on its own.

There were twenty-two men aboard the *Macaw* at the time: Paul Burton, his executive officer, Bud Loughman, and twenty enlisted men. There was a system of rotation between ship and shore among the *Macaw*'s crew at Midway involving "sections" of twenty or so enlisted men each, but not everyone participated in it. At least two men, deemed unfit, were deliberately excluded from it. As Bud Loughman noted years later, the salvage effort was critical and dangerous, and during it you wanted only good men aboard. You also wanted certain ratings more than others. There were, by official designation, no cooks among the twenty enlisted men left aboard that Friday evening, but there was a steward's mate, who might have done some cooking, as well as two radio specialists, three motor machinist's mates, two firemen, two shipfitters, and an electrician's mate. The other men represented a less generally industrial variety of nautical callings: four seamen, three bosun's mates, the chief pharmacist's mate, a quartermaster, and a gunner's mate.[27]

Six of the men were in their thirties, the oldest was thirty-six. Robert Vaughn, the steward's mate from Winston-Salem, North Carolina, had just turned sixteen. Nine of the men were married. One was an immigrant, from Germany, and two were the sons of immigrants, both parents from Poland in one case, from Ireland in the other. Three were college graduates, including both officers, and at least six were high school dropouts. Three had grown up on farms. Four were from New York State, three from Illinois, two from California, and one each from Kansas, Arkansas, Indiana, Ohio, Oregon, Missouri, North Carolina, Michigan, Colorado, Florida, New Jersey, Pennsylvania, and Texas.

Stanley Libera, the former submariner, was on board. He had grown up in Fulton, New York, twenty-five miles northwest of Syracuse, within blocks of Lake Neatahwanta on one side and the Oswego River on the other. He had found how dangerous being in water or on it could be. As a child, he said, he fell through the ice on the river one winter and was clawing at it from the underside when a neighbor fished him out with a pole. When he was fifteen, several friends wanted him to go sledding on the riverbank. His Polish immigrant factory-worker father said he had to chop wood and would get his ass kicked if he didn't, so he chopped wood. His friends' sled broke through the ice on the river, and everyone on it drowned. Had he gone with them, Libera said, he would have been at the front of the sled.[28]

Lawrence Mathers, thirty-six, was the oldest man aboard. He was not supposed to be there. He was supposed to have been replaced by fellow radio technician Harold Hayes. According to Hayes, he (Hayes) had accidentally been assigned to the wrong section. By the time he realized the mistake, Hayes said, his rightful section had set out for the ship without him.

If extra time on board meant having more to do, Mathers probably did not greatly mind. He was a doer. Born in Colorado in 1907, the son of a dry-goods merchant from Kansas, he attended Western State College of Colorado (since renamed Western State Colorado University), where he was president of the class of 1932, on the staffs of the yearbook and student newspaper, on the student council and basketball and track teams, in the Press Club, two fraternities, and something called Mask and Whig, and named to the All-Intramural basketball team. By 1940 he was living in Los Angeles and work-ing as a wholesale oil salesman—a "high-quality traveling salesman," in Hayes's words—making the rounds between Los Angeles and San Francisco. He enlisted September 29, 1942, in Los Angeles, spent about nine months there in electronics school, and got assigned to the *Macaw*. Hayes was a great admirer. Mathers was handsome and likable, with black wavy hair and "a face that stood out as having character," Hayes said. "He was one of those guys who coulda been a Hollywood star."[29]

One of the three motor machinist's mates aboard was Donald Whit-marsh, the "well liked, quiet guy" from far upstate New York whom Bob Jacobsen described as "one of the best Mo Macs on the ship," and the recent recipient of a crushing Dear John letter. Whitmarsh had replaced his friend Quinton Studer on salvage duty. Another was Richard Blaine Williamson, alternately of Kansas and Oklahoma, a married man in his early thirties with three children, a combine operator who seems to have combined a poetic streak with a tendency to drink too much. According to Dan Weber, before the war Williamson had four combines. He would start in north Texas, Weber said, and harvest wheat all the way to Canada. "He would paint the prettiest pictures" of wheat waving in the wind, Weber said. And he was sometimes less than entirely steady himself. Fireman Don Srack recalled Wil-liamson entertaining his shipmates in the crew's quarters with his struggles to climb into his upper bunk upon coming back from liberty drunk. If he was occasionally short on sobriety, Williamson apparently did not lack for cour-age. He was said to be among the *Macaw* sailors who responded at Funafuti to the call for volunteers to go ashore at Tarawa when it appeared the *Macaw* was to join the fleet supporting the invasion there. Fate had kept him out of harm's way at that fork in the road, but now, about three months later, it had put him squarely in its path.[30]

The third motor machinist's mate was Erwin Richard Knecht of Miller Place, New York, on the north shore of Long Island. Knecht was born in Germany in 1924. His father, Ernst Andreas Knecht, having immigrated to New York and lined up a job with the Knickerbocker Ice Company in Brooklyn, went back to Mannheim for his wife and infant son, and they celebrated Erwin's first birthday on the SS *Cleveland* en route back to New York, where Erwin and his mother swelled the rolls of immigrants, more than twelve million of them, who entered the United States through the processing center on Ellis Island from 1892 to 1954. Ernst had already done so.

They settled in Ridgewood in the borough of Queens, where Erwin, according to his future wife, née Gloria Loicano, grew up tough, a typical city kid, a "smart-alec angry kid with a chip on his shoulder." During the 1930s Erwin joined a youth group for German kids like the Boy Scouts, only with a fascist military twist. His father had been wounded in the face while serving in the German army in World War I. The experience may have soured him on German militarism. He was no fan of Hitler, and when he found out that his son was getting trained in the use of firearms, he went ballistic, yanked Erwin out of the club, and in the process gave the men who ran it an earful, something along the lines of where they could stick their swastikas. After the Knickerbocker Ice Company, Ernst went to work for the Rhinegold Brewery in Queens. Before the war Erwin worked as a mechanic at two gas stations and ran track (or cross-country, or both) in high school, from which he dropped out to enlist on February 23, 1942.[31]

When the Knechts landed at Ellis Island in 1925, they were slightly more than one mile from 108 Sussex Street in the working-class Paulus Hook district of Jersey City, New Jersey, the soon-to-be boyhood home of Erwin's future *Macaw* shipmate Edward James Wade. His Irish parents' third child and the first born in the United States, Wade would attend nearby St. Peter's Grammar School, and, as little reverence as he would subsequently display with regard to naval etiquette (it was Wade who cut in on Bud Loughman and his wife at the commissioning party), he would serve in his adolescence as an altar boy at St. Peter's Catholic Church, about two blocks from his home. If he was duly solemn in that capacity, he seems to have shed any vestige of solemnity by the time he enlisted on April 16, 1943. His shipmates' descriptions of him—"the ship's comedian," a funny guy with a reddish complexion, "kind of a comic little fella," a nice kid with some problems, "a fun-loving guy," a nice guy who talked too much, "a mutt"—corroborate the merry prankster image he projects from wartime photographs. Wade was still aboard the ship that Friday evening, and if the other men aboard with him were to be in need of comic relief, he would have been a likely source of it. "Wade I remember, about 5'5"," Bob Jacobsen wrote. "Always joking around."[32]

Another characteristically upbeat presence was Seaman 1/c Joseph Theodore Verkennes, aka Frenchie (his father's side of the family was actually from Holland), a married man and homeowner in his early thirties, like Dave Wallington an auto worker from Flint, Michigan, and like Wade notable in photographs for obvious good cheer, an attitude he seems to have sustained despite having suffered "severe crushing lacerations" of his right index finger when it got caught in a line wrapped around a bitt six days out of San Francisco Bay.

Augie Paul Koepke, the bosun's mate, raconteur, "sailor's sailor," and hapless drunk, was aboard, as were Shipfitters Nord Lester, prone to seasickness, and his friend Lewill Horsman, son of a café manager and cook from Lewistown, Missouri.[33] So were Bosun's Mate 2/c Charles Arnall Scott, son of a bakery sales manager from El Paso, Texas; Fireman 1/c Lewis Andrew Kingsley, thirty-one, married, a resident of Berkeley, California; William Roscoe Funk, the pharmacist's mate, also married, who lived across the bay from Kingsley in San Francisco; and Seaman 1/c George Washington Manning of Albany, Oregon, a former high school football player from a family with a less than savory reputation in their town as brawlers.[34]

Quartermaster Herman Ehlers owed his presence aboard the ship that evening at least in part to the navy's rejection of a request the previous April from the board of directors of the Farmers State Bank of Beecher, his hometown in Illinois, that he be relieved from active duty so he could return home and help run the bank—the death of his father, its president, three months before having left the institution with a critical gap in its executive ranks. The navy, deeming its own need of Ehlers's services greater than that of the bank, declined the request. Ehlers stayed in the navy, and his sister Garneta, a veteran of the bookkeeping department, stepped up to help fill the managerial void.

The navy of the 1940s operated largely along the lines of a rigid two-tier caste system, with little in the way of casual fraternizing between the two castes. As former enlisted man Bob Jacobsen recalled, "You did not talk to an Officer unless he addressed you [or] you were reporting to him." But Ehlers seems to have bridged the gap. His background as a bank manager, chess enthusiast, and classical musician—he played violin in a chamber group with his sister Viola (piano) and brother, Vernon (cello)—would seem to have suited him more to officer than enlisted status. He almost certainly spent more off-duty time with Paul Burton than did any other enlisted man on the ship. He seems to have been miscast as an enlisted man, but nothing in the photographic record or the remarks of his shipmates indicates he felt any envy toward the officers he served under, or superiority over the other enlisted men he served with. He seems to have had a smile for everyone, and friends of every stripe.[35]

Two Chicagoans were aboard that evening: Albert Bolke, from the South Side, the gunner's mate who didn't know how to swim, and Charles Kumler, from the North Side, an electrician's mate said to have sought submarine duty, like Paul Burton and Bud Loughman, and been denied it on the grounds that he chewed his fingernails.[36]

Robert Vaughn, the steward's mate from Winston-Salem, North Carolina, was aboard, apparently by his own choice. By and large, volunteerism played little or no role in determining who would undertake any given task in the navy of the time, or at least any standard sort of task. It's not surprising that for a job as extraordinary as going ashore at Tarawa there would be a call for volunteers. But for more mundane tasks, as former *Macaw* Fireman Don Srack put it, they pointed at men and said, "You and you and you." And by most accounts, that was how the men of its own crew were selected for salvage duty on the *Macaw*. But Bud Loughman said that Vaughn volunteered for more than his share of rotations aboard the stranded ship, and former Seaman Walter Eugene Voke seems to have said as much too. Within a couple of years or so, Voke, of tiny Ansonia, Ohio, would tell his wife, Dora Mae, about an African American sailor on the *Macaw* who, as she remembered it fifty-eight years later, signed up to be on the salvage crew, thought better of it and crossed his name off, then signed up again, then crossed it off again, then signed up again. She said she didn't know, based on what her husband (who died shortly after the war) had told her, whether Vaughn had finally made his mind up to leave his name on the list or simply hadn't had a chance to cross it off yet again when they requisitioned him.[37]

Seaman 1/c Curtis Wainscott, who grew up, like Lewis Kingsley, on a farm in southern Indiana, was aboard that day, and he may have volunteered too. It would not have been the first time. He was apparently in the detail that leapt amid heavy seas onto a barge that foundered six days out of San

Francisco Bay, to inspect it and set pumps on it. He may have comprised the whole detail himself. He and Wade were said to have swum to dummy torpedoes to retrieve them during torpedo practice. By one account, Adam Autin, a French-speaking bosun's mate from southern Louisiana, unversed in written English, relied on Wainscott to read his wife's letters and write the replies. Dave Wallington remembered Wainscott as "quite a brazen guy" and a risk-taker. His former shipmate Eugene Van Buskirk said of Wainscott, "If you was gonna do anything, you'd want him on your side."[38]

Another good man to have on your side, and another on board that evening, was Chief Bosun's Mate Tom Emmet Brown, a farmer's son from Arkansas. Brown was Regular Navy—he enlisted in 1933—and a newcomer to the *Macaw*, having, like Libera, boarded the ship at Pearl Harbor. As the newly arrived supervisor over the other bosun's mates, who were themselves supervisors, he encountered some initial resistance from at least one of his immediate subordinates, that being Bosun's Mate Ralph Mennemeyer, Augie Koepke's partner in overseeing the afterdeck division. Brown, apparently, was a man of few words, and he wasted few once things between him and Mennemeyer came to a head.

> Chief Brown, a tough man—physically and mentally. Most BMC's spend their time chewing out the seaman—not Brown. He told the boatswain mates under him what he wanted and held them responsible. If a seaman screwed up—he chewed out the BM for not having properly instructed the seaman.
>
> He never said anything to me. He would look over the boat deck[,] see it was ship shape and let it go at that. I seen him and Minimeyer in an argument; Minny was questioning Chief Browns qualifications and knowledge —The Chief told Minny to come back on the fan tail and they would find out who was the best man—Minny backed down. Minny was ten years younger and 50 lbs heavier—but he didn't want that Chief who was nothing but raw hyde.[39]

In another letter Bob Jacobsen wrote: "Chief Brown was like a piece of oak with lots of energy." Harold Hayes felt much the same way. Tom Brown was a good man, he said, "solid, like a good foundation." The support, moral and physical, Brown would soon be furnishing his new shipmates would prove instrumental in saving at least one life and arguably several more.[40]

9

Emergency Exit

Friday, February 11, 1944, was rainy and windy at Midway. A cold front passed through that evening, bringing moderately heavy rain and winds gusting to 45 knots. The rain lasted into the early hours of Saturday, February 12. The rain could have been of little consequence to the men on the *Macaw*—it could not have made things aboard the ship much wetter. For them, the critical factors were wind and sea state. The wind shifted about on Friday, from SSE (south-southeast) to WSW, picking up from 17 knots at 0100 to 28 knots at 0500, then gradually tapering off to 12 knots by midnight. By 0700 Saturday it was coming from the southwest by one account, from more or less due west by another, and had freshened back to 20 knots. The forecast was for 23 knots with gusts to 32 knots later that day and somewhat milder conditions the next—wind 18 knots, gusts to 26, from the northwest. But the seas that Saturday morning were coming in from the south or southwest, and they just kept getting bigger.

At about 0700 the *Macaw* sent a message to shore (A304AE was a storage room on the second platform, two levels below the main deck): "Heading 070 degrees true increased 30 degrees since yesterday X List 20 degrees X Pivot at bridge X Hauling wires too slack to hold us steady X A304AE flooded X No power X Will need six 100 ampere hour batteries X If 8-inch line could be passed to us and anchored east of #2 buoy we can try to decrease list X."[1]

The requests in that message went unfulfilled. Getting batteries or an eight-inch line or anything else to the *Macaw* at that point was essentially impossible. Conditions at the entrance had persuaded the brass ashore to close the channel by then. Of course they could have made an exception, but no one wanted another rescue vessel on the reef in need of rescue.

The *Macaw* sent another message about 0900, a mixture of good news and desperation. The coffee machine, apparently, had been knocked out by sea water, but now: "Coffee machine running again X Keeping water out of

A203AL with submersible pump X Please float 50 gallons diesel oil to us before sunset X This urgent X."[2]

A203AL was the chief petty officers' berthing on the first platform, one level below the main deck. The diesel oil was for the welding machine from which they had been drawing power. Previously they had been drawing oil for it from the ship's own tanks, but apparently the tanks by then were either dry or, more likely, no longer accessible. Commander Curtis proceeded at about 1000 at least far enough out the channel to size things up at its mouth, this aboard *YT-188*, the yard tug that had sought to escort the *Flier* into the lagoon almost four weeks before. He may have taken with him oil drums and an eight-inch line, and possibly batteries as well, but what he saw seems to have convinced him of the futility of attempting any resupply or rescue of the *Macaw* personnel pending the sea's settling down somewhat.

> 1000—The Salvage Officer inspected the channel in the vicinity of the MACAW and considered conditions unsafe to board or work on the MACAW. Seas were such that the boat would have swamped in any attempt to plant the anchor which was not considered feasible or useful. Seas prevented floating oil drums to the ship.[3]

That was how Connolly described Curtis's excursion. This is how Curtis himself described it (referring to himself in the third person):

> On Saturday, 12 February, fresh southwest winds, heavy sea. The MACAW took a 20 degree starboard list. The stern swung to the west and the port bilge worked higher onto the reef. The heading was 50 degrees. At 1000, the Salvage Officer proceeded out through the channel in YT-188 and surveyed the channel and the MACAW from the tug. Conditions of the channel were unfit for passage of vessels. Sea was breaking heavily on the starboard side of the MACAW but the ship was lying quietly and apparently receiving no additional damage.[4]

Connolly and Curtis, in their accounts of the day's events, both skip lightly over several hours around lunchtime, Connolly saying nothing about them and Curtis noting merely that "The sea increased during the day." Connolly's narrative resumes first:

1500—Although wind was from west at 20 knots, seas from the south seemed to be getting heavier around the MACAW. Heavy seas breaking over northwest reef and water in the lagoon rising.

1600—Sent the MACAW message "Sea conditions prevent delivery of oil X Will send out at first opportunity." Seas began to break over entire length of ship on starboard side and the list was about 20 degrees starboard.

By the time Curtis's narrative resumes, the *Macaw* was no longer "lying quietly."

At 1600, the MACAW was observed to develop more list estimated at 35 degrees. Heavy seas were breaking over the whole length of the ship and up onto the boat deck. The weight and force of seas continued to increase with crests higher than the boat deck.[5]

A list of 35 degrees was worrisome. It suggested the possibility of capsizing. In the next message in his account, Connolly addressed it:

1630—Sent message to the MACAW "Do you know what caused present list X Did you flood compartments above first platform."

1720—Received message from the MACAW "List became worse as generator room flooded to main deck as usual X Free water in motor room and compartment A304AE [X List] increased to 23 degrees X Small amount of water in A202L and A2–3AL X No power or pumps X Buda has gone X Personnel safe." Seas were increasing in height and force.[6]

Connolly's second question at 1630—"Did you flood compartments above first platform"—implies an assumption that the men aboard the *Macaw* still had some say in the matter of flooding compartments. By 1720, without power or pumps, they may still have, if only by way of opening or closing doors or hatches. That was all they could do—that and retreat upward as the ship went down. In theory they might have thrown things overboard, like Captain Cook off the coast of Australia, but it was too late for that.

The generator and motor rooms were in the hold, deep in the bowels of the ship. A304AE was a storage room on the second platform, one level above the hold and two below the main deck. It can have surprised no one aboard at this point that those three rooms contained water. But A203AL (misspelled in Connolly's entry), the chief petty officers' quarters on the first platform (A202L was a passageway communicating with it), was just one level below the main deck. Flooding there, even in small quantities, had to be alarming.

The Buda was an air compressor manufactured by the Buda Company of Harvey, Illinois, and probably the one Connolly cites in his narrative as having been placed aboard February 5. Had the Buda actually been gone at that point, instead of merely out of order, the men on the ship would have been better off without it, as would soon become evident.

Both Connolly (quoted first below) and Curtis noted a reduction in the ship's list early that evening:

1800—The MACAW list reduced to about 10 degrees starboard and appeared to have returned to original heading of 030 degrees true. Stern was under water but ship was sighted by land markers to be in same position as during day. Seas were still increasing in force and heighth. Since wind was still west at 20 knots, it now became apparent that these huge waves must have been caused by some disturbance at considerable distance from this station.[7]

At about 1800 the MACAW was observed to reduce the list and the stern submerged permitting seas to break on board as far forward as the pilot house. An urgent message was sent to the MACAW not to attempt to abandon ship. This because of darkness and wind and sea conditions. It was the Salvage Officer's considered opinion that the personnel were safer on board than to attempt to land through the breakers on the reef.[8]

Other things being equal, that reduction in the ship's list might have been good news, but the accompanying submergence of the stern was not. The sea was doing to the *Macaw* what the concerted efforts of Curtis and Connolly and all their supporting cast of men and machinery had failed to do—it was freeing the ship from the reef, pushing or prying or shaking it from its perch atop the coral backward into deeper water. The *Macaw* was sinking.

The seas, as massive as they got to be that day, may not have been the primary factor in dislodging the ship, or if they were, they may have applied to it only indirectly the force that actually moved it, an extraordinarily powerful seaward current they helped set up. The water level in the lagoon that evening was somewhere between one and two and a half feet higher than normal high tide, due largely to that day's huge waves pushing an enormous quantity of water over the relatively low west wall of the reef. Field engineer Maitland Dease of the Hawaiian Dredging Company, the firm that owned the *Gaylord*, testified later about water levels in the lagoon that day and their effects:

Q. Tell the board what the average water level as indicated by the tidal gauge in use at Midway reads.

A. The normal level at Midway reads from about 0 to about 1.2 feet plus, with zero being mean low water. On the evening of the 12th, there was an indication that she rose sharply between the hours of twelve noon to 6 p.m. or 1800 N.O.B. time to about 2.8 feet with surges indicated as high as 3.6 feet and the condition at high water shows it was very rough, very high surges, two foot swells being indicated in the sheltered boat haven where the tide gauge is located.

Q. What effect did this higher tide on the day of 12 February have on currents in the channel to Midway?

A. I am not a qualified expert on currents but I believe the whole Midway atoll is a bowl with one of the main outlets being the main channel, and the abnormally high tide tending to outlet through this channel would cause much higher currents than usual.[9]

The sheltered boat haven was an enclosure within an enclosure (the outer one being the lagoon), a sort of trapezoidal holding pen for small harbor craft at the eastern end of Sand Island, walled off on two sides by jetties with an opening about fifteen yards wide between them. Two-foot swells within the normally placid confines of the boat haven reflected extraordinary violence in the sea at large.

The lagoon at Midway occupies about 14,800 acres. A high tide 1.6 feet higher than normal there (the 2.8-foot tide Dease noted, minus the 1.2-foot normal high tide) would mean an extra 23,680 acre-feet, or roughly 7.7 billion gallons of water in the lagoon, much of which, as Dease suggested, would have sought to return to the sea by way of Brooks Channel. Given the southeast-ward set at the mouth of the channel that day, much of the water rushing from it was surging more or less broadside into the *Macaw*. Why the ship shifted in its heading to starboard as much as it did that morning is unclear—perhaps the brunt of the current struck it forward of the pivot that the message it sent at 0700 linked to the bridge. The more the ship pivoted to starboard, the broader a target it would seem to have presented to that current.[10]

"Around 1800," Bud Loughman would write, "it was apparent ship was slowly being forced into deeper water"—but not too slowly, judging from his next two sentences: "Water rose from main deck to boat deck in less than an hour. By 1800 water was coming up inside ladder to bridge deck."[11]

The bridge deck—aka the bridge, the navigation deck, or officers' territory—containing as it did the two highest enclosed rooms on the ship, it was there that the men congregated that evening as their ship sank. Burton ordered them there, but he might have saved his breath. As Nord Lester remarked fifty-seven years later, "There was no place else to go. . . . We were like rats being forced up by the water."[12]

The bridge comprised the pilothouse and chart room and the platform surrounding them. Its floor plan, or "footprint," reflected that of the two con-tiguous compartments that occupied most of it, the pilothouse forward and the chart room aft, the forward corners of each of which were beveled, mak-ing both compartments hexagonal and giving the two of them together, viewed from above, the profile of a pill bottle, the wider, squatter pilothouse representing the cap. Under normal circumstances they would have been at the same altitude above the waterline, but that evening, given the slope the ship was on, bow up and stern down, the pilothouse was actually slightly the higher of the two.

The pilothouse was about seventeen feet wide at the back and twelve feet deep at its deepest, the chart room a little longer and narrower. The pilothouse contained the wheel, a chart board, the quartermaster's desk, and various nav-igational fixtures including the annunciator, the control console, a magnetic compass, a radar console, and a sonar station. Together the two compartments comprised about 415 square feet of floor space, commodious enough for twenty-two men, all the fixtures notwithstanding, less so as the evening wore on and the sea began to encroach on them. But as cramped as their accom-modations got that night, they could have been worse. When salvage efforts were suspended Friday morning, Paul Burton had wanted to keep two "sections" of twenty men each aboard. Captain Connolly and Commander Curtis apparently persuaded or informed him that one would suffice.[13]

The pilothouse had three doors, all in the bulkhead aft, one at each corner and the third just inside its neighbor on the port side, hinge to hinge to it. The two outside doors opened onto the deck, the third door onto the chart room. The outer two doors were built to be airtight but not watertight. The middle door, being an interior feature, was neither. From the pilothouse, all three doors opened outward. On the port side of the chart room just aft of the pilothouse was a stairwell—in navy parlance, a ladder—leading down to the captain's cabin and the radio room on the boat deck one level down. It was that ladder, Bud Loughman said, that the water had started to climb by 1800.

The radio traffic between ship and shore seems to have intensified that evening as the ship's situation deteriorated. The following is from Captain Connolly's account:

1830—Seas became mountainous and the MACAW straightened up to about 5 degrees starboard list.

Searchlights played on the MACAW. The Salvage Officer stated that her negative buoyancy would keep her in this cradle, and that she could not possibly move aft. Realizing this negative buoyancy condition and from previous experience here, I agreed.

1834—Received message from the MACAW, "List has decreased to 5 degrees starboard X Deck housing pierced sea breaking over bridge X All hands are on pilot house level notify us if we drift off X Heading 050 degrees true." The Salvage Officer and I decided that added water would increase negative buoyancy and that the ship could ride out the heavy seas and that personnel would be safe so long as they remained on the ship.

1835—Sent message to the MACAW, "Keep all hands well secured X Under no circumstances try to leave ship."[14]

No one on the *Macaw* could have been keen to leave the ship under the circumstances, but they would soon have no choice in the matter. Sightings from the shore to the contrary notwithstanding, by the time Connolly and

Curtis agreed the ship could not possibly move aft, it had probably already started to. Not only was that movement possible, once it began it was probably unstoppable, and the negative buoyancy Connolly and Curtis counted on to keep the ship pinned in its cradle probably helped make it so. Things tend to snag, not slip, on coral, but the *Macaw,* in the path of a powerful current and battered by waves that by 1800 may already have exceeded the height of their biggest predecessors in January, was slipping backward off the reef, and whatever water was penetrating its pierced deck housing, instead of saving the ship, might just have helped drag it down.

What pierced the deck housing appears to have been the Buda air compressor. Perhaps it had not been properly secured, or if it had been, like other gear on the ship that day, it may have been set loose by the waves and either washed off the ship or shifted around loose on deck. In chronicling the evening's events five days later, Shipfitter Nord Lester assigned to some of them times later than those that other sources such as Connolly's narrative do. Here he suggests that the mishap involving the Buda happened after 2000. Connolly has the deck getting pierced by 1834. Nevertheless, it appears likely that the two incidents are the same.

> On Feb 12th, 1944, while on the U.S.S. Macaw (A.S.R. 11) The ship was laying with the Starboard Quarter to the sea. About 1800 it was noticed that the swells from the sea were increasing in size. All loose gear was taken higher or lashed down, and all door, and ports were dogged down. About 2000 there was electric fire on the ten (10″) inch pump in the passageway, between the crew's head, and mess hall. The fire was put out with a (CO_2) Extinguisher. Soon gear from the boat deck was being carried over the side, by the seas. The Buda Air Pump made a large hole in the side of the Recompression Room, and the ship started to fill.[15]

The fire Lester cites was not the only improbable outbreak of combustion that would plague the men that night as they were surrounded ever more thoroughly by water. Exactly how fast that water engulfed them depends on who's telling the story. The enlisted men who survived that night all wrote accounts of it within days afterward—they were required to—and Bud Loughman wrote one too, and the accounts, four or five of them, that assign more or less specific times to various developments tend to vary somewhat in that regard. By one account the water had climbed halfway from the boat to the bridge deck by 2000; by another it had already reached the bridge deck by then.[16]

It was about then (8:00 p.m.) that the after bulkhead at the back of the chart room sprung a leak, which the men plugged as best they could with mattresses and a brass rail from the navigator's desk. They probably used the rail to prop up the mattresses. It is unknown how many mattresses they used, where they got them, who got them, or how. The captain's cabin was on the boat deck just under the bridge. Most or all of the other berthing was lower in the ship and probably completely inaccessible. The captain's cabin itself must have been at least a problematic destination by then if not completely submerged.

How effective the mattresses were as a water barrier can be inferred from the establishment shortly thereafter of the next line of defense at the door between the chart room and the pilothouse. The water having started spilling over the coaming at the base of that doorway, Burton ordered the chart room abandoned but stayed in it himself, working the door as a valve, closing it against surges and opening it between them to let water drain out of the pilothouse. This strategy proved futile too. The door was not watertight. Closing it did not keep water from getting past it, and as Herman Ehlers would note, the water level in the pilothouse kept seeking the water level in the chart room, and that level kept rising. No amount of desperate exertion could defeat the laws of physics.

Befitting its function, the pilothouse was liberally furnished with portholes, fourteen of them, six at about head-and-shoulder level on each side and two in front, affording the man at the wheel a wide scope of vision. Plugging those holes were circular windows about two feet in diameter consisting of thick, unbreakable glass framed in heavy bronze casings hinged at the top to open inward. Each could be held open for ventilation in good weather by means of a chain from the overhead, or "dogged down" snug and watertight against a gasket.

The view that day through those portholes cannot have been reassuring. Given the ship's more or less north-northeastward heading and the northward set of the seas, the most nearly head-on view of the approaching waves would have been out the starboard ports. But given the *Macaw*'s starboard list, which ranged up to 35 degrees that Saturday, the view out that side of the pilothouse would have been correspondingly canted downward, constricting the men's horizon and perhaps mercifully sparing them a good angle on the monstrous waves sweeping up on them. At a 35-degree list they might have seen little to starboard but the water in their more or less immediate vicinity, and little to port but sky. But by 1830 the list was reported to have decreased to a mere 5 degrees, and there still would have been enough daylight by then to reveal the oncoming swells surging up to break on or just beyond the ship in all their terrifying grandeur.

The starboard side of the pilothouse flooded first because the ship was listing that way—not as far as it had earlier in the day, but far enough to drive the men to the port side of the room, where their struggles focused, and soon their lives would depend, on the forward port-side porthole. Someone produced what Charles Kumler would identify as a five-gallon can, and the men began bailing with it, working in pairs, one man holding the port open between waves, and the other dumping water out through it. They did not have to go far to fill the bucket. By 2200, according to Herman Ehlers, even on the upslope portside of the room, they were standing in water four feet deep.[17]

The water encroaching on them was coming from two directions, above and below. Inside the ship water would surge and ebb with the swells, but the real danger it posed was in its relentless upward creep, a reflection of the ship's gradual downward slide.

The *Macaw* was bathed in light that night from searchlights on both Sand and Eastern Islands, including mobile units at the south end of the south submarine basin breakwater and a twenty-four-inch light mounted on the base signal tower, some of them trained on the ship as early as 1830, seven minutes before sunset. Other lights shone on the reef and on the beach on Eastern Island in search of refugees. The light no doubt came as a blessing to the men trapped on the ship, but perhaps a mixed one insofar as it revealed in gleaming black and white the monstrous waves assaulting them every thirteen seconds or so. The men may have supplemented the outside illumination with flashlights or cigarette lighters.[18]

Captain Connolly conferred at about 1900 with the marine defense officer, a Lieutenant Colonel Tingle, who deployed on the west and south shore of Eastern Island a double beach guard consisting of fifty marines, one naval officer, and ten enlisted men from the Naval Air Station and Construction Battalion. Then, at 2030, there was good news for the *Macaw*: "Weather moderating X Wind northwest 15–20 knots X Barometer rising."[19]

That message might have been more comforting to the men aboard the ship if it had been true of the waves as well as the weather at large, and if they had gotten it. Apparently they did not get it. The batteries for the TBY radio had the strange property of combusting when they got wet, and as much as the men no doubt struggled to keep them dry, they did get wet and started smoking. The men in the pilothouse were probably about waist deep in water by then, completely surrounded by it when waves engulfed the ship, and among the dangers they faced was that of fire, or at least of toxic smoke inhalation. As they ignited, the batteries were tossed out the same port the men had been bailing through, and through which, since earlier that day, they had hung the antenna for the radio. They seem to have made their last attempt to use the radio about 2030, the same time Connolly says the cheerful weather report was sent the other way. Apparently neither message got through. Shortly afterward the last battery ignited and went out the port, and with it the last hope the men aboard had of communicating with the shore.

Captain Connolly was monitoring the situation from the signal tower, a converted water tank standing 170 feet high by one official account, 200 by another, near the southeast edge of Sand Island overlooking the seaplane basin, about a mile and a half away. Between the *Macaw* and that tower there was nothing but the seaplane basin, the more southerly of the two breakwaters that enclosed it, and open water.

In the basin were probably all eighteen PB2Y Coronado seaplanes that had been operating out of Midway over the preceding two weeks, making bombing runs on Japanese-occupied Wake Island, about 1,200 miles to the southwest. Alongside the breakwater there might have been some equipment or small craft, and on the water beyond it there might in theory have been a small boat or two, but given the height of the tower, the view from within it of the *Macaw* would have been obstructed by nothing but the waves sweeping over the ship. That is not to say that in the intervals between waves that view would have been entirely clear. The lingering spume from each wave probably continued to obscure the ship even after the wave broke, and meanwhile in the glare of the searchlights the mounting front of the next wave must have made for a difficult backdrop. But the view from the tower was good enough that by 2100 the men in it could see that things were looking grim. The *Macaw* was submerged to its boat deck and—the supposed impossibility of its moving notwithstanding—it had moved aft half a ship's length, about 125 feet. A radio communication check about then showed no message received by the *Macaw* or from it. By 2130, Connolly wrote, "Water breaking green seas over pilot house and estimated to be waves 30–35 feet high reaching to top of foremast."[20]

Connolly's estimate of the height of those waves was probably about right. Under normal conditions, to break over the top of the *Macaw's* foremast, a wave would have had to top out at just over a mythological hundred feet. Given that, by numerous accounts by the men inside it, the pilothouse was more or less underwater by about 2130, it seems that by then it had sunk about forty feet. If the whole ship had sunk that far purely vertically, a wave would still have had to come in at more than sixty-three feet to clear the foremast. But the *Macaw* was not sinking straight down; it was angling bow up and listing. By itself, the bow's angling up might have slightly elevated the top of the mast, but the list would have lowered it, far more than offsetting any lift produced by the ship's altered trim.

The sharpest list estimate for the *Macaw* before midnight was 35 degrees. Bud Loughman wrote of a 50-degree list at an unspecified time, inferably after midnight. A list that sharp in combination with a vertical descent of forty feet might have brought the top of the foremast within range of forty-foot waves. Whether waves were actually breaking that high that night, no one can say. No one was out there with a tape measure, and if anyone had been, he would not have known exactly where his base was to measure from.[21]

Capt. Charles D. Edmunds, USN, who had replaced Captain Connolly as acting commander of the submarine force at Midway three days before, testified later about waves twenty-five to thirty feet high. Bud Loughman would write of fifty-footers. Edmunds described "an extraordinarily high sea . . . with mountainous groundswells breaking in the immediate vicinity of the vessel." Commodore G. E. Short, the commandant of NOB 1504 at the time, who was also in the signal tower that night, used some of the same language, citing "mountainous groundswells" and "extremely high rollers," some of which "foamed up to the top of the Macaw's foremast." That was probably an accurate description, though from a mile and a half away at night, even with good binoculars and powerful searchlights, it cannot have been easy to discern where a wave stopped and its foam began. In any case, it seems safe to say the waves that night ranged in height somewhere between Edmunds's estimate of twenty-five to thirty feet and Loughman's of fifty. By all accounts they were huge.[22]

Judging from Curtis Wainscott's account, it was about 2300 when a wave tore loose a section of the steel spray shield along the starboard side of the bridge deck about thirty feet long and estimated by Bud Loughman at one inch thick. The wave, Loughman wrote, bent the shield "like cardboard" and tossed it about twenty feet in the air, where he said it wavered and seemed likely to crash down against the pilothouse ports. Instead, according to Wainscott, it fell onto an antenna wire, then over the side.[23]

By about that time it appeared to the men in the signal tower that the pilothouse had carried away, and Captain Connolly, by his own telling, requested permission of Captain Edmunds to go out to the ship in an LCM, a mechanized landing craft. "The answer," Connolly wrote, "was definitely in the negative." So, as he noted, were the prospects for the men on the ship: "2300—2400—The situation looked hopeless as it was now manifestly impossible for any one to have successfully left the ship without being killed either clearing the ship or in the tremendous surf."[24]

The pilothouse had not in fact carried away, and the men inside it had not given up hope. They had, however, given up bailing. They had had to, either because, as Bud Loughman wrote, they had lost their bailing cans (plural—apparently there were two) or because continued attempts at bailing would have meant more water coming in than going out. But even then the forward portside port remained vital to their struggle to survive. Oxygen depletion was shaping up as an issue by about midnight—having disposed of the problem of fire, they now faced the threat of asphyxiation—but as long as the seas were submerging that port only intermittently, they were able to drain water out through it during the gaps between waves, much as Paul Burton had done earlier with the door to the chart room, and to let fresh air in.

But those opportunities gradually became shorter and less frequent, and it became increasingly difficult to hold the port shut between them. One man had sufficed for that task earlier in the evening. As the night wore on and the seas lowered their shoulders more and more against the ship and brought more and more pounds of water pressure to bear upon it, even on what amounted to the lee side, by at least one account it took three men at a time. The window of opportunity to use that window was shutting, and finally, when it seemed there wasn't time enough to use it profitably anymore, the men shut it themselves.

The water continued to rise and we started to drain it as the water dropped outside every so often, through the port we had open. The port was held closed when the water level rose above it outside Eventually the water level seemed to be above the pilot house over

two thirds of the time so the port was dogged down just tight enough
so that air came in through it as the water level dropped below it
every now and then, sort of a breathing effect.[25]

The breathing effect Herman Ehlers refers to was a product of the fluctu-
ating air pressure within the ship as the waves surged into and drained out of
it. When a wave swept into the ship, water poured in through the gouged hull,
displacing the air inside and forcing it up, some of it into pilothouse, enough
with each wave to increase the air pressure in the room by three-tenths of 1
percent, an increment registered by the aneroid barometer in the room and
one just powerful enough to push shut the forward port-side port (and
maybe one or more of the ports aft of it as well), which had been "dogged
down," or secured, on an opening of about a quarter of an inch—just tight
enough, as Ehlers noted, to respond to this barometric shove. In this way,
each wave in effect shut the door on itself. Or the doors—Bud Loughman
suggests that all three ports in the port-side forward bulkhead may have been
enlisted to serve this valve function. When the wave drained out of the ship
and the air pressure in the room dropped, the port, or ports, either popped
open under the now comparatively greater pressure of the air outside or were
reopened manually (it's not entirely clear which), in either case once again to
about a quarter of an inch—any greater an opening might have let too much
water in—and the room sucked in fresh air from outside, not much air
because there wasn't much of an opening, but enough to sustain the men
within. The ship itself was breathing after a fashion, and enabling the men in
the pilothouse to breathe, even as it was drowning, and even if its exhalations
were blocked. And the driving force behind this God-sent pulmonary mechanism was the same one that was dragging the *Macaw* down. The following is
how Bud Loughman described the process, referring to ports in the plural:
"They were cracked just enough to respond to the inboard pressure of the air
when compressed by rising seas inside as well as outside the ship. In this way
the ports admitted no additional water through them and when the seas went
down below the level of the ports, the pressure in the room would correspondingly decrease & the ports would crack sufficiently to admit air."[26]

It was a remarkable arrangement, and it couldn't last. It relied on two
things, one being the wrench the dogging down was done with, whether after
every wave, as some accounts suggest, or only occasionally by way of tweak-
ing a system that basically worked on its own, as others indicate. In either

case, that wrench had done vital service for hours that night when finally, according to Bud Loughman, the man wielding it dropped it. The water in the compartment had gotten deep enough by then that the attempt to retrieve it meant diving for it and groping in the dark. Several men reportedly did just that but couldn't find it.[27]

If they had found it, it wouldn't have done them much good. Loughman said it was about 0100 Sunday when the wrench was lost, and by then the seas were covering the ports so much of the time that there would have been little or no use for a wrench anymore anyway. It got to where even in the troughs between waves, the water was staying above the ports—there was no more air outside them to admit. The ship by various accounts had resumed a sharp starboard list by about midnight—Lawrence Mathers estimated it at 30 to 40 degrees. About two hours later, Bud Loughman wrote, it was 50 degrees. The *Macaw* was in its death throes. "All I know is the ship was tilting more and more," Stanley Libera said. "Water was getting higher and higher and higher and higher." Bud Loughman wrote: "You could hear the ship straining as she slipped into deeper water. The ship's list would increase to such an extent, it was thought she would go over."[28]

Albert Bolke, five feet four inches tall, was probably the shortest man in the pilothouse that night, and depending on where he was standing and whether he was able to find a perch of some sort, probably among the first to have the water flirt with his chin, and to resort to a tactic Bud Loughman described from that night, that of hanging from the steel I-beams that ran along the overhead (i.e., the ceiling). Edward Wade, at five five and a half, would have been literally and figuratively in the same boat.

Once the forward port subsided even below the troughs between waves, it was just a matter of time before twenty-two pairs of lungs exhausted the oxygen in the room and replaced it with carbon dioxide. That oxygen, the breathable kind, was confined to a triangular space under what amounted to a peaked ceiling, the apex of which was the juncture between the portside bulkhead (i.e., the left wall) and the overhead—the latter of which, for the men closest to that bulkhead, would no longer have been quite overhead—and the men were crowded into the strip of space along that bulkhead underneath the trapped pocket of air. By 0230 Sunday, February 13, that air was becoming unbreathable.

Bud Loughman wrote of their last minutes in the pilothouse to his lifelong friend Jack McCarthy about a month and a half later:

After the ship had settled so deeply as to no time have the ports above water then the CO_2 content began to build up. . . . [A]t 0230 12–13 Feb . . . we had no more than 18 inches of air space between ourselves & the overhead. The ship being on a fifty degree list to starboard, forced us to breathe in our little equilateral air pocket. The CO_2 content became unbearable. . . . It was like being under an overturned canoe.[29]

By his own earlier account, Loughman's estimate of an air pocket of as much as eighteen inches may have been generous. In an official report submitted eleven days after the sinking, he wrote that, after holding at chest level for several hours, by 0230 the water level had risen to within twelve inches of the overhead: "Occasional lurches would fill that space with water. The carbon dioxide content became untenable."[30]

Sixty-five years later, in what may have been a manual understatement, Stanley Libera indicated by hand that the water at its worst got to somewhere from upper-chest to chin level. But, he said, he didn't think he would die. And he may not have been alone in that sentiment. No one panicked. "Everyone was cool headed," Richard Blaine Williamson would write. Nord Lester confirmed that judgment: "There were no noises, or words of frightened men." So did Lewill Horsman: "We stayed in the pilot house until the water was up to our chins and the air was filled with CO_2, everyone was breathing in short heavy breaths," he wrote. "Every one was calm and never said much."[31]

At that stage no one would have wanted to say much. No one had any breath to waste. By a hearsay third-party report fifty-eight years after the fact, William Funk, the pharmacist's mate, expended a little about then, wondering aloud in a state very understandably matching his name: "God damn, why am I here? We shouldn't be here. We should never have been on this rock." But that was the only reported expression of unhappiness in about eight hours among almost two dozen young men trapped on the very brink of mortality. Lawrence Mathers wrote days later that Paul Burton and Bud Loughman worked throughout the ordeal to keep the men's spirits up. At first that would not have been a hard job. Bud Loughman described the spirits of the men that Saturday evening as "excellent." Nord Lester recalled joking and smoking, and said they kept smoking until their cigarettes got wet. There was probably some gallows humor as the night progressed, but less of it as the ship settled down, the proximity of death settled in, and the means of avoiding it dwindled. Whatever shows of youthful bravado they may have put on for one another, none of them can have been happy about their plight as the night wore on. But with that one possible fleeting exception, no one seems to have let on otherwise. But neither, it seems safe to say, by about 0200 was anyone feigning devil-may-care jollity. As the oxygen waned, so presumably did the youthful raillery. What conversation there was in those grim last few minutes in the pilothouse was apparently, and not surprisingly, sparse.[32]

The historical record is not entirely clear on whose idea it was to leave the pilothouse, or exactly when they did. By most accounts they left about 0230. Bosun's Mate Charles Scott, whose watch was still working at the time, wrote that it was 0300. Paul Burton may have been thinking of trying to hang on until daylight, but it had become obvious by about 0200 that they couldn't. "At approximately 0200, the water was so high that it was very hard for every-one to keep their head in air," wrote Charles Kumler, the electrician's mate from Chicago. "At about 0230 the air gave out altogether. Most of the men who could get air, couldn't breathe."[33]

According to Bud Loughman, Kumler passed out around 0230, where-upon he, Loughman, suggested to Burton that they had better go, and Burton in turn ordered the men to leave the pilothouse and make for the flying bridge and the foremast atop it. Blaine Williamson credited the proposal to William Roscoe Funk. "At about 2.30," he wrote, "Chief Funk said to the Cap-tain don't you think it is about time to open the hatch & abband ship & the Captain said Yes." But Stanley Libera insisted it was Loughman who broached the idea. His exact words, Libera insisted sixty-seven years later, were, "We better get outta here or we'll die in here like a bunch of rats."[34]

Whoever proposed the idea, Burton endorsed it and ordered the door opened. The door in question was in the aft bulkhead, just inside the portside aft corner of the room. The door opened out onto the bridge deck, and it was hinged, as you faced it from the inside, on the left. The port side was the lee-ward side that night, spared the worst of the ocean's violence. But that com-parative advantage probably subsided somewhat as the ship itself did and the starboard side of the ship, the protective barrier, slipped into the sea. In any case, by about 0230 Sunday, even if relatively mild, the beating the portside pilothouse door had taken had apparently been enough to damage it, for when Burton ordered its dogs (or latches) released, and the men near it—including Bosun's Mates Tom Emmet Brown and Augie Paul Koepke, the lat-ter about to abandon his third ship in just over a year and a half—sought mightily to shoulder it open, it budged only about two inches. Koepke then enlisted more help. "I put my fingers in the crack trying to pull as well as push a wave caught the door and forced it shut mashing my fingers," he wrote. "I remarked then that the door wouldn't open & hollered come on everybody shove on this door."[35]

Stanley Libera was not sure sixty-seven years later whether he was among those who responded to Koepke's call, but if he wasn't, it was only for lack of space or access. No one there required persuasion to help. "If we didn't get that hatch open," Libera said, "all of us would have been in one little grave together." Koepke's recruiting was effective. Lots of brute force was brought to bear on the door, and it yielded at last. As Libera said of this effort, "When you're under distress, you're twice as strong."[36]

For Herman Ehlers, the quartermaster from Illinois, it opened none too soon, even if only on another predicament.

> The port hatch was then, after some difficulty, opened and the water level outside just happened to drop at this time allowing us to file out. Just prior to the hatch being opened the water where I was, forward in the pilot house, reached the overhead, cutting off my air but as the hatch opened the water dropped quite a bit and gave me an opportunity to reach the hatch with little difficulty. After clearing the hatch I commenced climbing to the signal bridge having in mind to reach the fore mast if at all possible. After maintaining my hold on the signal bridge through several breakers I reached the mast and had just started to climb up when a large wave broke my hold and carried me off.[37]

Motor Machinist's Mate 3/c Richard Blaine Williamson, too, describes in his survivor's account a harrowing final few moments before the door was opened: "The men next to the hatch tried to open it but they couldn't get it open. At that time the water level was above the top of hatch and the water level was about 1–1/2 foot from the over head. At this time the ship rolled & every one was under water but it rolled back & that give all of us a chance to get our breath then we all pushed & the hatch came open."[38]

At least part of the port side of the pilothouse still had a thin band of what passed for air under the overhead when the door opened, and when the first of the seas that proceeded to surge into the room receded, it left that same little pocket behind, only cleaned out and refreshed. The experience of drinking in that delicious fresh air after hours of inhaling an increasingly dense concentration of human exhaust left on Bud Loughman an impression he was to record in more than one written account of the night. One was in his letter to his friend Jack McCarthy: "The CO_2 content became unbearable & we forced the port door open to the bridge deck. The seas were then at their highest. Fortunately due to the list of the ship & to the coaming over the door, the seas rushed in, covered the entire area to the overhead and when subsided left clean air in that pocket of 18"."[39]

Another was in the narrative he submitted to the subsequent board of investigation: "Before leaving a wave forced me back into the pilot house. That wave cleared the foul air and permitted several of us to get fresh air in the space formed by the top of the door to the overhead."[40]

Paul Burton by various accounts ordered the men to make for the foremast, but that was another objective mere necessity would have directed them to. The foremast was the higher of the ship's two masts; it offered two horizontal surfaces to stand on in the form of the forward searchlight platform, about ten feet above the flying bridge, and the crow's nest, another forty feet or so up; and it was close at hand—it emerged from the superstructure of the ship at the midpoint of the forward edge of the flying bridge, just atop the pilothouse, within about eight vertical and fifteen horizontal feet of a man standing at the portside pilothouse door. The searchlight platform, about six feet in diameter, could hold many more men than the little crow's nest but at a far lower elevation. There was a ladder by which men climbed from one to the other. In a pinch they could cling to that. The searchlight platform was where Seaman 1/c Stephen Miller had delivered his Shakespeare recitations. The flying bridge, about ten feet below it, was about to become the scene of some real drama, including a tragedy.

As near as the foremast was, it would not prove easy to get to, and not everyone who got to it climbed it, or climbed it very far, Herman Ehlers being a case in point. Robert Vaughn and Augie Koepke got to it, Vaughn with Koepke's help, but neither of them ended up on it. Koepke, by his own account, was the third or fourth man out the door. (The radio guard he refers to was a fixture, described by Bob Jacobsen as an arc-shaped steel tube, that served as an anchor for antenna cables. It was mounted outside and just above the portside pilothouse door. Curtis Wainscott in his account calls it an antenna bar.)

Two or three fellows went out before me. As I went out I hit my head on a Radio guard above the door & made my way to the Ladder leading to the Flying Bridge. I went up this ladder and on to the [flying] bridge deck & was working my way forward to the Mast. The Chief Bosin Mate Brown, Called to me & asked me to give Vaughn a hand. I didn't know if he was injured or what, but I stopped & reached over the Flying Bridge deck & pulled him up & to geather we made our way to the foot of the Mast. (From the time we left the pilot house up until this time the Waves were not as strong as they had been & we seemed to be in a sort of lull.) A Big wave hit me & I was washed off the Flying Bridge. My Submarine jacket caught on the Starboard 20 MM gun & when the wave subsided I was dangling on the gun barrel which was in a upright position, I threw my arms over my head & slipped out of my jacket. My life belt was unhooked in this proceedure but I was free. I rose up on the next wave & saw Vaughn standing on the flying Bridge next to the Mast. I hollered for him to give me a hand & he did succeed in grabbing my arm, but another wave hit & I was washed over the Starboard side.[41]

The *Macaw* had eight 20mm antiaircraft guns, four of which were on the bridge deck, two on each side, one forward and one aft. It was probably the forward starboard gun Koepke found himself dangling from the barrel of like a rag doll, that being the closer of the two on that side to the foremast. In attempting to return the favor Koepke had done him in hoisting him onto the flying bridge, Vaughn almost certainly left the mast—the odds that the wave he almost succeeded in plucking Koepke from would have delivered Koepke to within even two arms' reach of the mast are low. After the next wave broke his grip on Koepke and swept him overboard, Vaughn apparently made his way back to the mast, or tried to. He was on or somewhere near the flying bridge and in need of help when Curtis Wainscott arrived there.

When the door opened everyone started to leave one by one. When I got outside the door, I reached up and caught hold of the antenna bar on the bulkhead. There were two beside me on the same bar and there was someone hanging on my shoulders. I asked the Chief Boatswain [Brown] to help me and at that time there was a breaker come over the ship and that is the last I saw of him or the fellows on the bar. I went from there up to the signal bridge where I stood for a moment. I saw the colored mess attendant. I made my way forward to help him but at that time a breaker hit me and I went over on the port side by the main mast and around the bow of the ship and then started to sea.[42]

Ship's Carpenter 3/c George Washington Manning got to the flying bridge a little later and found Vaughn "hanging on to the rail around the platform forward." It's not entirely clear from that description which side of the rail Vaughn was on—whether inside it, standing on the platform and clutching the rail, or outside it, hanging by his arms from the rail—but it was probably the latter inasmuch as Manning wrote that he stopped there to give Vaughn a hand. Had Vaughn been standing on the platform, he probably would not have needed one. If he was outside it, hanging from the rail, he clearly did. That more perilous position also fits better with what happened next: "When a large wave hit us and tore Vaughn loose and knocked him against the forward 3-inch gun barrel and knocked it down. It was the last I saw of him. I believe that it killed him instantly."[43]

The forward three-inch .50-caliber gun stood on a mount at the forward snub nose of the boat deck, overlooking the forward stretch of the main deck and the bow, and was overlooked in turn, about fifteen feet aft and ten up, by the flying bridge. The barrel of the gun was about thirteen feet long. When Vaughn hit it, it was in its locked, upright position. It may have been the combined impact of Vaughn and the wave that propelled him that dislodged it and left it horizontal. Manning proceeded up the mast to the crow's nest, where he encountered Edward Wade and Charles Scott. According to Manning, the two of them repaired into the crow's nest, asking him to alert them in the event the ship should start to roll over, and he obligingly said he would. If that seems inhospitable of Wade and Scott, a third man could probably not have fit into the crow's nest, Manning would be better able to monitor things outside it than they could in, and it would probably have done no one any good for two or all three to cling to the mast instead of just one. The crow's nest, as long as it stayed on the mast and the mast stayed intact, offered a haven it would have been foolish for no one to take advantage of.[44]

From his vantage point about forty-five feet above the flying bridge, Manning saw Radioman Stanley Libera swinging below on what Manning identified as an antenna cable and two or more signal halyards, which are lines on which a ship can run signal flags up and down a mast. Libera, having like Koepke and lots of other men been swept off the flying bridge while trying to get to the foremast, had managed to grab onto what he identified only as antenna cables and, as he described it, he "hung onto them for about a half hour swinging from one end of the ship to the other" and repeatedly banging his legs on one of the searchlight platforms, presumably the forward one. Whether one or more cables or lanyards or some combination of the two, whatever Libera was swinging by had apparently torn free at the lower end— any cables, probably from the antenna bar Augie Koepke bumped his head on and Curtis Wainscott and others clung to upon exiting the pilothouse. It was likely the foremast that the cables and/or lanyards in question dangled from, or one of two service spars that crossed it, one below the crow's nest and one above it; and given the ship's list, they probably dangled, and Libera probably did his swinging, on the ship's starboard side. Manning descended the mast— how far he doesn't say—and tried to grab Libera or whatever it was he was swinging by to rein him in, but a large wave struck, knocking Libera's head against the searchlight platform, breaking his grip, and dropping him into the sea.[45]

In the pilothouse, Libera had been optimistic—he hadn't thought he would die. Now he figured he probably would. He had twice narrowly avoided drowning as a kid, once through the good offices of a neighbor, once through those of his father, but he was on his own now, and to the extent that he could see anything, he could that see that his prospects looked bleak. A devout Catholic, Libera said his prayers: "When I was out there . . . I'm calling it swimming. I didn't see anybody. I didn't know where the hell I was at. . . . All I saw was waves, kept swallowing the water, swallowing the water. I said to God, 'I'm blessing myself because this is the end.'"[46]

He did, actually, per other recollections, see a few people, including, just after he was washed overboard, a man hanging from something above the deck—probably either Vaughn dangling from the railing at the edge of the flying bridge just before the wave that likely killed him, or Koepke, moments before that, snagged on the barrel of the antiaircraft gun from which he escaped at the cost of his life vest. Libera said he always wondered whether that man made it.

Manning meanwhile climbed back up to the crow's nest and saw Motor Machinist's Mate 3/c Erwin Richard Knecht, probably atop the tripod, a three-legged structure aft on the boat deck that supported the mainmast, which stood atop it, and the ship's forty-five-thousand-pound boom, which projected from it at an angle toward the stern. A wave had hit Knecht as he emerged from the pilothouse and washed him to the base of the structure, dragging him against lines for the smaller aft boom on the port side en route. Resembling a child's erector set construction writ large, the tripod stood about forty-five feet above the boat deck and, like the foremast, offered at least temporary sanctuary from the huge breakers. Knecht described what he saw while on it:

> The next thing I knew I was holding on to a plat form or something and looking up I saw the tri pod. There was a voice calling Help me! Help me! while I was climbing up the ladder. When I reached the peak of the tri pod, I sat down to regain some of my strength. Look-ing down I saw Kingsley holding on one of the tri pods. I tried encouraging him by yelling "You can make it Kingsley." Just as I started down the ladder to help him, a wave came over, after it passed I looked down and Kingsley was gone.[47]

Radio Technician Lawrence Mathers, the former traveling oil salesman who was supposed to have been safely on shore that day, was one of two men (the other was Brown) to report being swept right over the ship from one side to the other. (One account by Loughman suggests that he might have made such a crossing too.)

> At approximately 2 a.m. the water level had risen to the point where there was barely room for the heads of the officers and men between the surface and the overhead of the pilot house. At this point the fact became apparent that we must try to open the port hatch of the pilot house and attempt to reach the flying bridge. Some difficulty was experienced in getting the hatch open, during which time all hands were in peril of their lives. The hatch was finally forced open by the combined efforts of all those near it, and the incoming rush of water submerged the entire pilot house. As soon as the water receded, all hands moved out onto the bridge deck as soon as possible. I seized the bar outside the hatch on the port side on which antennae were normally secured. Beside me was Funk, CPh.M, and on the ladder to our right was Bolke G.M3c. Above us, on the signal bridge railing,

was Wainscott S2c. In this position, we were struck by the first large breaker to come over after we left the pilot house. When the force of the wave subsided, Funk was gone from my side, and Wainscott was gone from the railing. Bolke climbed up the ladder, and I climbed up so that my feet were on the bar and I was holding onto the signal bridge railing. The next large wave swept me away from the ship and to port for about fifty yards. The current there swept me back over the ship at a point about amidships and out on the starboard side. Here I found Kumler, EM2/c, and we hung onto each other. At a point farther out on the starboard side, we met Ehlers, QM2/c, and the three of us hung together. Within a few minutes we met Brown, CBM, and Wainscott, S2/c, supporting between them Koepke, BM2/c, who was injured and without a life belt. We joined forces with these three, and formed a circle, supporting Koepke among us.[48]

It was Koepke's good fortune to find the company he did in the water. Having suffered smashed fingers, a blow to the head, and coral abrasions and lost his life vest to the 20mm gun, he would almost certainly have drowned if he had had to fend for himself. Once he found himself in the water, he removed his shirt and shoes, tried to swim back to the ship, and failed. He couldn't overcome a contrary current. Then he found Wainscott—the guy, "If you was gonna do anything, you'd want him on your side"—and Wainscott was now at Koepke's side when Koepke was finding his third unscheduled departure from a ship even harder than he had the first two. Wainscott was not in perfect health himself—he had suffered a deep gash to his heel, having cut it, Loughman thought, on the ragged remaining edge of the bridge deck spray shield that had been torn apart (or of one of two that had, as Loughman would later suggest). But his own injury notwithstanding, Wainscott was able to hold Koepke up. Wainscott had been swept overboard as he was trying to assist Vaughn, and was drifting out to sea when he heard Koepke hollering in distress:

> While going out someone called and said they didn't have a life jacket. I swam over and we got together. It was Koepke, BM2c. We were going out to sea all the time. A little ways out we met the chief boatswain's mate [Brown]. We stayed together. Just a little farther out

we saw the Captain. We tried to get to the channel buoy but couldn't make it. We then headed out to sea.[49]

In keeping with naval protocol, it seems that officers Bud Loughman and Paul Burton were the last two men to leave the pilothouse. Shipfitter 2/c Lewill Horsman wrote of pushing Loughman and Seaman 1/c Joseph Verkennes toward the door—this by way, no doubt, not of stampeding them but of helping them make headway against a wave—and of Loughman's stepping aside as they neared the door and standing by Burton. More than one survivor has claimed to be the last to leave the pilothouse that morning, but you would expect that man to be the captain, and it seems clear that it was. Nord Lester stated so unequivocally shortly afterward in writing, and Bud Loughman did too, twice. Loughman also claimed years later to have gone back into the pilothouse in search of the ship's log. If he did, he did not find it.[50]

Loughman wrote a number of sad letters to wives and parents of missing men after that night, and among them was one to Paul Burton's wife, Betty, dated February 22, 1944. "We all managed to reach the topmost deck," he wrote her, "but Paul and I were seemingly swept overboard by the same swell. He went his way and I mine."[51]

Neither man's path would be smooth. Loughman described his a month and a half later in a letter to his friend Jack McCarthy:

I left with the captain, nos. 21 & 22 respectively. We went topside or rather due to the listing to starboard walked on an even plane to the flying bridge hoping to make the foremast. We both simultaneously reached that deck only to meet up with a 50 footer & Loughman began what he thought was his last great struggle. I was under for a long time but escaped injury. The entire spray shields had been torn off & their remaining members were dangerously ragged. I tried for the ship again and made the rim of the stack, this being visible in the trough of a wave. I held onto it with all my force but was carried away again. I later felt myself being swept at a great rate towards the mainmast, which was atop tripod legs which supported our 45000 lb. boom. I doubled up around the ladder leading up and was then streamed aft like a wind vane. When that pressure let up I was going up a cable hand over hand when another incoming 50 footer took me off. Next time I remembered coming up and being shot through the mainmast section. I hit another shroud and hung on. I remember getting air once & then was carried out & under. When I did come up I was 150 feet aft of the ship heading swiftly out to sea. I was fine however & managed to keep my head above water from then on. I heard my skipper answer when I called there was an object capable of supporting us on my left. He kidded with me & I with him. I never heard from him again. He and that group were carried away from me and I was carried toward the beach. A strange whim of the sea carried me back out, this time near enough to that object That I was able to make it after considerable exertion. I found another of my shipmates there & we clung to it til the following morning.[52]

"That object" to which Loughman refers so cryptically was buoy No. 2, the one the *Macaw* had maneuvered so close to, and possibly overridden, on another rough day at Midway during its last few moments of freedom four weeks before—four weeks that must have felt like so many centuries to Paul Burton, if he gave them any thought that day. The reason for not calling a buoy a buoy was censorship, in this case self-censorship. Loughman knew better than to identify the No. 2 buoy any more specifically than he did.

Judging from this letter, after getting swept off the ship his first time, Loughman succeeded in what Koepke and later Whitmarsh tried and failed to do—he swam back to the ship—but he didn't stay there long, and he probably should not have gone back at all. The ship was not a bad place to be if you were in the crow's nest, like Wade and Scott, or on the foremast near it, like Manning, or atop the tripod, like Knecht. But anywhere else the combination of hard and sometimes jagged surfaces and huge waves made for a very hazardous environment. Loughman was lucky to have returned to it and been expelled a second time from it without serious injury. He did much better, once he saw the buoy, to swim for that, and having grown up on Long Island Sound and spent much of his childhood in and on water, he was a strong enough swimmer to get to it.

So was Nord Lester, who had grown up in the San Diego area and done lots of ocean swimming as a kid. That had been fun, but he hadn't relished the prospect of doing more that morning. As he left the pilothouse, he recalled fifty-four years later, he said to himself, "Oh shit, I'm gonna hafta swim." Both Lester and his buddy and fellow diver Lewill Horsman, like so many of the other men that day, made it to the flying bridge only to get swept off it. Lester, like Loughman, would return to the ship, though not apparently by choice, and there he would have an encounter with the aft counterpart to the three-inch-fifty gun that Vaughn was hurled into.[53]

> I made my way to the Flying Bridge, and was hanging on to the Port Signal gun. There I saw L.E. Horsman S.F.2/c at the bottom of the foremast. The following wave I was washed overboard. I was caught in the Channels out going tide. A wave came and I was washed against the stack, as the water receded I hit the tripod, or main boom, as the water receded there I saw Knecht M.M.Mo.3/c in the rigging, again as the water receded. I cleared myself, and hit the after three inch, and cleared the fantail. As the tide was going out to sea, I saw the Channel Buoy, on the port side going out. On making my way to the Bouy I saw Kingsley F.2/c who appeared to be all right, as I spoke to him a wave hit us, and that was the last I saw of him. I spoke to some one behind me, and said "make for that Bouy" and after Lt. Loughman arrived.[54]

Lester was one of four men who reportedly saw Kingsley after they left the pilothouse. Erwin Knecht from his perch on the tripod saw him clinging to one of its legs and started down to help him when a wave carried Kingsley off. Motor Machinist's Mate Richard Blaine Williamson testified that Kingsley floated between him and his fellow MoMM Donald Whitmarsh and that Whitmarsh talked with Kingsley. There's no record of what they said. If Williamson was able to make out any of their exchange, he neglected to say so in his survivor's report, and neither party to the conversation lived to recount it.

Buoy No. 2 was a popular and elusive destination that morning. At least ten men tried to get to it; only two, Lester and Loughman, succeeded. Among those who tried and failed were Williamson and Whitmarsh. The paths the two of them and Gunner's Mate 3/c Albert Bolke followed from the pilothouse intertwined. Those paths led two of them to safety and one to his death. The following is from Williamson's account:

> When I got out [of the pilothouse] a wave came over & I was under the railing as soon as it passed I reached down to help Bolke who was holding on to Whitmarsh & another wave came over & threw me over board on the port side I came up back by the booms the

current was very swift there it then carried me out toward the buoy on the starboard stern There I met Whitmarsh We were floating around to-gather until a big breaker came & we were both taken under Whitmarsh & I were both trying to get to the buoy Soon after the first big breaker came over another one came & I was carried toward shore. I hollered to Whitmarsh twice but didn't get any answer. After that there was one breaker right after the other until I land in shallow water next to an old barge that is sunk I thot of getting on it but I was so cold I kept right on toward shore. Liberia came up next to me while in the shallow water & I ask him how he was making it & he said ok after I left the post. where the water was shallow & swam from there on to the shore I came out next to the crane on eastern Island There were several Marines waiting for me they were holding hands & standing in the water about neck deep to pick me up from there I was taken to the hospital with Bolke who beat me ashore a few minutes this is all I remember other that the Marines sure treated us fine at hospital[55]

With the aid of a life vest, stern necessity, and Lewill Horsman, Albert Bolke had learned to swim. Or if he hadn't swum, he had at least floated successfully. Improbably enough, Bolke was one of the first men ashore. Horsman, upon taking his turn at getting swept off the flying bridge, caught hold of a rod of some sort, possibly a ceramic-clad antenna cable, and was trying to fight his way back to the foremast when another wave took up where the first one left off, tore him off the ship and submerged him. After what seemed an inordinate amount of time underwater, he realized that he had lost his life vest and had the presence of mind to divest himself with what must have been great haste of much of his clothing, and thus unencumbered he broke the surface at last. There he happened upon Bolke, whose pants he helped him shed in turn for greater mobility and buoyancy, and then they made their way separately to Eastern Island, Bolke the first-time swimmer making the better time. By the time Horsman made his way through the barbed wire on the beach and got an escort to the infirmary, Bolke and Williamson were already there. Before long Stanley Libera was brought in too.[56]

Asked afterward how he had done it, Bolke is said to have replied that he just hit bottom and started walking. Fifty-eight years later his former shipmate Howard Rechel quoted Bolke addressing the subject of his survival in different but similarly lighthearted terms: "I couldn't swim. I didn't know what I was gonna do. Then I was the first one ashore." Then he'd laugh, Rechel said. "An easygoing guy."[57]

Stanley Libera was asked sixty-seven years later how *he* had done it.

"Don't ask me how I got to shore," he replied. "All I know is the Lord in heaven there said it's not my time."

"I swam all that time, I never saw anybody. I didn't know where the hell I was going. . . . I told them I was swimming. They said bullshit, the wind blew you in."

"They" were apparently his shipmates, but whoever they were, he seems to have embraced their thinking, for he himself on another occasion expressed the exact same sentiment—that for all he knew he might have been heading out to sea, and that the winds blew him in.

Had he swallowed any water?

"Swallow water, oh Christ, I must have swallowed half of the ocean."

He said he had no recollection of actually getting to the beach. The last thing he remembered was seeing a hand reaching out for him. "The only thing I remember is I had my hand up in the air and somebody grabbed it." And the next thing he knew, he was waking up in the infirmary.[58]

Having descended the tripod in his futile attempt to assist Kingsley, Erwin Knecht climbed back atop it and spent the rest of the night there. "I went to the top of the tri pod where the commissioning pennant was and held on while the waves broke over and under me," he wrote. "About 4 o'clock in the morning I saw Whitmarsh coming toward the tri-pods. The waves were carrying him between the tri-pod and the mast. Manning was gathering up rope to try to aid him from the mast but a wave came along and dragged him away."[59]

Manning tried to warn Whitmarsh off, but Whitmarsh either failed to hear him or paid him no heed. "I then saw Whitmarsh MoMM1/c trying to swim back to the ship," Manning wrote. "I yelled and told him to head for the open sea that he would be picked up in the morning. I guess he didn't hear me for he kept trying. I grabbed a hold of a signal hal[y]ard and cut it loose and threw it to him. He tried to catch it but couldn't a large wave hit him and that was the last I saw of him."[60]

If Knecht's reckoning of time is roughly accurate, Whitmarsh by then had been struggling for his life an hour or more, during which, according to Williamson, he had tried and failed to get to buoy No. 2. This after an ordeal of almost eight hours in the pilothouse. He must have been thoroughly exhausted. He may have felt his only chance lay in getting out of the water as expeditiously as possible, and he may have been right. Trying to reboard the ship may have been a calculated risk. Or he may have been beyond the rational stage at that point and just going on instinct, drawn irresistibly to anything offering any chance of a solid surface to climb onto. The wave that carried him away from the ship and Manning's lifeline may have been the one that drowned him.

Bob Jacobsen figured that William Roscoe Funk's physique ill equipped him for the struggle he faced that night. "Funk, Pharmacist Mate was the skinniest guy I ever knew. Just bones with skin pulled over them," he wrote. "Those hours in the pilot house in the cold water must have really drained his body heat. When he went out the WT door to face the raging sea he would have had little energy to fight for survival."[61] If anyone saw Funk after the wave that swept him from Lawrence Mathers's side when they had just gotten out of the pilothouse, there's no record of it.

Charles Kumler, in getting bandied about the ship before he was torn off it, had gotten his coat snagged on one of the 20mm guns much as Koepke had, but unlike Koepke, Kumler was able to extricate himself without losing his life vest. Swept off the ship to starboard, he congregated with five other men in the floating maritime support group that would arguably save two men's lives.

> I believe I was about the fifteenth man out, I was washed back aft, and my coat was caught on the No 6 20 Millimeter. After freeing myself, I came to the surface and was washed back over the stack and back between the booms to the after starboard side of the ship. I then saw MATHERS RT1c. We swam toward each other and clung together. After a while we saw EHLERS, QM2c so then we all three stayed together. About five minutes later we saw BROWN, CBM, WAINSCOTT S2c, and KOEPKE, BM2c, so we six clung together from then on. We made a circle and drifted out towards sea. Once we sighted a channel marker buoy and tried to get to it, but the current was so strong it was impossible.[62]

This excerpt from Koepke's memorandum picks up after his failed attempt to swim back to the ship after he was washed overboard:

I then saw Wainscott & told him to come over by me & he did. I then told him I was without a life jacket & he said, "That's O.K. You stick with me, my jacket will hold us both up." As we floated by the after part of the Ship we met Brown CBM & he joined up with us. I called to Mathers & Ehlers & everyone I saw to join us & stick to geather. We then Saw the Captain & I asked him to join, but he said he Could make out alright by himself. we floated out the Channel & as we neared the Starboard Entrance Buoy we tried to swim for that but Couldn't make it against the Current. We saw two fellows who did make it & presumed one to be the Captain because he had been pretty close to us. Then we floated to sea & the Current carried us in Circles but always farther to sea.[63]

The starboard entrance buoy was buoy No. 2. Paul Burton was not on it. Bud Loughman and Nord Lester were, and would spend the rest of the night there. En route to it Loughman talked to Paul Burton in the water too. Loughman had spotted Koepke's group and called to them to point out the buoy, and Burton heard him and asked him how he was. Loughman, employing a nickname or mock title they apparently addressed each other by, quotes himself in his letter to Burton's wife as replying, "Fine 'ting' you." And he quotes Burton as saying the same back to him, and that was apparently the extent of their conversation. Forty-seven years later Loughman recalled being carried under at about that point by a wave, and when he came back up, he saw no sign of Burton. Burton, he said, had mentioned to someone in Koepke's group, probably Brown, that the strap of his life belt was broken. That, apparently, provided him his rationale for declining the invitation to join their group—he didn't want to be a burden to them. He reportedly told them it was every man for himself—by way not of discouraging their cooperative arrangement but of excusing himself from joining it—and was last seen swimming out to sea with his broken life belt under his arm.

10

Business on Great Waters

Bud Loughman and Nord Lester were on buoy No. 2 no more than about four hours that night, but for both men, clinging to it and cold, those hours passed slowly. "It was cold and I had the shakes," Lester said fifty-five years later. "I wished they'd come and get me off that buoy. . . . It was a long night."[1]

It was not a comfortable perch. Loughman would recall that the buoy, having snapped a mooring line, would spin like a corkscrew one way as it rose on a wave and the other as it fell, and Lester said it came to the top of each wave with a jolt that could have thrown them off. Although Lester himself did not recall it, he apparently had another bout of seasickness on the buoy. Loughman recalled his buoymate vomiting repeatedly on his back. "It felt good," Loughman said—it provided the only warmth he felt all night long.[2]

It was a long night for the men in the water too, and longer for none of them than for Augie Koepke, on whom the multiple injuries he had sustained in leaving the ship, in his encounters with the pilothouse door, the antenna bar above that door, and the coral reef, had taken an obvious toll. So, probably, had hypothermia. Koepke was clearly not a man of weak will except when it came to alcohol, nor was the water frigid. But it was cold enough, and the prospect of rescue in those long, slow hours before dawn remote enough, to chill his will to live. By his own account he asked twice that night to be let loose to drift off—and, by plain implication, to drown—but Chief Bosun's Mate Tom Emmet Brown had a hold of him and would have none of it. "Then we floated to sea & the Current carried us in Circles but always farther to sea," Koepke wrote. "We stayed out until we were picked up. I hung onto Broun's Coat by the collar & also had my other arm around Wainscotts waist & my feet I wrapped around Mathers between these three . . . I was kept afloat. Two times during the night while we were floating I wanted to give up & asked them to turn me loose but Brown had me by my belt & wouldn't let me go."[3]

Neither, it seems safe to say, would anyone else on hand have let him go, but if he had made a determined effort to get away, it's not entirely clear anyone but Brown would have had the physical wherewithal to restrain him. Ehlers or Mathers might have, but Wainscott had a serious injury of his own, to his heel, probably worse than any one of Koepke's injuries, and as the night crept slowly into morning, Kumler started showing signs of shock.

It was a long night in the signal tower, too. Captain Connolly appears to have stayed there all night, probably most of it clutching a pair of binoculars and much of it in the company of Captain Edmunds, his recent replacement as senior officer present afloat. Commodore Short, commandant of the base, was in the tower as well. At about 0100 on Sunday someone there made an encouraging discovery: the pilothouse, thought to have carried away, was intact after all. About an hour and a half later, Connolly would report, there was a sign of life from the ship.

> 0230 (about)—Seas slightly decreased in frequency but continued to roll in at the heighth of the mast. A watcher in the Contractor's Tower said he saw a man climb the mast about this time but I did not see him. Waves between shore and the ship and searchlight shadows frequently cast shadows and obstructed the view.[4]

By 0330 the waves, while still, by Connolly's account, propelling "forceful green seas" right over the pilothouse and mast, had begun to subside, and by about 0400, three men (Bolke, Williamson, and Horsman) had swum ashore at the western tip of Eastern Island. At about 0550 Lt. Elisha K. Kane, the duty officer in the flight control tower on Eastern Island, notified his counterpart at the Port Director's Department, Lt. R. M. Hardy, that men from the *Macaw* had been spotted in the water on both sides of the reef and at least one man on either Spit or Goony (aka Swan) Island, tiny scraps of sand flanking the channel more or less directly between Sand and Eastern Islands.

The eighteen PB2Y Coronado seaplanes in the seaplane basin that morning were preparing to take off for Hawaii's Kaneohe Bay Naval Air Station, having over the preceding two weeks made four 2,100-mile-roundtrip bombing runs to Wake Island to keep the Japanese there from providing aerial support to their countrymen trying to fight off US amphibious landings in the Marshall Islands. There were at least two (and apparently just two) rearming boats on hand at NOB Midway at the time, Nos. 1 and 3, and probably both had been engaged in the predawn darkness in ferrying men and supplies to the Coronados over the troubled waters of the lagoon.[5]

Rearming boats are sturdy, open boats, about thirty-five feet long and eleven or twelve wide, designed for conveying ammunition to seaplanes. Rearming boats Nos. 1 and 3 each carried a two-man crew. In boat No. 1 were Seaman 1/c LeRoy Benny Lehmbecker and Seaman 2/c Howard Eugene Daugherty. Lehmbecker was from Hopkins, Minnesota, a suburb of Minneapolis, the elder by about a year of two sons of a machinist for a farm implements firm and his wife, both of German descent. Five feet seven and a quarter inches as of the time he enlisted, LeRoy was nicknamed Pee Wee. He enjoyed tinkering with radios. His family hunted. During the Depression they dined frequently on blackbird. For five years in his teens LeRoy delivered the *Minneapolis Tribune,* which awarded him a certificate of merit for making his deliveries "in the face of actual physical danger, and with great bravery and determination" during a blizzard on Armistice Day, 1940. During or after, probably after, what may have been an abbreviated turn at Hopkins High School, he completed a course in aircraft sheet metal at the Minnesota Aircraft School in Minneapolis, where he was commended for proficiency in riveting and assembly. In April 1942 he went to work for the Despatch Oven Company of Minneapolis, a manufacturer of industrial ovens, apparently as a truck driver.

When he enlisted on August 20, 1942, LeRoy Lehmbecker had a girlfriend of recent vintage, Shirley Hutchenson, the daughter of the man who ran the local feed supply store. They had had, as she recalled sixty-four years later, exactly one date, on which they went to a movie (she couldn't recall what it was), and almost a year and a half later he had sent her exactly one letter, in which he confided that he had a ring for her. He apparently enclosed some money with that letter, and news of that money transfer apparently reached his father, for his father let LeRoy's brother, Gene, know that he took a dim view of LeRoy's sending money to Shirley Hutchenson. LeRoy trained at San Diego, spent fourteen months at the naval air station at Pearl Harbor, and was transferred in December 1943 to NOB Midway. He was twenty-two years old.[6]

Howard Daugherty, from Caryville, a small town in northeastern Tennessee, was one of five children of a coal miner, and was himself, at age seventeen or eighteen, a coal miner—he worked twelve weeks in 1939 and made $225—and a junior high school dropout, making him one of the more educated members of his family. Neither of his parents had completed fourth grade. He went by his middle name, Eugene. As of the time he enlisted in Nashville on October 17, 1942, he had been dating a young woman for about a year. His younger brother Lonzo served in the navy during the war too. Family lore has it that Lonzo enlisted, under a pseudonym and duress, when given a choice of doing that or doing time for rape. Lonzo is said to have served in the North Atlantic. Eugene, like LeRoy Lehmbecker, trained in San Diego and came to Midway after a posting in Hawaii. His exact date of birth is unknown. He was about twenty years old.[7]

In rearming boat No. 3 were Seaman 1/c Ernest David Samed and Fireman 2/c Edward Anthony Pitta. Samed was from the Cincinnati area. His father, David, originally Daoud, had immigrated in 1905 from Syria, then part of the soon-to-implode Ottoman Empire. As of 1917 David Samad (the spelling varies) was working as a barber in Tracy, California, a Central Valley town about fifty miles east of San Francisco. He enlisted in the army that October in Stockton and served briefly with the 91st Division at Camp Lewis, Washington. The men of the 91st went to France in June and July 1918 and fought there in the last few months of World War I, but David Samad did not go with them. For reasons that are unclear, he had been discharged in February. By 1920 he was in Cincinnati, where he had family connections in the sizable Syrian community and where on May 21 of that year he married the former Fannie Phelps of McCreary County, Kentucky, who had moved to the big city, apparently in search of work as a domestic after the failure of her first marriage, one she had gone into at the age of fourteen. About five years later they produced their only child, Ernest, and five years after that they were living near Fannie's family in Whitley City, Kentucky, in the southeastern corner of the state just over the line from Tennessee (and about thirty miles from Caryville), and David, who apparently worked as an auto mechanic in Cincinnati, was once again cutting hair. Fannie died of tuberculosis in June 1931, and it was apparently after that that David and Ernest took up residence in the Old Soldiers' & Sailors' Orphans' Home in Xenia, Ohio.

Ernest enlisted in the navy in Cincinnati on November 24, 1941, did his boot camp at Great Lakes, and that New Year's Eve joined the crew of the battleship USS *Pennsylvania*, Anthony Tomkovicz's former ship, at San Francisco, where it had gone to repair damage sustained at Pearl Harbor three and a half weeks before. One year and a week later, Samed (the navy spelling) was tried at deck court on charges of resisting arrest by the shore patrol, found guilty, and docked forty dollars in pay. He was transferred to Pearl Harbor in February 1943, and then to NOB Midway. Samed's exact date of birth, too, is unknown. He was nineteen or twenty.

Edward Anthony Pitta grew up in Oakland, where the *Macaw* was built, and in the Delta region between San Francisco Bay and Sacramento. His great-grandfather Amaro Pitta immigrated, apparently in 1906, from the island of Madeira, a Portuguese possession in the Atlantic about 460 miles off the coast of Morocco, and set himself up in the bar business in San Francisco. His bar, on the present site of the Transamerica Pyramid, promptly burned down in the fire that destroyed much of the city after the earthquake on April 18 of that year, whereupon he removed across the bay to West Oakland and opened a bar there. One of his twelve sons, Jose Amaro, inherited the business and reportedly expanded it to include hotel accommodations, prostitution, and asparagus. His customer base is said to have included Portuguese mill-workers from Massachusetts he recruited by offering to pay their cross-country train fare. He would reportedly meet them at the depot in Oakland, issue them work clothes, impound their street clothes, and send them to work on the family's asparagus farm on Bradford Island in the Delta about fifty miles away, then truck them back to Oakland on weekends, loan them back their civvies, and direct them to his various West Oakland establishments, where he would recoup at least part of their wages before swapping out their attire again and sending them back to the farm.[8]

The family business prospered and branched out. Jose Amaro's sons grew up "wealthy and wild." One of them would become a member of the so-called Stardust Gang, named after the San Francisco bar in the basement of which gang members conspired to import heroin and opium from Mexico. Another son, Manuel, was Edward Pitta's father. Born in Oakland in 1925, Edward was reportedly sent off to the asparagus farm when his parents' marriage unraveled and raised there by fieldworkers. His older brother had drowned in the Delta at age fifteen months, seven months before Edward was born, and the Delta would prove hazardous to Edward too. He was in a brothel owned by one of his uncles in Stockton one day when one of that uncle's two girlfriends came in intending to shoot the other and accidentally shot Edward instead. There was, however, at least one aspect of growing up in the Delta, laced as it was by waterways, that would prove to be greatly beneficial. As his son James put it, "My dad was just a strong strong strong swimmer," one with a penchant as a young man for jumping off bridges. If he missed the ferry that took him to school, James said, he would swim.[9]

Pitta enlisted in San Francisco on June 12, 1943. Within about four months he too had been assigned to NOB 1504. He was eighteen.

When Lieutenant Hardy, the Midway Port Director's duty officer, received word of men in the water, he relayed the news by telephone to his boss and Captain Edmunds, then ordered that rearming boat No. 3, manned by Samed and Pitta, be broken out and dispatched to tiny Spit Island to pick up any survivors they might find there. At the same time he ordered the crew of the No. 1 crash boat to proceed out the channel and gather what survivors they could without unduly putting themselves at risk. That was a tall order. The waves by then had subsided somewhat but were still enormous. But if any boat on hand that day was equal to the task of navigating those waves, it would have been a crash boat. Crash boats are designed to rescue pilots whose planes have crashed at sea (or they were—they have largely been supplanted in that role by helicopters). They vary in size but tend to be bigger and faster than rearming boats—a crash boat might run to eighty-five feet or more with a top speed of 25 knots, as opposed to thirty-five feet and 10 knots for a typical rearming boat (the rearming boats at Midway were thirty-three-footers)—and crash boats feature closed construction, with a deck and a cabin atop the hull, whereas rearming boats are open, like rowboats. Rearming boats are sturdy enough, but their design makes concessions to the protected waters seaplane pilots like to land on. They're not designed for rugged surf. So it made sense for Hardy to assign Samed and Pitta the less challenging task of proceeding only as far as Spit Island, a fifteen-acre patch of sand on the east edge of Brooks Channel about a half mile north of the mouth, far enough north that the waves propagating past it might have spent enough of their fury to be manageable for the smaller craft. But Samed and Pitta failed to comply with Hardy's instructions. They proceeded all the way out the channel and made straight for the *Macaw*.[10]

The courage it took them to do that defies comprehension. Perhaps they couldn't see all that clearly what they were getting themselves into. According to Commodore Short, Lieutenant Hardy received word of men in the water at 0550. If that was the case, Pitta and Samed were probably under way by 0600. Astronomical dawn, before which there is no sunlight, is not until 0609 at Midway on February 13, and morning nautical twilight, deemed sufficient to navigate by, does not start until 0636. Maybe Short's chronology was off a bit. Maybe they set out a little later and had a little more light. George Manning wrote within days afterward that they came out at daybreak. But if Short's timeline is more or less accurate, the searchlights would still have been in full play, and what with the breakers gleaming under those lights and throwing off crests of illuminated spray, the men in the boat probably had a good enough and maybe even an exaggerated view of what awaited them. If they didn't, the progressively more violent roller-coaster ride out that channel must have conveyed some idea. It would have been bad enough if their task had been merely to break through the surf, but the *Macaw* had gone down within, or within a stone's throw of, the break zone. They would have to maneuver perilously close to the breaking surf or within it.[11]

From his perch on the foremast, George Manning saw them coming. He and either Wade or Scott, or all three of them, all still on the foremast, foresaw disaster and tried, and failed, to do for Samed and Pitta what Manning had tried and failed to do for Whitmarsh, to warn them off. "When day break came we sighted a rescue boat laying out," Manning wrote. "They circled the bow and put there stern to the waves. We told them to get the devil out of there and to come in at the stern. They must not of heard us for they tried to back down to us. A large breaker came in and capsized the boat. We saw them trying to make the beach but lost sight of them in the breakers."[12]

According to Commodore Short, who based his account on a statement from Pitta, the instruction from one or more of the men on the foremast was to come around to the port side of the ship. With the waves approaching from the south (if they still were—that's how Connolly described them the previous afternoon) and the *Macaw* bearing something on the order of 30 to 50 degrees true (i.e., angling on something like a 45-degree angle to the right of due north), the port side would have offered a comparatively protected area to maneuver in. Samed and Pitta had apparently cut across the bow or rounded the stern and approached the ship on the starboard side, and it may have been while they were trying to round or reround the bow in compliance with the instructions from the men on the foremast that the boat capsized.

Samed, according to Short, was thrown from the boat, and Pitta carried under it. When Pitta got out from underneath it, he found Samed atop the overturned vessel hanging onto the propeller shaft. Pitta tried to join him on the hull but couldn't manage it. He grabbed a piece of driftwood instead and hung onto that until he saw that he was drifting out to sea, then let go of the wood and swam to a little island —probably Spit Island. Swimming to it about half a mile against a current that might still have been running at six to ten miles per hour, he might have needed all the stamina he developed swimming in the Delta channels as a boy. The waves at his back may have helped him overcome that current. If they did, they were not as kind to Samed.

According to Short, Pitta was the last man to see Samed. That may have been true, but it seems a bit more likely that Manning, Wade, or Scott was, or possibly Knecht from his vantage point atop the tripod. Manning wrote of seeing "them," presumably both Samed and Pitta, trying to make the beach and of losing sight of them in the breakers. That suggests that when Manning last saw Samed, Samed had left his perch atop his capsized boat and tried to swim for it. If he did, he didn't make it. Rearming boat No. 3 was swept over the reef and recovered. Samed was never seen again.

Connolly in his statement seems to take credit for Pitta's rescue.

0600—Report received from the Port Director's Office that men were in the water and boats enroute. I sent out one contractor's tug and another proceeded to the channel north of number three buoy. Saw man who was member of crew of overturned rearming boat in the water to eastward of MACAW and rescued him from the eastward side of the sandpit. Saw crash boat outside the channel picking up men.[13]

The crash boat not surprisingly fared better outside the channel. That may have been due in part to the fact that once out of the channel it proceeded a short but significant distance out to sea, where there was no shortage of men needing rescue and less danger from breaking surf. The first stop apparently was the No. 2 buoy. A spotter plane had found Bud Loughman and Nord Lester on it shortly before and buzzed them. Loughman pointed toward the men in the water, and the pilot waggled his wings to indicate that he had seen them too. When the crash boat arrived—manned, as Loughman recalled it, by a crew of three, including a seasick pharmacist's mate—what Loughman later termed "a Laurel and Hardy affair" ensued in which the boat made several passes attempting to pull alongside the buoy and overshot it every time. Someone aboard the boat, Loughman recalled, almost beaned him with a monkey's fist, a line-throwing weight, in trying to toss them a line. Finally, he said, he told the boat crew to cut their engine, he and Lester would swim to them. They did so, and then the boat picked up Brown and his companions. According to Connolly, that group boarded the rescue craft about a half mile from the *Macaw*. If that half mile extended south or slightly southwest of the *Macaw*, that would put them just about where the *Flier* had begun its ill-fated approach to the channel four weeks before.[14]

By the time the crash boat got to Brown's group, Kumler was in shock but able to follow instructions. Thrown a line, he reportedly held onto it with one hand so tightly they were able to pull him aboard just by hauling on it. It took some doing to coax him into relaxing his grip. Kumler later had no recollection of the proceedings. "At about 0530, I believe, I was out of my head," he wrote, "because I don't remember anything from then until I was drinking coffee in the hospital at 1130 that same morning. It has been said that I was picked up by a crash boat at about 0630 with five other men."[15]

Surface water temperature in the vicinity of Midway in February, as noted previously, generally ranges from 66 to 72 degrees Fahrenheit. Water being denser than air, it conducts heat more readily. That's why cold water feels colder, and hot water hotter, than air at the same temperature, and why immersion in cold water can drain a human body of heat about thirty times faster than comparably chilly air. For humans, core body temperature is typically about 98.6 degrees. If it falls below 95 degrees, the result is hypothermia, which can be deadly. Water temperatures like those at Midway in February may not sound cold, but immersion in water of 60 to 70 degrees will induce exhaustion or unconsciousness in a typical adult in two to seven hours. Counting their time in the pilothouse, by 0530 that morning Kumler and his companions had been at least partly immersed for most of eight hours. Confusion is symptomatic of mild, and amnesia of severe, hypothermia. Kumler, subsequently unable to recall his rescue, apparently experienced the latter.[16]

According to Bud Loughman, the seasick pharmacist's mate on the crash boat prescribed brandy for all hands. (Whether he partook himself is unclear.) The brandy apparently flowed pretty freely that morning. Loughman recounted getting five small medicinal doses of it from what he suggested was an equal number of donors, none of whom knew of his other sources, and Loughman wasn't letting on. He consumed it all, he wrote, "without a murmer."

"They had me in the hospital for several days," he wrote. "The truth of the matter was I had a terrible hangover."[17]

Meanwhile, their work in loading the Coronados completed, LeRoy Lehmbecker and Eugene Daugherty in rearming boat No. 1 were heading back to the shelter of the boat haven at the eastern end of Sand Island when they noticed the activity around the mouth of the channel. At least seven boats participated in the rescue attempt that morning, including a mechanized landing craft, or LCM, two tugs, the two rearming boats, the crash boat, and a patrol aircraft rescue boat, or PARB, a close relation to a crash boat. On the PARB was Lieutenant Hardy, who had gone out on it to direct the rescue operation. Lehmbecker and Daugherty pulled alongside and offered him their services. Hardy and the PARB's commander, a Lieutenant (jg) Patton, gave them instructions much like the ones Hardy had given Samed and Pitta: they were to patrol for survivors along the channel and in the lagoon to the north of the *Macaw* but not to approach the reef or get into the surf. They responded to this injunction just as Samed and Pitta had: they ignored it. Manning described what ensued:

> An L.C.M. Layed out of the channel and went around our stern and waited. Knecht dove in and swam to it. It then went farther out. Another boat came around the bow and I dove in and swam to it. I got a board and then Wade dove in. We were starting to bring him into the boat when the motor conked and we went broadside to the breakers. Where a large breaker hit us and capsized the boat. I came up and saw Wade he was trying to help one of the crew. Another breaker hit us and I lost sight of Wade and the crew member. I then saw the cox of the boat and tried to get to him. I got within reaching distance when he was caught in a current and was swept down and away. I looked to see if he might come up but he didn't so I started to swim for the beach. I was picked up on a sand bar by a crew of a small boat and then was transferred to a crash boat where I was treated we waited until they brought Wade in. Then we were taken to the hospital.[18]

As Manning suggests, what apparently doomed rearming boat No. 1 was engine failure. Short in his report confirmed as much: "Lieutenant Hardy and Lieutenant (jg) Patton observed the number one re-arming boat alongside the masts of the MACAW. It appeared to proceed for a short distance as if it were maneuvering to come about into safer water when suddenly it seemed to stop and lie dead in the water. A moment later a large breaker rolled head on into the bow throwing the bow into the air and flipping the boat completely over."[19]

According to Short, by the time rearming boat No. 1 flipped, Lehmbecker and Daugherty had been unable to get Wade into the boat, but they had managed to get a line to him and were trying to drag him into calmer water. Wade later told Short that after capsizing, the boat overtook him and drove him to the bottom, but that he managed to recover and make it, like Pitta, to one of the little islets in the channel, from which he was rescued at last.

All four of the men who had weathered the night high atop the *Macaw* would eventually jump off it. As Manning suggests in his account, Knecht was apparently the first, followed by Manning himself, Wade, and Scott, in that order. Manning was the only *Macaw* sailor to actually board either of the rearming boats. Knecht and Scott were picked up by the LCM.[20]

Of the four men who went out in the rearming boats, only Edward Pitta survived. Ernest Samed, Eugene Daugherty, and LeRoy Lehmbecker died. So did five men from the *Macaw*.

Robert Vaughn's body washed ashore, or was recovered just offshore, four days later, and Eugene Daugherty's within a day after that. Vaughn's skin, according to Bud Loughman, had retained its pigmentation only under his belt. After a partial autopsy on Vaughn, Lieutenant Duff, the submarine base medical officer, declared the cause of death to have been drowning. Loughman, in a letter he wrote to Vaughn's father, implied the same, but that may have been because he figured Vaughn's parents would find drowning a more palatable cause of death for their son than blunt force injury. Loughman, who had some idea what it would take to dislodge the barrel of the forward three-inch fifty gun from its locked upright position, stated more than once years later his conviction (one he shared with eyewitness George Manning) that Vaughn had died the instant he hit it. Duff, in a subsequent report, makes no mention of even a partial autopsy on Daugherty.

Both Robert Vaughn and Eugene Daugherty were buried at sea on February 18. The sides of the old volcano Midway comprises the top of fall off not far beyond the hundred-fathom curve the *Flier* had drawn up to, more or less, upon its arrival from Pearl Harbor thirty days before. The boat (or boats) that carried Vaughn and Daugherty on their final, short sea voyages did not have to go far to reach a spot of suitable depth. The burial craft retraced the path Samed, Pitta, Lehmbecker, and Daugherty had followed out the channel five days before, and passed the ship that had been their destination that day, buried itself now all but for its masts and booms and tripod, with maybe a bit of the aft portside corner of the flying bridge peeking through in the troughs between waves, all listing to starboard something like 40 degrees. The sea, as if by way of acknowledging the solemnity of the occasion, had grown a great deal calmer by then.

Like David Samed and Frank and Elizabeth Lehmbecker, Daugherty's father probably received little notice beyond the standard Western Union telegrams from the Navy Department deeply regretting to inform him, first, that his son was missing in the performance of his duty, and later, that he was confirmed dead. There's no indication that Bud Loughman, the senior surviving officer of the *Macaw*, wrote to any of them. He may have, or may have wanted to but just not had the time. But he did take the time to write to his deceased shipmates' families. In writing to Robert Vaughn's father, William Vaughn, he may have had more concern for family feelings than for strict historical accuracy. Among a few other deviations, he has Vaughn getting "pinned" against a gun, not smashed into it, and (at least briefly) surviving the encounter, and says Vaughn's body was "in good condition" when found four days later, when per other reports the coral and salt water had worked to disfigure it badly. If the original letter bore a date, the surviving copy does not, but it was probably written within a few weeks of the sinking.[21]

U.S.S. MACAW
c/o Fleet Post Office
San Francisco, Calif.
Mr. Vaughn,

I know that the Navy Department has already notified you that your son Robert has died. There is little to be said to help you in your great sorrow, but I was with Robert the night he went overboard and thought my telling you what happened would be of some help. Our ship, on January the sixteenth, struck a reef on an island in the Pacific Ocean.

We were in a safe enough way and had every expectation that the ship would soon be freed. Salvage operations were carried on and we all took turns at staying on board doing what we could to free the ship from the reef. The men who went ashore were invariably glad to come back on board because we broke out the best foods and received ice-cream, cake and the like from the beach. Our living conditions were normal—had lights at night, Steak and eggs for breakfast for instance. Robert was always doing his work, never had to be asked to do anything twice, always seemed to know what to do and did it well. He whistled a lot and had a funny shy like laugh when a joke was cracked or when we kidded him about something. He was going to be advanced in rating to cook third class on the first of March. To show you how sure we all were that we were in no danger, I had my wife's picture and my little girl's picture sent out to me along with other articles of a personal nature which I had left on the beach when I had my turn there.

On the night of February twelfth, the seas became extremely high. A weather man was on the island sent us weather reports every day. This storm had started a way out at sea and weather conditions around the island were not at all unusual. The weather had been a little rough during the day, but the ship was well secured and we had had some heavy weather on several previous occasions and had no trouble coming through. This storm caused the ship to move into deeper water. We had to leave the inside of the ship around two thirty the thirteenth of February and go topside to try to get up the foremast. Robert managed to get out with the rest of us but a wave pinned him against a gun. One of his shipmates went to his rescue, got him clear of the gun and helped him to the foremast some distance away. This man that helped him lost his own life belt and was injured by a wave carrying him back against the gun where Robert had been pinned.

Robert was seen climbing the ladder on the foremast and had reached a platform well above the flying bridge deck. He seemed to be doing all right when a tremendous wave hit him and carried him forward across the bow of the ship. The wave was followed by several others in quick succession and I feel that this is when he went to his God. Several other men were caught in this series of waves and they too were never again seen alive.

I feel Robert went quick and didn't suffer. He was cool-headed throughout.

He lived clean, both from a physical as well as from a moral standpoint and I feel he's up there now praying for you.

His body was found on the seventeenth of February in good condition. I personally identified him. He was buried at sea the following day with full military honors. Six of his shipmates were pallbearers and the remainder of his shipmates were at the funeral. A United States Navy band played, a contingent of Marines fired a volley of shots three times in the air and his flag draped body was taken out to sea on a PT boat. He was clad in his uniform, was carefully wrapped in heavy canvas, and a heavy weight was placed at his feet. When quite a ways off shore we gently slipped him into the calm sea.

Very Sincerely Yours,
Gerald F. Loughman,
Lieutenant, USNR.
Acting Commanding Officer

11

Aftermath

A board of inquiry into the loss of the USS *Macaw* convened at Pearl Harbor on Monday, February 21, 1944, aboard the USS *Bushnell*. The board consisted of the same four officers who had met aboard the same submarine tender three weeks before to inquire into the grounding of the *Flier*. Two days after convening, the *Macaw* panel reconvened at Midway. They heard testimony over six days from twenty witnesses, including twelve from the crew of the *Macaw*, reviewed various exhibits such as weather records and salvage plans, deliberated for several more days, and on March 1 announced their findings of fact and their opinions.

Among the facts they found were that "from the time of getting under-way on January 16, 1944, until the time of grounding, the Commanding Officer, Lieutenant Commander P. W. Burton, U.S. Navy, was conning the ship and was, himself, the Officer of the Deck"—in other words, he was the one directly supervising the navigation of the ship—and that buoy No. 4 was missing.

Among their opinions were that Captain Connolly's order to Burton to proceed to the rescue of the *Flier* was proper; that Burton "handled his ship in a seamanlike manner" during the initial attempts to get a line to the *Flier*, but that on the way back to the channel the *Macaw* "did not proceed a sufficient distance to seaward to permit rounding up on the channel axis prior to passing between the entrance buoys, and in so doing, the Commanding Officer did not display good seamanship"; "that the absence of channel buoy number four deprived [Burton] of a valuable navigational aid"; that the performance of the small-boat crews in the rescue operation was "outstanding and in some cases . . . above and beyond the ordinary call of duty"; "that the comparatively large number of survivors was due to compliance with [Connolly's order to Burton] to keep all personnel on board"; and that "the

Commanding Officer, U.S.S. MACAW, Lieutenant Commander Paul Willits Burton, U.S. Navy, is responsible for the grounding of the U.S.S. MACAW."[1]

Captain Connolly was the first witness. Promptly advised that he was an interested party, that is, a suspect, he declined legal counsel. He was exonerated.

There's at least a little irony in the board's opinion that the survivors owed their survival to compliance with Connolly's order to stay on board: "Keep all hands well secured X Under no circumstances try to leave ship." Strictly speaking, when the men in the pilothouse left it that night, they did not intend to leave the ship altogether, only to get to and climb the foremast. A photograph taken later that day shows about fifty feet of the foremast projecting from the water. The searchlight platform is just visible at about wavetop level. Between the searchlight platform and the ladder and crow's nest above it, all the men might in theory have managed to ride out that night. The searchlight platform might have accommodated most or all of them (all of them only if very tightly packed), but whether it would have offered a tenable refuge amid the huge waves that night is doubtful. Even if all the men had made it that far, they might have had no choice but to keep going up the mast, and whether they could have all fit on its upper reaches, high enough not to get swept off, is also doubtful. Clinging to the ladder and perhaps to one another through all the rest of that dreary night, they could hardly have been "well secured." It was impossible to stay well secured on a sinking ship. Obviously Connolly meant well, but if they took his order to mean they should stay within the ship, they did not comply with it, and if they had, they would all have asphyxiated or drowned.

A better description than "valuable" for buoy No. 4's role as a navigational aid might have been "critical." It was buoy No. 4 that marked the corner Burton was in effect found guilty of cutting. Presumably buoys No. 1 and 2 should have been valuable aids to navigation too, but by the navy's own account, their value to Paul Burton that day may have been compromised as well. A wartime document titled "Midway Mission" contains a warning about them: "NOTE: The channel entrance buoys #1 and #2 are out of position, being eastward of the dredged channel. They should not be used as aids to navigation until further notice."[2]

This document, largely an inventory of military facilities, is undated but was clearly produced after the *Macaw* sank—it notes the presence of an obstruction buoy marking the location of a wreck at the entrance to the channel. The *Macaw* itself may have had a lot to do with displacing buoy No. 2 if the ship did in fact overrun it on January 16, 1944, as Chief Commissary Steward Albert Homer Jones insisted it did. But the *Macaw* was in no way to blame for buoy No. 1 being out of place. If it was out of place after the ship ran aground, east of where it should have been, it might well have been so at the time, and so might buoy No. 2.

The board does not seem to have taken this possibility into account. It was told, but in its findings makes no mention, of the dredge that, according to Worth Windle, obscured the rear channel range light on January 16. Nor does it mention Captain Connolly's browbeating Burton that day. No one told them about it. Its first of twenty-three opinions was that Connolly's order to Burton to proceed to the rescue of the *Flier* was proper. The board asked one witness, Windle, one question regarding Burton's attitude about going out that day. As far as Windle knew, did Burton feel any apprehension about it? Windle's answer was less than categorical:

> Well, the Captain did not, to the best of my knowledge. But he said to me, "We're getting underway" and myself, I didn't think it was impossible to bring the ship in. I'd never seen conditions as bad as they were that day, but I believe in my own opinion that a ship could be brought in. And then the Captain didn't say a word to me regarding danger or anything like that going back into port.[3]

As noted earlier, for Windle never to have seen conditions as bad as they were that day is significant. He had enlisted in 1919.

The board's critical conclusion about Burton's role in the grounding— that, in attempting to reenter the channel, he did not proceed far enough out to sea to "round up" on the channel axis—amounts basically to saying he cut a corner he should have gone around. Of course, had the No. 4 buoy not been missing, or the rear channel range light obscured, or one or both of buoys No. 1 and 2 out of place (if either was), it would have been a great deal easier to determine where that corner was, and where the axis down the middle of the channel was. If Paul Burton made a mistake approaching the channel the way he did, he had a lot of help making it. Missing, misplaced, and obstructed navigational aids aside, Connolly's browbeating may have impaired Burton's judgment, causing him to rush things, to reach for the channel too soon.

Other things being equal, the sea alone that day would have challenged any-one's seamanship. Plenty of factors contributed to the destruction of the *Macaw*. Paul Burton's seamanship may have been the least of them, if it was one at all.

Among the witnesses who testified before the board of inquiry was the salvage officer, Cmdr. Lebbeus Curtis, who summed up in the following exchange about as neatly and poetically as anyone could have what finally did in the *Macaw*:

> Q. What weather and sea conditions were, in your opinion, respon-sible for the final shifting of position of the MACAW so that she became totally submerged?
> A. The sea that maintained on the night of 12 and 13 February was probably twice the height and weight of anything that had been experienced while the ship had been grounded. These seas broke over the reef on all sides of the lagoon and filled the lagoon to a height not seen before. This head of water in the lagoon, which was several feet higher than the normal outside level, could only escape through the dredged channel. This caused an unusual and terrific current which expended its full force on the port side of the MACAW as she lay aground. This, combined with the lifting power of the seas breaking on the wreck, caused her to slide astern.[4]

All seventeen sinking survivors were promptly hospitalized, all suffering, according to Lieutenant Duff, the medical officer, from shock and exhaustion. Within a day Ehlers, Libera, and Bolke developed bronchopneumonia. Verkennes came down with acute bronchitis. Koepke, Lester, Horsman, and Wainscott were treated for coral lacerations and abrasions. Within days everyone had been released, but Koepke and Wainscott were subsequently readmitted because their wounds had not healed satisfactorily.[5]

Group photos of the *Macaw* crew at large and of just the sinking survi-vors were taken on bleachers at Midway on the occasion of a beer party on March 12, one month after the ship sank. Wainscott is in them. He looks chip-per enough, but in the survivors photos his right leg is draped over a pair of crutches, and his right foot appears to be heavily bandaged. For reasons unknown, five of the survivors—Koepke, Horsman, Scott, Brown, and either Lester or Knecht, apparently Lester—do not appear in these photos.[6]

With the death of Paul Burton, Bud Loughman assumed command of a sunken ship. With the sinking of their ship, its surviving crew assumed more or less officially the status of supernumeraries, a status most of them had already assumed in fact. From the time of the grounding, they remained at Midway exactly two months, during which the men ashore were given some work to do, but generally not much. There just wasn't much to do. Some of them helped unload a cargo ship. Shipfitter Lloyd George Fox continued in his postal duties as a clerk in the Midway post office. Bob Jacobsen bunked, and presumably did some work, with the base carpenters. Howard Rechel was assigned the task of lighting the boiler of the furnace for the mess hall at 0400. That was his only task in an eight-hour shift. For that, he said, "the suckers had me up from midnight to eight in the morning."[7]

On shore at Midway the *Macaw* sailors did not lack for recreational opportunities. On Sand Island alone during the latter stages of the war there were four boxing arenas, sixteen handball courts, nine tennis courts, twelve volleyball courts, about three dozen horseshoe pits, at least three badminton courts, three indoor and three outdoor basketball courts, five bowling alleys, a softball field, archery facilities, several recreation halls (including a small one for mess stewards—in other words, African Americans), three movie theaters, an officers' club, and a three-hundred-man beer hall.[8]

And there was always bird-watching. For all its amenities, Midway was still a few scraps of coral and sand in the middle of the Pacific Ocean. There were few if any women. Drinking was restricted. It was a far cry from Pearl Harbor or San Francisco. But in lieu of the charms of a more civilized place, what Midway did have, in fabulous abundance—what it still had, even after all the massive violence of the Battle of Midway—were gooney birds. They were always good for a laugh, with their lengthy, lumbering takeoff runs and wing-and-a-prayer landings. You could even pet them if you knew how. You could twirl your finger in front of them to more or less mesmerize them, former Gunner's Mate Ralph Enzweiler recalled, then you could scratch the backs of their necks. They enjoyed that. But you had to be careful. They had strong beaks, and if you didn't do it just right, Enzweiler said, if you didn't lull them into a proper state of acquiescence first, "they could dadgum nearly bite your finger off."[9]

And of course there was gambling. Quinton Studer recalled one-hundred-dollar-a-hand blackjack games at Midway with six to eight men at a table. Stanley Libera prospered there playing blackjack. There being nothing to spend it on, "just sand and goony birds," he said he sent his winnings to his fiancée to buy a hope chest. Sixty-seven years later she was gone, but the hope chest still sat in her old bedroom in the home they had shared in New Britain, Connecticut.[10]

Not all gamblers at Midway, even winning ones, fared so well. Not long after the sinking, Bud Loughman was shown another body that had washed ashore to determine whether it too was one of the *Macaw*'s missing men. It was not. The body, Loughman said, turned out to be that of a submarine sailor whose boat had left without him after he missed muster. He had won five thousand dollars at poker and was found to have a bullet hole in his head.[11]

The USS *Nautilus* (SS-168) was the biggest submarine in the US fleet and played a correspondingly large role in the war, notably at the Battle of Midway. It was an attempt during the battle by the *Nautilus* to torpedo the battleship *Kirishima* that drew a futile counterattack with depth charges from the destroyer *Arashi*, and it was the wake the *Arashi* cut in returning to its station that pointed Wade McClusky and his dive bombers the way to the Japanese carriers. Twenty-one months later, just before midnight on March 11, 1944, the *Nautilus* was on its way to Midway, returning from its eighth war patrol, when it was ordered to proceed straight to Pearl Harbor instead. It changed course accordingly on March 12 but had to change it back two days later due to engine trouble and a shortage of fuel. So the *Nautilus* went to Midway after all, entering the channel past what little of the *Macaw* remained visible about 0830 on March 16. About seven hours later, having taken on fuel, water, thirty-two warheads, and 102 passengers with luggage, it got back on its way.

The passengers were what remained that morning at Midway of the crew of the *Macaw*, and as big as the *Nautilus* was, with 102 extra bodies aboard it was crowded. In the words of *Macaw* radar operator Harold Hayes, "They put us in wherever they could find a place to hang us by the collar."[12]

Lloyd George Fox did not relish his time aboard the *Nautilus*. Sixty-six years later he recalled the sub as a "dirty, stinking old thing." His clothes reeked so badly of diesel by the time they got to Pearl Harbor, he said, he threw them all away but his shoes.[13]

Fox was apparently not the only one those fumes got to. Two tales of something like insanity have been told about that trip, tales similar enough to suggest they might be variant accounts of the same incident. As told by Bud Loughman, the central character was Alfred Homer Jones of Zanesville, Ohio, the chief commissary steward aboard the *Macaw,* who held that status under what is called an acting appointment, a sort of temporary, revocable promotion, one that confers a less than fully secure hold on the rank in question. He had come up for permanent assignment, and Loughman had been instrumental in denying it to him.

> I remember there was an incident on this ship. The . . . I forget what his rate was, but I know he was a chief, he had an acting appointment . . . I think he was a chief commissary steward or something like that. He was white, and I had no use for the man. . . . [T]he commanding officer, skipper, called me to the bridge . . . or his cabin and told me that Jones had apparently gone berserk and he was in the crew's mess and would I please go in and quiet him down. . . . [W]hen I got into the crew's mess, he was all by himself in there . . . he had a case of catsup bottles, and . . . anyone who came in, he was throwing a catsup bottle. Well, I'd be the one that he would most like to hit, I'm sure, because he had come up for a permanent appointment . . . but I had turned him down. . . . [W]hen I walked in there, I really thought the guy was going to konk me. . . . I was scared stiff. But I walked over to him, he had a couple of bottles there, and I went over and I said, "Jones, give me those bottles." Fortunately, he gave them, handed them to me. He didn't konk me with them.

Loughman said he ordered Jones handcuffed. What became of him thereafter Loughman did not recall forty-seven years later, but he thought the matter had been handled more as one of mental health than of mutiny.[14]

Bob Gonnoud told the parallel tale. He was in what he termed the combination mess and rec room aboard the *Nautilus* when someone from its crew (Gonnoud thought it was the chief of the boat) came in and started talking about lighting up the Christmas tree and making other bizarre remarks. Then he picked up a circular knife-sharpening stone of a sort a chef might wear on his belt and started smashing things. The *Nautilus*'s XO (executive officer) grabbed him, Gonnoud said, then they gave him a shot, strapped him to a metal gurney and put him in officers' quarters.[15]

On the fifth day out of Midway the men of the *Macaw* were back at Pearl Harbor. They were treated to a stay at the Royal Hawaiian Hotel, a swank hostelry on Waikiki requisitioned by the military as an R&R center during the war; then they scattered to wherever the navy saw fit to send them. Or stayed put if the navy saw fit to have them do that. Richard Williamson and fellow "bilge rats" (i.e., motor machinist's mates) George Keehn, Vernon Zeigler, and Dan Weber stayed at Pearl Harbor on a six-man submarine maintenance team, working on hydraulics, hatch openers, exhaust pipes— whatever needed fixing.[16]

Ship's Cook Anthony Tomkovicz stayed at Pearl Harbor and worked as a meatcutter. Among his colleagues and mentors there were several cheerful German POWs. They were happy to be in Hawaii. It was so much nicer than the Eastern Front. "They were singing and jovial and glad to be prisoners," he said.[17]

Bob Jacobsen stayed at Pearl Harbor too and worked at the submarine base. It was during his second stay there, early in 1945, that Jacobsen got his Dear John letter from Colleen, his girlfriend back in Oakland. "This handsome soldier had swept her off her feet and they had married. So she said it would be best if we quit writing to each other." He never saw her again.[18]

Lyle Webb stayed at Pearl Harbor, though exactly how long is unclear. According to Jacobsen, Webb resumed doing laundry there, sold chances on a diamond ring that would keep mysteriously ending up back in his possession every time he raffled it off, and took to acquiring whole stacks of the *Honolulu Advertiser*, a daily newspaper, and selling copies on the base, presumably at a healthy markup. Business, as Jacobsen described it, was brisk— the papers would sell right out. Within about a year Webb was aboard the USS *Sitkoh Bay* (CVE-86), a newly commissioned escort aircraft carrier that supported combat operations in the Philippines and on Iwo Jima in the early months of 1945. Webb was probably aboard for at least one such voyage. He was honorably discharged on March 20, 1945.[19]

Dave Wallington worked at Pearl Harbor cleaning corroded submarine guns, then after a summertime furlough back in Michigan he was assigned as a quartermaster to a section of *ABSD-1*, the prefabricated dry dock the *Macaw* had escorted eight sections of to Espiritu Santo. By then *ABSD-1* was at Leyte in the Philippines. The captain, Wallington said, wore his hat backward and seemed "a bit psycho." Fearing the end of the war would cost him his men, that they'd get news of Japan's surrender and their repatriation orders over the radio, Wallington said, he had radio contact with the rest of the world cut off. But his best efforts at prophylaxis notwithstanding, that news and those orders got through eventually. Wallington got sent back to the States and discharged.[20]

Jack Vangets was assigned to guard duty at the receiving station at Pearl Harbor, then served aboard the battleship USS *Iowa* (BB-61), aboard which he rode out Typhoon Cobra, the storm that ravaged a US fleet east of the Philippines on December 18, 1944, sinking three destroyers and claiming the lives of almost eight hundred men. Typhoon Cobra was the inspiration for the storm that drives the crisis in Herman Wouk's *The Caine Mutiny*.[21]

Lt. William Herman Smith, the communications officer, "Pat" to his family, "Snuffy" or something worse to some of his shipmates on the *Macaw*, was assigned after the sinking to the USS *Fulton* (AS-11), a submarine tender. After the war, Smith, who had never gone to high school, served as flag secretary to an admiral. He mustered out after thirty years in 1958, took a job with Boeing in Seattle, and ran cattle near Yakima, Washington. At about age ninety he moved to a care facility in Fort Belvoir, Virginia, outside Washington, DC. Having mellowed out considerably (a fact attested to by his son Gordon, who had run afoul of him in their younger years once or twice himself), Smith died there, as beloved of his family as he was unloved on the *Macaw*, on May 13, 2013, at the age of 104.[22]

After the *Macaw*, Bob Gonnoud went to the *Florikan*, the *Macaw*'s sister ship that had had such a harrowing time towing the *Flier* from Midway back to Pearl Harbor. For his part in averting the disaster that almost claimed the submarine on that trip, the *Florikan*'s captain, George Sharp, got what he and Paul Burton had both so deeply desired, to get back into a submarine. Within five months of maneuvering so adeptly to reestablish the towline that day, Sharp was given command of the *Nautilus*. By the time he died of a brain tumor in 1957 at the age of fifty-one, Sharp had risen to the rank of rear admiral.

The *Flier*'s skipper, Lt. Cmdr. John D. Crowley, got a second chance too. The board of inquiry into the *Flier*'s grounding concluded that Crowley should have undertaken to negotiate the channel at more than 10 knots, but that otherwise he had done nothing wrong. They deemed him responsible for the grounding but absolved him of "culpable negligence." In reviewing their findings, Vice Admiral Charles Lockwood struck down even the charge of going too slow—the channel at Midway, Lockwood wrote, was too narrow to negotiate at anything over 10 knots. (This seems to have been distinctly a minority opinion.) Lockwood did, however, fault Crowley's judgment in choosing to attempt the channel amid conditions as rough as they were that day. That was a mistake, he wrote, but given various "exigencies" in operation at the time, an excusable one.

As noted above, the boards that investigated the grounding of the *Flier* and the loss of the *Macaw* comprised the same four officers. They seem to have assigned to Mother Nature more of the blame for the *Flier*'s grounding than they did for the *Macaw*'s. Given that the circumstances of the two were so nearly identical, the disparity in the judgments is pretty striking. If Paul Burton were alive to compare the results, he might have felt put upon.

In any case, John Crowley kept his command. The *Flier* underwent repairs at Pearl Harbor sufficient to make it back under its own power to Mare Island. Thoroughly reconditioned by that May, the *Flier* did its first war patrol at last and put in in early July at Fremantle in Western Australia for a refit. Fremantle was a major US submarine base during the war, and it was not uncommon for American servicemen on liberty in nearby Perth to engage in hostilities with their Australian or New Zealand counterparts, the issue typically being Australian women and the charm the Americans, with their exotic accents and their money, seemed to have for them. It was to prevent such hostilities that the American command imposed a 5:00 p.m. curfew around the beginning of August 1944. All US servicemen were to be back on base by then, and it was to enforce that curfew that James Alls of the *Flier*—the former fireman, now motor machinist's mate 3/c, whose insistent badgering of a Washington, DC, recruiter had broken down the man's resistance to Alls's obviously underage enlistment a couple of years before—was pressed into the shore patrol. In his capacity as a law enforcement agent, Alls entered a bar in Perth and found an American Army Ranger and a group of New Zealanders about to do what Alls was there to prevent— they were about to fight. Alls got there just in time to hear the Ranger tell the New Zealanders, about five of them, that he could lick them all. Alls was trying to impress upon his countryman the advantage of leaving the bar and leaving the New Zealanders inside it unlicked when one of the latter hit him, Alls, with what he thinks was a beer mug, broke his jaw, and knocked him out.

Alls was convalescing in a medical facility when the *Flier* left days later on its second war patrol. It was on that patrol, on August 13, 1944, exactly six months after the *Macaw* sank, that the *Flier* hit a mine in the Balabac Strait between Borneo and the Philippines and followed suit, taking all but fourteen of its crew down with it. As a motor machinist's mate, Alls would almost certainly have been trapped deep in the bowels of the ship and killed. His assailant in Perth had saved his life.[23]

The story of the eight men who ultimately survived the loss of the *Flier* is one of the great epics of the war in the ironically named Pacific, and is told in at least three books and a website (regarding which, see the suggestions for further reading in this volume). Commander Crowley was among the survivors. Both he and Alls would do additional submarine service, and both would survive the war.

Bud Loughman was offered command of another submarine rescue vessel after the *Macaw* but declined the offer. His heart, like Paul Burton's, had always been set on submarines themselves, and he made it known that if he couldn't be in one, he wanted out of the submarine service altogether. That spring he was granted his wish at last (the eye test he had reportedly failed years earlier notwithstanding) and assigned to the USS *Seal* (SS-183). Later he served aboard the *Searaven* (SS-196). The *Macaw*, after it sank, was his only command, and of his wartime postings he spoke most fondly of the *Macaw* and its crew. Of all his experiences in the war, the one he revisited most was clearly the *Macaw*'s sinking.

Loughman remained in the Naval Reserve for more than twenty years after the war. He raised a family and pursued a career in the glass industry, first as a corporate sales executive, later as the proprietor of a glass shop in Morro Bay, a small town on California's Central Coast. In his retirement, he and his wife, Patricia (née Sheils), delivered Meals on Wheels, and he distributed literature for a group seeking to foster world peace. For his last ten years or so Loughman and former *Macaw* Fireman Donald Srack lived within about five miles of each other, and neither knew it. Loughman died December 28, 1998, of complications following a stroke. He was eighty-two.

Capt. Joseph Connolly served as the naval commandant of Okinawa in 1946–47 and as a senior staff officer attached to Gen. Douglas MacArthur's Far East Command the following two years. He retired from the navy as a rear admiral in 1951 and took an active part in civic affairs in his adopted hometown of San Jose, California. He died of cancer in 1978 at the age of eighty.

Herman Ehlers returned to the family bank in Beecher, Illinois, and ran it with the assistance of his sister Garneta. He told her that Paul Burton played a good game of chess. Ehlers never married. He died of colon cancer in 1975 at the age of sixty.[24]

The sinking of the *Macaw* left Stanley Libera with a case of pneumonia in his left lung. On an extended survivor's leave shortly thereafter, he married Anna A. Andruskiewicz, who had accosted him as a stranger, apparently on a dare, on a street in New London, Connecticut, with "Hiya, sailor" about two years before. Libera had one employer after the war, a zipper manufacturer in Kensington, Connecticut, for whom he was in charge of quality control. He retired in 1981 and died September 16, 2015, at the age of ninety-two. Anna had died about twenty years before.

Libera spoke passionately about the *Macaw,* and highly of Paul Burton, more than seventy years after the ship went down. As the end neared and he slipped into dementia, he talked about Midway, asked his niece where she had come from, as in what training facility, whether San Diego or Hawaii, remonstrated with an imaginary fellow sailor who had gotten fresh with her, advised her that she couldn't sleep in a men's barracks, and warned her to watch out for the rats and the gooney birds.[25]

Charles Scott owned a service station in El Paso, Texas, after the war. Scott, like Libera, revered Paul Burton. "According to my standards," he wrote, "there never was a better or more courageous man." Dan Weber returned to the Houston area and started a dredging business with his father. Charles Kumler, drawing on his navy experience, pursued a career as an electrician in the Los Angeles area and wired the home of 1950s sitcom stars Ozzie and Harriet Nelson. Kumler, a smoker, died of cancer in 1964 at the age of thirty-nine.[26]

On July 9, 1944, the radio program *Ohio, These Are Your Sons,* sponsored by Standard Oil of Ohio, designated Curtis Wainscott "Ohio's Fighting Man of the Week" and presented a fictionalized dramatization of the destruction of "the ill-fated warship, the Macaw" and of Wainscott's role in coming to the aid in the water of an injured shipmate by the name of Eddie Adams, the author's stand-in for Augie Koepke. The transcript, by Gilbert Kingsbury, an editor at WLW-WSAI in Cincinnati, places the men accurately enough in the pilot-house before they're swept overboard, and has the ship, at an unspecified location "on the far reaches of the seven seas," being battered by "great waves, mountain high." But when push comes to shove and the decision is made to leave the pilothouse, the officer (by implication, Paul Burton) issuing the order says, "Let's get below." That would have been the wrong direction. Moments later, after Adams and Wainscott have been swept overboard, the commanding officer tells another sailor, Myers, "Quick! Signal the engine room. Reverse the engines." Of course the engine room was deep underwater by then, and the engines hadn't worked in four weeks. But if they were working, reversing them would not have done much good either unless they were already in reverse, seeing as the whole problem was that the ship was sliding backward. Dan Biss narrated the program.

Wainscott worked after the war at Fisher Body in Fairfield, Ohio, outside Cincinnati, repaired lawnmowers on the side, and played an active role in his Masonic lodge. He died of a heart attack in 1975, one year shy of retirement.[27]

Augie Koepke stayed in the navy until 1956, twenty years after he first enlisted. His last ship was the USS *Midway* (CV-41), an aircraft carrier named after the battle and commissioned September 10, 1945, eight days after the surrender of Japan. From then until 1955 the *Midway* was the biggest ship afloat. It was the first US carrier too big to transit the Panama Canal. Perhaps for that reason it was based, for at least part of the time then Chief Petty Officer Koepke served aboard it, at Norfolk, Virginia, where the Koepkes rented a house off the base, and where on Sundays the whole family—Koepke, his wife, and their two daughters—would have dinner aboard the ship, and the girls, under the supervision of sailors assigned babysitting duty, would play tag and hide-and-seek under the wings of the planes parked on the deck.

After Koepke mustered out, they settled back in Palm Beach, Florida, where Koepke followed his father into the employ of the exclusive Bath and Tennis Club—the senior Koepke served as general manager there; Augie Paul tended to the vegetation and grounds—and established himself as a fixture in the local golfing scene, frequently participating in tournaments at the West Palm Beach Country Club, occasionally winning them, and twice shooting a hole in one. He died on May 5, 1984, at the age of seventy.[28]

Albert Bolke served after the *Macaw* aboard two minesweepers, the USS *Towhee* (AM-388) and the USS *Peregrine* (AM-373). He was home on leave in Chicago in December 1945 when his sister arranged a blind date for him with a fellow employee at Ritchie's, a South Side box factory. They had four dates in four days. On the first they went bowling. On the fourth they saw a Maureen O'Hara movie (probably *The Spanish Main*, a swashbuckler costarring Paul Henreid), he proposed, and she accepted. They raised five children while he pursued a career as a sheet metal worker. Albert Bolke died of lung cancer in December 1993, also at age seventy.

Lawrence Mathers went (or went back) to work for the Richfield Oil Company in California and settled in Redwood City, south of San Francisco, after the war. George Manning returned to Albany, Oregon, and went to work in a planing mill. An avid bowler, he declined an offer to bowl professionally in favor of a career in the lumber industry, one that would afford him a more predictable income on which to raise a family. He suffered after the war from a chronic sinus condition his son Don attributes to his inhaling fumes aboard the *Macaw* the night it sank. Manning died in 1972 at the age of fifty.[29]

Erwin Knecht, the immigrant from Germany whose father had yanked him out of a sort of homegrown Hitler Youth society before the war, returned to Long Island after it, studied diesel mechanics on the GI Bill, worked briefly in Detroit, and settled in 1962 with his wife, dog, and four children in Southern California, finding employment along the way in electrical work, carpentry, silversmithing, photo processing and sales, and making and furnishing doll houses as a hobby. Knecht spent several hours early on February 13, 1944, atop the tripod. He told his family he had a vision that night in which the whole ship lit up and Jesus appeared. The vision conveyed a message. Whether Jesus actually articulated it or merely endorsed it by his presence is unclear, but the message itself was clear enough. It was to do what Knecht did much of that night to the tripod—to hang on. Knecht died in 1992 at age sixty-seven.[30]

Richard Blaine Williamson returned to Cedar Vale, Kansas, and to his agricultural pursuits and raised a large family. Fellow former Motor Machinist's Mate Dan Weber and his wife stopped by Cedar Vale on their way back to their Houston-area home from Colorado circa 1969 and were informed by Williamson's aunt at the local post office that he had died the week before. Directed to his grave in a small cemetery, Weber said, they found it surrounded by wheat fields like the ones Williamson had harvested with his combines and described in such lovely terms to his shipmates. Williamson was fifty-eight.[31]

Howard Rechel, like Williamson and Weber among others, spent the rest of the war at Pearl Harbor repairing submarines, some so thoroughly banged up, he said, that every light bulb inside was broken. He and his crew worked on everything but the main engine—everything "from torpedo tubes to toilet bowls." After the war he returned to New Jersey, raised a family, and pursued a career as a telephone technician.[32]

Eugene Van Buskirk ran an antiques store in Calhoun, Georgia, for forty years.[33] Lloyd George Fox raised wheat, barley, oats, and pigs for forty-five years on a farm just north of Arnegard, North Dakota. It was hard work, but he loved it. "Plant that stuff in the spring and hope it rains," he said. "Cross your fingers and hope it grows." Fox, an obviously decent man, looked back with regret more than sixty years later on his reading of Paul Burton's mail. "I had no goddamn business doing it," he said.[34]

Jack Vangets worked, as did his father, for the General Motors Guide Lamp Division back in Indiana after the war. In his eighties he was shooting his age in golf.[35] Joseph Throgmorton returned to Paducah, Kentucky, and pursued a career as a pipefitter.[36]

Harold Hayes worked in the radio shop at the submarine base at Pearl Harbor for the rest of the war, then for forty-six years in the Central Meter Shop of the Illinois Power Company in his hometown of Decatur, Illinois. Like fellow Illinoisan Albert Bolke, Hayes could not swim. His daughter Susan thinks that after the war he never again ventured off dry land. She recalls being out for a spin on a lake on her uncle's boat with her mother as a child and waving to her father as he stood watching from the shore. He had declined to go along. Hayes, father of eight and a devout Methodist, died in January 2014 at age ninety-three.[37]

William Hale Wantz, the Royal Executioner at the equator-crossing festivities, worked at a bakery in Petersburg, Virginia, after the war. Stephen Miller, the Shakespeare aficionado Wantz brought to tears with his paddle during those rites, settled in Brentwood, Missouri, a suburb of St. Louis. He was married briefly and had a daughter. His daughter thinks he contemplated entering a seminary but changed his mind, got a teaching degree, and taught school. His health failed early. He was in an iron lung in a VA hospital when his niece Jane Anne Martin and sister visited him there at one point, and could see them only by way of looking in a mirror. "He was a good person . . . a gentle man," Martin said. Miller died in 1967 at the age of forty-three.[38]

Clyde Isbell, who was monitoring the fathometer when the *Macaw* ran aground and subsequently attributed the ship's destruction to misleading readings he reported to the bridge, read light meters for a Texas utility after the war, then reenlisted, in the air force this time, and later put in twenty years with the US Postal Service.

Ship's Cook Anthony Tomkovicz, the former coal miner, pin setter, and Hollywood stagehand from Charleroi, Pennsylvania, traded on the experience he gained with his happy German POW colleagues at Pearl Harbor in a roughly fifty-year career as a meatcutter for Safeway in Southern California. Nord Lester returned to the San Diego area after the war and ran a plumbing company. Fifty years after his time on the *Macaw*, he was still getting seasick on fishing trips. His friend Lewill Horsman settled in Fort Worth and would eventually head up the environmental resources section of the Fort Worth branch of the US Army Corps of Engineers.[39]

Al Muti, who cut hair on the fantail of the *Macaw*, worked as a barber back in San Francisco before settling into a career in discount grocery marketing. Bob Gonnoud worked for thirty years as a Los Angeles fireman. Lyle Webb returned to Southern California and the newspaper business. By 1955 he was publisher of the *Redondo Reflex*, a weekly in Redondo Beach. Gonnoud dropped in on Webb once after the war. Webb did not seem particularly happy to see him. "When I approached him, he just brushed me off real quick," Gonnoud said. "He kind of shooed me out the door." It seemed to Gonnoud that Webb wanted no airing of his wartime past. Webb died in 1964 at the age of sixty-five.[40]

Joseph Verkennes returned to his wife in Flint, Michigan, and if, as seems likely, to his old job at the Fisher Body plant there, he was colleagues once again with his old shipmate Dave Wallington. Wallington worked there briefly postwar, got married, went to school on the GI Bill, got a job in the loan department of a bank, raised a family, and ended up in nearby Grand Rapids.

Worth Thomas Windle, the navigation officer who struggled with Paul Burton to guide the *Macaw* into Brooks Channel the day it grounded, took command in October 1945 of the USS *Falcon*, the submarine rescue vessel George Sharp had commanded during the *Squalus* rescue in 1939. Windle died in 1954 at age fifty-one.

For his role in keeping his floating support circle intact and Augie Paul Koepke alive the morning of February 13, 1944, Chief Bosun's Mate Tom Emmet Brown was awarded the Navy and Marine Corps Medal, the navy's highest award for bravery in a noncombat situation. He was still in the navy as of 1952. He died September 17, 1993, in Pearcy, Arkansas, at age seventy-nine. What became of him in the meantime is unclear.[41]

Edward Wade was assigned to the navy's amphibious forces command at Pearl Harbor after the *Macaw*, then in April 1945 to *LST40*, a tank-landing vessel, aboard which he was demoted, for reasons unknown, from seaman first class to second class on May 12, 1945, off Okinawa, on and around which the bloodiest battle of the Pacific war was raging at the time. Wade appears to have mustered out on December 3, 1945. He died in 1970, three days shy of forty-four. What he died of and what he had been doing over the preceding twenty-five years are also unknown.

Ten days after the *Macaw* sank, Bud Loughman sent the secretary of the treasury a memo with the subject line "VAUGHN R. A. STM1c Heroically gave his life trying to save a shipmate." The memo cites Robert Vaughn's leaving the foremast and its promise of safety to go to the aid of Augie Koepke when Koepke had just slipped out of his life jacket and off the upright barrel of the 20mm antiaircraft gun he'd been dangling from—a move by Vaughn that did little for Koepke and probably cost Vaughn his life. Loughman named Koepke as a corroborating witness. Apparently Loughman hoped Vaughn would be posthumously awarded a medal for valor, one issued by the Treasury Department. This initiative does not seem to have borne fruit.

Frank and Elizabeth Lehmbecker received a telegram from the Navy Department three days after the *Macaw* sank informing them that their son LeRoy was missing. Within about a month he had been confirmed dead and the local paper had published his obituary, but his mother refused to believe it. She kept writing him letters, and they kept coming back, stamped

> Returned to Sender
> Unclaimed

She wrote twenty-one of them from February 17 through March 25, two on March 4, and then, apparently, she stopped. The letters sit now in a file drawer, unopened, sealed testimony to a mother's fierce, undying love for her son. "My grandma always felt he'd be coming around the corner," LeRoy's nephew Gene Lehmbecker said. LeRoy's disappearance left his parents bitter toward the Japanese. "If something was made in Japan, they just had a fit. It couldn't be in the house," Gene said. LeRoy's death "basically just ruined their life."[42]

Shirley Hutchenson, the girlfriend LeRoy left behind after their whirlwind romance, married an army veteran in 1956 and raised a family with him, but she said sixty-two years after LeRoy died that, had he brought her the ring he said he had for her in the one letter he wrote her, she probably would have accepted it.[43]

Robert Daugherty, Eugene Daugherty's father, lost two of his three sons in the war. Eugene's brother Lonzo, said to have enlisted under a pseudonym rather than do time in prison for rape, died in it too. He was reportedly buried at sea like Eugene, the sea in Lonzo's case apparently being the North Atlantic. A local 2003 newspaper article about Campbell County, Tennessee, war dead lists him by his real name. Robert Daugherty, according to his daughter Vickie, would talk about neither of them afterward, though it seems he may have made an exception with the young woman Eugene was dating before he enlisted. The two of them, Vickie said, came together in their shared grief, got married in 1955, and produced one child, Vickie, born in 1959, about thirty-six years after her half brother Eugene was born and fifteen years after he died going to the rescue of the men of the stricken *Macaw*.[44]

Ernest Samed died with his dues paid up on a government-issued life insurance policy that paid a death benefit of ten thousand dollars. That money presumably went to his father, David, the Syrian immigrant, barber, and US Army veteran, and his second wife, the former Sadie Lashuay. Samed's father died in 1948.

When Edward Pitta returned to California after the war, his uncle Joe, drawing on funds of dubious provenance, presented him with a shiny new Cadillac, its trunk liberally stocked with liquor. Edward, accompanied by five navy buddies, promptly wrecked it. The car was so thoroughly mangled, it was reportedly featured as a cautionary image on a roadside billboard promoting driver safety alongside the grim message "Six sailors killed"—though in fact no one actually had died. Pitta proceeded through a series of jobs—gas station hand, factory worker, cannery worker, produce buyer, construction foreman, fisherman—in the Bay Area and Northern California, lost multiple fingers in another unsuccessful rescue attempt, trying to free a coworker's arm from machinery in a rubber products factory, and survived another shooting, this by one of his six wives at their home in Fort Bragg in 1977. Husband and wife both told the police the shooting, like the prewar incident in the brothel in Stockton, was accidental, and no charges were pressed. Edward Pitta, who threw himself in harm's way in war and peace alike and seems to have suffered more of it in peace than in war, died in November 2009 at the age of eighty-six.[45]

Cmdr. Thomas Lincoln Wogan, formerly of the USS *Tarpon*, presided over the commissioning of the USS *Besugo* (SS-321) on June 19, 1944, in New London, Connecticut, and commanded the new boat on its first three war patrols, from September 1944 to February 1945. On July 10, 1945, he assumed command of Submarine Division 362. In September 1948 he was posted as inspector-instructor to the Naval Reserve Training Center in Albuquerque, New Mexico, where on January 15, 1950, his wife, Helen, having reportedly suffered a lengthy illness, was found dead of carbon monoxide poisoning in the family garage.

That July Wogan was transferred to San Diego. He served there as chief staff officer of a submarine flotilla. On March 17, 1951, the day before he was scheduled to take command of Submarine Squadron 5, he shot and killed himself while sitting in his car, similarly in the garage at his home. He was reportedly despondent over his wife's death. He was to have been feted that evening by members of his new squadron at the Admiral Kidd Commissioned Officers Club on San Diego Bay, where reservations had been made for 150 people. Wogan left two daughters, fifteen and seven, and a son, five.

Betty Burton never remarried. As far as her granddaughter Traci Burton knows, she never so much as dated anyone after Paul died. She raised her two children by herself with the help of a maid in Haddonfield, New Jersey, across the Delaware River from Philadelphia, working at the Haddonfield Public Library and translating books into Braille for the Library of Congress. She was not given to talking about her husband. Whenever anyone would mention him to her, Traci said, it was as though a shade closed over her face. She was still wearing her wedding ring when she died on March 8, 2003, at the age of ninety-three.[46]

Given the circumstances of his death, it was inevitable that there would be speculation as to whether Paul Burton had committed suicide. Opinion among the men who served under him was divided on that score. Bud Loughman, who apparently never suspected the contempt Burton held him in, angrily rejected that theory. Burton's other chess partner on the *Macaw*, Herman Ehlers, heard the speculation about suicide and, according to Ehlers's sister Garneta, he was disinclined to believe it. "Doggone," she said, quoting him, "I thought I saw him on some part of the ship. . . . I can't believe he didn't make it."[47]

But others found the suicide theory at least plausible. As William Smith noted: "He was quite a swimmer. . . . If anyone aboard a small ship should have survived it, he should have."[48]

Don Srack didn't know whether to believe the suicide speculation, but he noted that Burton, having lost his ship and several of his men, would have faced a terrible administrative ordeal. Lloyd George Fox thought that between his marital and naval troubles, when the *Macaw* went down, Burton figured the easiest thing to do would be just to swim out to sea.[49]

But his doing that does not by itself necessarily indicate self-destructive intent. The sea was, typically, less violent offshore that night than in. Nor should Burton's reluctance to make for buoy No. 2 with Lester and Loughman or to join up with Brown's group in the water necessarily be construed against him. Bob Jacobsen may have been a bit confused as to who was where that morning, but he makes a good point when he writes of Burton: "He was a loner. His drifting out to sea, past the group on the buoy saying he didn't need help would have been his way."[50]

Jacobsen was a rather harsh critic of Paul Burton, so it's not surprising that he laid out the case for the prosecution in some detail . . .

My memory is a bit hazy but I believe there were 26 or 28 articles for the government of the US Navy. Among them . . .

Hazarding a ship or grounding a ship through neglect, poor navigation, poor seamanship or poor reasoning can result in reduction of rank and a Dishonorable discharge from Naval Service.

Paul Burton knew of this article and it must have been a heavy load on his conscience all those days he lived after the Macaw grounded. He knew that his Navy career was over and he had put a huge black blotch on his military families proud name.

In the pictures I have seen of P. W. Burton he looked to have lost a lot of weight. I think that suiside is very likely—though his physical condition would also say he was a good subject for hypothermia.[51]

. . . or that he made it twice:

Burton was from an old Naval family. I imagine his whole life he heard: Honor and duty—Leaving the Tarpon under what seems to be a bad fitness report—causing the grounding of the Macaw—Seeing the end of his ship—Seeing men in the water fighting for their lives—I am now convinced that Paul Burton did not plan to be a survivor—I think he felt he had deeply tarnished and pitted the family honor—[52]

Speculating about what might have ensued had the salvage effort succeeded in getting the *Macaw* off the reef and into the lagoon, Jacobsen wrote:

Paul Burton would have likely been removed as CO of the Macaw. The day the Macaw was brought in the lagoon he would have had to go to the Court of Inquiries into the grounding of the vessel. I think Burton was just doing some wishful thinking that he would sail the vessel to Pearl. I think with all the "black marks" on his record—he would never command even a garbage scow. Would have probably spent the rest of the war in command of a LMD—Large Mahogany Desk—shuffling paper work or counting mess kits with the knowledge that at the end of the war he would be discharged— No career![53]

Former Seaman 1/c Joe Throgmorton put it more succinctly: "I believe in my soul he jumped in that water, swam out to sea," he said. "I don't think he wanted to live after that ship went down."[54]

Though the Japanese were still engaging in it as recently as the Battle of Midway, the supposedly honorable practice of a captain's going down with his ship seems largely to have lost its allure over the last three hundred years or so. For Paul Burton to have gone down with his, he would have had to stay in the pilothouse. The Macaw sank, but never the whole way. When the huge seas of the night of February 12–13 subsided at last, the Macaw, as noted above, was submerged only to about the flying bridge—the masts and tripod still projected at an angle above the surface. Even by the harshest pre-modern reading of the traditional sea captain's honor code, the suicide requirement did not apply. Whether Burton exercised his option that way that morning, no one will ever know. But his behavior that morning, when he declined an offer of sanctuary from his men and swam past them out to sea, begs the question why. By the time he was within hollering range of Brown and his companions in the water, he was well outside the surf break, probably far enough that there would have been no percentage in going any farther, except perhaps a negative one in that, the farther out he went, the bigger the haystack for the spotter planes to spot the needle in when it started getting light.

Burton certainly had inherited a proud military tradition, and he had made no secret of the importance he attached to upholding it. A poem he composed, titled "A Sailor's Lives," appeared in the January 27, 1933, edition of The Log, a student publication at the US Naval Academy. This is the first stanza:

Sometimes I wish I had two lives to lead.
One life gives hardly all the time I need!
There's first the life to live of work and fame—
In order to give credit to my name—
For after all it's only fair return
To try to have my loved ones look with pride
On him whom they've endeavored to have learn
That "in all things let honor be your guide."

Eleven years later, deemed unfit for submarine service, captain of a ship that had, on his watch, run aground and sunk without the dignifying assistance of the enemy, Burton may indeed have felt that he had disgraced his family, or at least himself in their eyes. But his seamanship on January 16, 1944, was arguably no more blameworthy than that of either Captain Connolly, who compelled him to put his ship at risk, or Commander Crowley, who faced basically the same navigational challenge and did much as Burton did under much the same conditions at the same place and almost the same time. Burton's taking the line he did in attempting to reenter Brooks Channel may have been a mistake—one made greatly more likely by the absence of buoy No. 4—but it was hardly shameful. If it was a mistake, it was the mistake of a man doing his utmost under exceptionally difficult circumstances. If a sense of shame supplied the incremental weight that finally dragged Paul Burton down that morning, that really was a shame.

Family matters of any stripe aside, Burton probably did figure as he swam away from his ship that his prospects for a satisfying naval career had gone down with it. At the very least, as Don Srack would remark years later, he faced a terrible bureaucratic ordeal, and as Bob Jacobsen suggested, an abbreviated naval career confined to a desk. Burton obviously had his faults, some of the deficiencies as an officer Tom Wogan laid to his charge perhaps among them. But just as obviously he was a man of pride and action. He may have found the prospect of spending the rest of the war, and of his time in the navy, in an office building intolerable. As of the morning of February 13, 1944, things had not gone well for him for about a year. When his ship all but vanished beneath the waves, and his prospects not just of submarine duty but of any sea duty at all vanished completely, as he may have thought they had, he may have felt once again like that boy whose ice cream had fallen off the cone. Only now the irrecoverable ice cream may have represented not just the thing he wanted most in life but life itself. He may have felt his life was over, and that by swimming out to sea he was merely acknowledging a fact. Paul Burton was thirty-two.

Any story can always be reframed with what-ifs. One intriguing what-if regarding the *Macaw* concerns Cmdr. John Crowley of the *Flier* and whether he helped do in both his ship and the *Macaw* by way of an act of kindness. The recommended starting point for a submarine's approach to the channel at Midway was about two miles offshore. While awaiting the motor launch that was to have brought him the harbor pilot on January 16, 1944, Crowley, by his own account, brought the *Flier* in almost two miles to reduce the smaller craft's exposure to the heavy seas running that day. So Crowley started his approach considerably closer to the channel entrance than he would have otherwise. Had he started it farther out, he would have conducted it within a frame of greater space, meaning probably more space between the sub and the tug that tried to lead the way in, less concern on Crowley's part about running the tug down, less constraint that way on the submarine's speed, less time spent exposed to the same southeastward current that would help dislodge the *Macaw* four weeks later, better steerageway for the sub as it penetrated the surf zone, and a better chance of passing through that zone without incident and safely into the lagoon. As it was, the *Flier* was "cabin'd, cribb'd, confined" in its approach, and the sea, constrained by nothing like Crowley's consideration, put his ship on the reef.[55]

Another what-if concerns the number of men aboard the *Macaw* the night of February 12–13, 1944. According to Captain Connolly, when the salvage efforts were put on hold yet again the morning of February 11, Paul Burton wanted to keep two sections of twenty men each on board, and it was only after conferring with Connolly and Commander Curtis, the salvage officer, that he agreed that one would suffice. If Burton had had his way, the pilothouse would have been almost twice as crowded as it was and the oxygen in it depleted almost twice as fast. For better or worse, the men in it would have had to leave it sooner, likely about when that night's huge waves were at their peak, and almost twice as many lives would have been at risk.

On January 14, 1944, two days before the *Flier* and *Macaw* ran aground, the submarine USS *Albacore* (SS-218) sank the Japanese destroyer *Sazanami* three hundred miles southeast of Yap in the Caroline Islands. The *Sazanami* was one of the two Japanese destroyers that had shelled Midway the morning Pearl Harbor was attacked. On February 18, at the conclusion of that war patrol, its eighth, the *Albacore* stopped off briefly at Midway. The men topside as it entered and exited the channel would have had a close view of the upper reaches of the *Macaw*'s masts and tripod, poking out of the waves just off the eastern flare of the channel entrance, very nearly where buoy No. 4 was supposed to have been. The *Albacore* and its crew of about sixty went down in turn ten months later, having apparently hit a mine just off the coast of Japan. The *Ushio*, *Sazanami*'s shelling partner on that fateful December 7, survived the war, the only one of the twenty-two combat ships in Japan's Pearl Harbor assault fleet to do so. It was scrapped in 1948.

The ships in Convoy PW 2294 had a better survival rate. Both minesweepers, all three tugs, and all eight Liberty ships survived the war. Two of the Liberty ships were purchased after the war by Greek shipping firms. By 1973 all eight had been sold for scrap.

All four Kaiser shipyards in Richmond, where four of the convoy's Liberty ships were built, shut down shortly after the war, having during it produced 747 ships, more than any other complex in the country, in two-thirds the time and reportedly at one-fourth the average cost elsewhere. The four yards are now part of the Rosie the Riveter/World War II Home Front National Historical Park, where visitors can tour the SS *Red Oak Victory*, a product of Yard No. 1, launched November 1944 and one of a very few Liberty or Victory ships still afloat.

Employment at the Moore Dry Dock Company in nearby Oakland peaked circa 1943 at about thirty-eight thousand. The company built more than eighty ships during the war and converted or repaired more than two thousand. After the war, the firm's fortunes and payroll declined along with those of much of the rest of the nation's shipbuilding industry as government orders plummeted and production shifted to yards in Asia. Moore launched its last oceangoing ship within about a year after the war and closed up shop altogether in 1961. Schnitzer Brothers, a metal-recycling firm based in Portland, Oregon, bought the property and conducted what at the time, in October 1961, was the largest auction of industrial equipment ever on the West Coast. Much of the scrap they proceeded to recycle went to Japan.[56]

After he mustered out, Bob Jacobsen rafted logs in his old hometown of Garibaldi, Oregon, then moved to Long Beach, California, and took the advice of the self-styled career counselors on the fantail of the *Macaw* and got a job with a utility, in his case Southern California Edison—but all that only after another ten years or so in the navy, during which he revisited Midway twice, the first time aboard a transport four years after the war.

In 1949 we hauled a load of tanks and artillery to Yokahama Japan—on the way back to the states we stopped at Midway Island. It was being decommissioned. All the planes were gone—The gooneyville submarine base was deserted. Was a crew of Sea Bees—who were piling a mountain of stuff on the dock for us to haul to Pearl Harbor. We helped all we could to reduce the stock of liquor at the old Navy base rec center. They wanted to get rid of all the booze. Beer was 5¢ a can—Bourbon or Scotch was 10¢ a shot of scotch or a high ball. They had magnums of champaine for 50¢—We bought it and poured over each other—Some of the worst hangovers in my whole life.

In 1954 I went into Midway on [a] tanker. During the Korean war they reactivated the Navy air field. The chanel had shallowed up—We had to anchor outside. A small yard tanker shuttled back and forth hauling aviator gas and jet fuel to the Island. All the old sub base barracks, galley, rec hall and shops were gone. Not a sign of any remains of the Macaw—They must have had to use a tremendous amount of explosives to destroy her. She was a very heavy built ship. God it must have taken a lot to reduce that tri-pod mast to little pieces of rust.[57]

The *Macaw* had indeed proven hard to dispose of. In fact the job was never more than half done. Much of its equipment was salvaged, including its McCann rescue chamber, which had been torn loose and swept overboard; but shortly after the sinking, Lebbeus Curtis, the salvage officer, deemed the ship itself a lost cause, whereupon it was declared a hazard to navigation and ordered demolished. That task fell, ironically, to a salvage ship, the USS *Shackle* (ARS-9), and it is a testament to the Moore Dry Dock Company and the quality of its workmanship that it took two and a half tons of demolition charges to blast away just what remained of the *Macaw*'s superstructure, tripod included. The ship's hull remains largely intact. It lies now about where it came to rest the night it sank, probably a little farther offshore, still heading inshore. As of 2005, it had taken on a sharp list to port. Encrusted now with invertebrates, the *Macaw*'s remains are home or hangout to lobsters, turkeyfish, and octopuses, who dwell in the many nooks and crannies demolition left it with, and graced inside and out by a never-ending swirl of sea life, including monk seals, manta rays, turtles, dolphins, Galapagos sharks, and rarities such as Steindachner's moray and the yellowtail parrotfish, the latter of which might plausibly feel right at home under the bow or in the bowels of a ship named the *Macaw*. Perhaps it feels a bond of kinship.[58]

Midway was designated a national wildlife refuge in 1988. The navy closed up shop there five years later. Today the atoll is part of the Papahanau- mokuakea Marine National Monument, jointly managed by the US Fish and Wildlife Service, the National Oceanic and Atmospheric Administration, and the State of Hawaii. Public access to the atoll has been periodically restricted in recent years in the face of government agency budget cuts and in the hope of Mother Nature's undoing as fully as she might the environmental harm 160 years or so of occasionally violent human habitation have done to it. The *Macaw*, or what's left of it, remains in theory government property, but pos- session being nine-tenths of the law, it belongs now in fact to the sea.

Appendix

Crew Photo Roster

Front row (including men on ground), from left: Donald Srack, Daniel Weber, Robert Phelan, Charles Shook, Quinton Studer, Raymond Toth, Anthony Tomkovicz, Joseph Tibor, Virgil Anderson, Edward Bronson, John Leigh.

Second row: [Floyd Harvey or Dwight Harvey], John Parsons, Ralph Enzweiler, William Gibbs, Frank Spoonamore, Worth Windle, guest officer Cullen, Bud Loughman, guest officer Brad, William Smith, John Stout, Leroy Warner, Russell Francis, Erwin Knecht [or, possibly, Nord Lester].

Third row: Curtis Wainscott, Edwin Goetsch, Alfred Jones, George Baker, Joseph Calligan, Dean Jewell, George Keehn, Robert Gonnoud, Robert Bloom, Nathan Turner, George Manning, Robert Jacobsen, Harry Vance, Jack Vangets, Edward Wade, Arthur Springs, Jack Moore, Albert Muti.

Fourth row: Stephen Miller, Lyle Webb, Lawrence Mathers, Robert Blinn, E. J. Nations, Vorie Darling, Luther Fry, Meredith Keene, Stanley Libera, George Gritton, Ernst Luders, Hughey Lindsey; (*behind Lindsey*) Victor Auble; (*to Auble's left*) Leonard Mayer; (*to Mayer's left*) Joseph Verkennes; (*to Verkennes's left*) Adam Autin; (*behind Verkennes*) Lewis Vickers; (*in front of Verkennes*) Walter Voke; (*in front of Autin, with Voke's hand on his shoulder*) James Main.

Back row: Bert Maas, Robert Mathews, Richard Williamson, Herman Ehlers, Claude "Toby" Hannah, David Wallington, John Paul Graaff, Albert Bolke, Elmer Ganstine, J. T. Strickland, Charles Kumler; (*in front of Kumler*) Robert Friend; (*to Kumler's left*) Charles Brasier, Myron Froehlich, Peter Semotuk.

Brief Glossary of Nautical Terms

abeam	At a right angle to the keel
aft	Toward the stern
amidships	In the middle of a ship
ballast	Heavy material carried aboard for stability or to control the draft
bearing	Direction of travel
boat deck	Deck one level above the main deck
bower	Anchor deployed from the bow
bridge	Deck from which navigation is conducted
brig	Shipboard jail cell
bulkhead	Wall
bullnose	Circular aperture at the prow of a submarine through which a towing line can be rigged
cans	Depth charges
captain's mast	Shipboard disciplinary hearing
commission	(*verb*) Put into active military service, or confer officer status on; (*noun*) warrant conferring officer status
conn	(*verb*) Supervise navigation; (*noun*) supervision of same
designer's waterline	Waterline of ship bearing full load on even keel in still water
draft	Depth at which a ship sits in water
fantail	Usually open overhanging section of main deck at stern

fish	Torpedo
fit out	Prepare newly launched ship for sea trials
flying bridge	Uppermost deck, typically comprising at least in part the roof of the pilothouse
fore	Toward the bow
general quarters	Battle stations
groundswells	Broad, deep undulations of the sea
gunwale	Upper edge of the hull, typically projecting several feet above the main deck
halyard	Line or tackle for hoisting and lowering
head	Toilet
keel	Longitudinal timber or plate extending along midline at base of ship's hull and often below it
knot	One nautical mile per hour
ladder	Staircase
leeward	Side opposite the direction the wind is coming from
liberty	Free time
line	Rope or cable
list	Lean
mess	Dining facilities
messenger	A smaller line passed from one vessel to another and then reeled back connected to a bigger one
muster role	Ship's roster
nautical mile	6,080.2 feet, or approximately 1.1 miles
officer of the deck	Officer responsible for operation of ship in absence of captain and executive officer
overhead	Ceiling
petty officer	Enlisted man promoted to subordinate officer status
pilothouse	Room containing the wheel and other navigational equipment
port	1. Left. 2. An opening for a window (i.e., a porthole) and/or the window itself
quartering seas	Waves approaching a ship at an angle from behind
rating	Rank

relative	Measured (as degrees of bearing) from a vessel's fore-and-aft alignment
screw	Propeller
seas	Swells or waves
shakedown cruise	Preliminary, probationary excursion by newly launched ship
ship seas	Take on water
sick bay	Shipboard dispensary and medical treatment facility
starboard	Right
steerageway	Speed sufficient to make ship respond to movements of rudder
take the range	Align ship with pair of guide markers so as to take proper line in entering narrow waterway
three sheets to the wind	Drunk
trim	Longitudinal attitude of vessel; i.e., the difference between the forward and aft drafts
true	Measured (as degrees of bearing) from north on a compass
waterline	Line along which ship's hull breaks the surface
wheel	Steering wheel
windward	Side the wind is coming from

Acknowledgments

Thanks to James Alls; Marjorie Anderson; the staff of the Archives Room at the library of the US Naval Academy in Annapolis, Maryland; Richard Baeza; Greg Barker; Admiral Bert Bensen, USN (retired); Martha Bolke, Marcia Nowaczyk, and Penny Goll; Larry Boyd; Melvyn Brown; Henry Burke; Traci Burton; Howard P. Byers; Vickie Cannon; Henry J. Casaburi, Jr.; Kerry Cassell and the staff of the Alumni Office at the Haverford School, Haverford, Pennsylvania; Sean Connelly; Amy Davidson; Jack S. Dawson; Alfred Dobbins; Garneta Ehlers; Ralph "Shorty" Enzweiler; Ehren Epstein; Cheryl Faulkner; David Faulkner and family; Karylee Feldman; Lloyd George Fox; Jayne Freeman; Myron J. and Ginger Shannon Froehlich; Capt. Adrian A. Garcia, USN; the staff of the Genealogy Room at the New York Public Library, Stephen A. Schwarzman Building; Helen Golen; Robert and Patricia Gonnoud; Jack Graves; Harold, Alice, and Susan Hayes; the staff of the Hennepin County (Minnesota) Historical Society; the staff of the Hennepin County Library; Kim Hillison of the Garland County (Arkansas) Library; Charles Hinman; Shirley Hirschey; the staff of the Hopkins (Minnesota) Library; Rebeka J. Hughes; Clyde and Alice Isbell; Pat Jacobsen; Alvin, Mary, and Nelson C. Jacobson; Gloria Knecht; Christine Kingsley Kozima; Harry Kumler and Charlotte Kumler Bellsmith; David Laine; Gene and Patricia Lehmbecker and Kelly Keller; Nord and Betty Lester; Stanley Libera; the staff of the Linn (Oregon) County Clerk's Office; Joanne Lord; Gerald F. "Bud" and Patricia Sheils Loughman; Don Manning; Jane Anne Martin; the staff of the McCreary County (Kentucky) Clerk's Office; the McCreary County Historical and Genealogical Society; Lisa McKeon; Stephen Mennemeyer; Dora Mae Mikesell; Carole Montague; Director Kay Morrow of the McCreary County Public Library; Tami Paddock; Chelsea Parker; the staff of the Newspapers and

Microfilm Center at Parkway Central Library in Philadelphia, Pennsylvania; Gloria Manning Perkins; Charles Wayne Phelps; James Pitta; Robert Pitta; Jerry, Joan, and Joel Podgorski; Howard Rechel; Naturalist Keith Robinson of the Clermont (Ohio) County Park District; the staff of the Sacramento (California) Public Library, Central Branch; Gloria and Dennis Samad; Jack Scovil; James and Ginger Shaw; Dan Sicardi; Frank Siraci; Amy Smith; William, Gordon, and Sharon Smith; Kenneth and Sharon Sorrick; Lou Ann Speulda-Drews of the United States Fish and Wildlife Service; Donald R. and Catherine E. Srack; Shanna Stevens; Quinton Studer; the staff of Chicago's Conrad Sulzer Regional Library; Joe Tegeder; Joseph and Claribel Throgmorton; Anthony Tomkovicz; Eugene Van Buskirk; Jack, Lois, and Dale Vangets; Lee Alma Vaughn; Gary Voke; Terry Wainscott, Jim Wainscott, Brenda Carter, and Peggy Wainscott Handley; Mary Wall; Dave and Nancy Wallington and Joy Markiewicz; Donald Warner; Dan and Betty Weber; Mark T. Weber and the staff at the US Navy Memorial Foundation in Washington, DC; Donald F. Whitmarsh; Wanda Worley; and Margaret Alice Zuroweste.

Thanks to Douglas A. Campbell and Michael Sturma, whose books about the USS *Flier* both give vivid accounts of the events at Midway on the afternoon of January 16, 1944, and were greatly helpful to me in reconstructing them.

Thanks to those who wrote deck logs, war diaries, and/or war patrol reports, or who compiled muster rolls, for the USS *Bootes* (AK-99), *Bushnell* (AS-15), *California* (BB-44), *Clamp* (ARS-33), *Flier* (SS-250), *Florikan* (ASR-9), *Ganymede* (AK-104), *George F. Elliott* (AP-13), *Henderson* (AP-1), *Lipan* (AT-85), *Lynx* (AK-100), *Lyra* (AK-101), *Macaw* (ASR-11), *Sailfish* (SS-192), *Sculptor* (AK-103), *Tarpon* (SS-175), *Token* (AM-126), *Triangulum* (AK-102), and *Tumult* (AM-127), and for the *Lakatoi*, *LST-40*, Submarine Squadrons Four and Eighteen, NOB Midway, NOB Pearl Harbor, and both the Atlantic and Pacific submarine commands.

NARA, the National Archives and Records Administration, is a vast treasure trove of documents about and photographs of all things American. I'm deeply grateful to the staffs of the NARA facilities in College Park, Maryland, and San Bruno, California—especially to Nathaniel Patch, Michelle Bradley, and Alicia Henneberry—for helping me plumb its mysterious depths. Thanks, too, to the staff of the National Personnel Records Center in St. Louis, and to the US Census Bureau and all the unsung census takers whose careful labors over the decades have contributed so greatly to telling the story of the American people.

Thanks to the providers of the following online resources: American Merchant Marine at War, FamilySearch, Fleet Organization, Fold3, Geology. com, History, Historycentral, HistoryNet, Hullnumber.com, HyperWar, National Ocean Service, The National WWII Museum, Naval History and Heritage Command, NavSource Naval History, Newspapers.com, Officer of the Watch, The Pacific War, the U.S. Naval Institute's Naval History Blog, uboat.net, Wikipedia, and the World War II Database.

Thanks for logistical, moral, and in more than one case financial support to Bradley D. and Roberta Allen; Jim and Sheila Barry; Katherine Burger; Jodi Compton; Ruth Corkhill Daneman; Terry Dyke and Marilyn Fenn; Michael Filipiac; Marty Friedman; Cres Gilbert and Natalie Thiele; Joan Gilbert; Stefanie Goebel; Delbert Guilfoy; Mary Katherine Hall; Trevor and Rebecca Higgins; Galen Kirkland and Natalie Chapman; Rosemary, Gerald, William, Mary Lee, Gregory, and Michael Loughman; Joe McIntire; Thomas J. O'Brien; Joan and Jerry Podgorski; Scott and Juli Rinefort; Richard Schwarz; Duncan Searl; Olya Segal; Gloria Smith; Richard Stevenson; Jeff and Scottie Twine; Bob Winston and Susan Negrete; and Lily Witham.

Special thanks to Lavinia Schwarz, who put her genealogical research skills and boundless enthusiasm at my disposal many times and housed, fed, and encouraged me; to Laurie Searl, for her patience, good humor, and expert editorial assistance; to Kathleen Ryan, whose friendship and some good luck led me to Bob Jacobsen; to Traci Burton, whose generosity in opening her family archives helped me sketch at least a rough outline of her intriguing grandfather; to cartographer Richard Gilbreath; to Hans K. Van Tilburg, PhD, Maritime Heritage Coordinator, Pacific Islands Region, National Oceanic and Atmospheric Administration, for his encouragement with this project; to Natalie O'Neal Clausen, my editor at University Press of Kentucky, for believing in this story and for dissuading me, by way of enforcing a word limit, from getting in my own way in telling it; to her assistant, Allison Webster, and the rest of the staff at UPK; and to Susan Murray, for her sharp-eyed and judicious copy-editing.

Greatest thanks and smooth sailing to Robert Clyde "Bob" Jacobsen (July 31, 1922–February 23, 2012), logger, sailor, "wood butcher," family man, Los Angeles Dodgers fan, University of California alumnus, pen pal extraordinaire, and last survivor of the Garibaldi (Oregon) High School class of 1941.

If I have forgotten anyone I should be thanking here, please impute that to a faulty memory, not ingratitude.

Notes

1. Rough Start

1. "Midway Mission (Enclosure 'A' serial co 011100): Naval Operating Base, Naval Air Station, Submarine Base, PT base, plane refueling base, and cable station," undated (inferentially ca. 1944–45) USN document, 102.

2. "Midway Mission," 105; "RECORD of PROCEEDINGS into a BOARD of INVESTIGATION . . . into the grounding of the U. S. S. FLIER (SS250) at Midway Islands, T. H. on January 16, 1944": Dalton, 19.

3. *as one or both of the two offshore buoys*—"Midway Mission," 102; *even the range lights*—"RECORD of PROCEEDINGS into a BOARD of INVESTIGATION . . . into the loss of the U. S. S. MACAW (ASR-11) at Midway Islands, T. H. on February 13, 1944": Windle, 28.

4. *Flier* Investigation: Dalton, 20.

5. "Midway Mission," 105.

6. "*Stand by for pilot.*"—*Flier* Investigation: Crowley, 2.

7. "Actual Wind Conditions for 16–19 January, 1944," Aerological Office, Midway Naval Air Station; "Monthly Aerological Record, NAS Midway—January 1944," handwritten transcription, apparently by Bud Loughman; *"extremely large quartering seas"*—*Flier* Investigation: Crowley, 12; *waves that day at twenty feet*—*Flier* Investigation: Adams, 22.

8. *almost two miles*—*Flier* Investigation: Crowley, 2–3; *"Follow me."*—*Flier* Investigation: Crowley, 3.

9. *He said later*—*Flier* Investigation: Crowley, 13.

10. "*Starboard ahead full*"—*Flier* Investigation: Crowley, 3–4.

11. James Alls, telephone interview, 1 March 2014. Unless otherwise noted, all interviews have been conducted by the author.

12. *inside the channel*—*Flier* Investigation: Crowley, 3; and Liddell, 15; *a better job himself*—Alls telephone interview, 1 March 2014.

13. *Macaw* Investigation: Connolly, 2.

14. Robert Gonnoud, telephone interview, 23 January 2013.

15. Robert Gonnoud, telephone interview, 21 February 2015; *Macaw* Investigation: Windle, 29.

16. *Macaw* Investigation: Windle, 29; Quinton Studer, telephone interview, 25 June 2008; Gonnoud telephone interviews, 21 February 2015 and 23 January 2013.

17. *Macaw* Investigation: Windle, 30.

18. Jacobsen letter No. 4.

19. *Macaw* Investigation: Connolly, 3.

20. Ibid.

21. Harold Hayes, personal interview, 18 September 2012.

22. *Macaw* Investigation: Loughman, 26, and Windle, 28; Gonnoud telephone interview, 23 January 2013.

23. Windle, "U. S. S. MACAW 16 January, 1944," memo to executive officer; *Macaw* Investigation: Windle, 28; G. F. Loughman, "NARRATIVE OF U. S. S. MACAW: 16 January 1944," 1.

24. Loughman "Narrative," 1; Bosun Joseph S. Albin, "Memorandum for Executive Officer," undated; *Macaw* Investigation: Albin, 41; Robert Gonnoud, telephone interview, 2 June 2002; Dave Wallington, personal interview, 11 June 2004; Dave Wallington, telephone interview, 6 March 2011.

25. *Macaw* Investigation: Graaff, 38; Dunn, memo for executive officer re *Macaw* grounding, undated.

26. *Macaw* Investigation: Jones, 35–36.

27. *kapok life jackets*—Dunn and Ens. George F. J. Crocker memos re *Macaw* grounding, undated; *"You couldn't notice"*—*Macaw* Investigation: Windle, 32.

28. *Macaw* Investigation: Windle, 28.

29. *Macaw* Investigation: Ehlers, 33, and Windle, 30.

30. Harry Kumler, telephone interview, 10 March 1999; *Macaw* Investigation: Loughman, 26, Windle, 32, and Kumler, 48.

31. *Macaw* Investigation: Windle, 32; Robert Gonnoud, telephone interview, 16 April 2016.

32. *Macaw* Investigation: Windle, 30. Having just provided that harrowing account to the board, Windle was asked whether at any time prior to the grounding he felt the ship was in a dangerous position. He replied, "No sir."

33. *Macaw* Investigation: Albin, 42.

34. Nord Lester to author, 29 July 1999.

35. Crowley and Liddell narrative: "War Patrols and Loss of U. S. S. FLIER," recorded 2 October 1944; Gritton, memo for executive officer re *Macaw* grounding, undated.

2. On the Rocks

1. Clyde Isbell, personal interviews, 26 April 2002 and 30 April 2004; *the ship's draft*— "RECORD of PROCEEDINGS into a BOARD of INVESTIGATION . . . into the loss of the U. S. S. MACAW (ASR-11) at Midway Islands, T. H. on February 13, 1944": Fact No. 7, 67.

2. Jacobsen letter No. 4.

3. Quinton Studer, telephone interview, 25 June 2008.

4. Dan Weber, personal interview, 24 April 2002.

5. *Macaw* Investigation: Windle, 28.

6. Jacobsen letter No. 5.

7. *Damage Control Book: ASR11,* 16; Lightner, Dunn, Windle, Crocker, Gritton and Albin memos re *Macaw* grounding, all undated, all probably written by 20 January 1944; *Macaw* Investigation: Kumler, 48.

8. Albin grounding memo.

9. *Macaw* Investigation: Connolly, 4.

10. Robert Gonnoud, telephone interviews, 2 June 2002 and 18 November 2014.

11. "RECORD of PROCEEDINGS into a BOARD of INVESTIGATION . . . into the grounding of the U. S. S. FLIER (SS250) at Midway Islands, T. H. on January 16, 1944": Crowley, 6

12. Ibid.

13. Dave Wallington, personal interview, 11 June 2004; Dave Wallington, telephone interview, 26 April 2010.

14. *Macaw* Investigation: Connolly, 4.

15. *Flier* Investigation: Banchero, 45–46, Crowley, 8, and Liddell, 37; Douglas A. Campbell, *Eight Survived: The Harrowing Story of the USS* Flier *and the Only Downed World War II Submariners to Survive and Evade Capture* (Guilford, CT: Globe Pequot, 2010).

16. *Macaw* Investigation: Connolly, 3, 5.

17. Comm. William A. Sullivan, narrative re organization of Naval Salvage Service, Office of Naval Records and Library film No. 165, recorded 9 December 1943; "Jap Ships to be Salvaged," *Circleville (OH) Herald,* 27 July 1944; "Lebbeus Curtis, 83, Navy Rear Admiral," *New York Times,* 8 February 1964.

18. *Flier* Investigation: Crowley, 8.

19. "Memorial Services for Southern Pacific Hero," *Riverdale (IL) Pointer,* 10 February 1944.

20. James Alls, personal interview, 14 April 2015.

3. Troubled Waters

1. Clay Blair, *Silent Victory: The US Submarine War against Japan* (Philadelphia: Lippincott, 1975), 331–32.

2. *"anything you want"*—William R. Anderson, *The Ice Diaries: The Untold Story of the Cold War's Most Daring Mission* (Nashville, TN: Thomas Nelson, 2008), 6–7. Anderson served aboard the *Tarpon* in World War II.

3. Wogan to COMSUBPAC (CO USS TARPON Conf. Ltr. SS175/P17–2(1) Serial 06), 10 March 1943.

4. Gerald F. "Bud" Loughman, personal interview, 29 November 1997.

5. Burton Second Endorsement to BUPERS, Officer Performance Division (Pers-3204:ge, 72367), 13 November 1943.

6. Robert Gonnoud, telephone interviews, 2 June 2002, 18 November 2014, and 21 February 2015.

7. Gerald F. "Bud" Loughman, personal interview, 30 December 1991.

8. "About the International Platform Association," Platform, internationalplatform. org/about-the-international-platform-association; "The Warren Memorial Presbyterian

Church at Louisville, Ky.," *Frank Leslie's Sunday Magazine* 17 (January-June 1885): 560; "Return of U. S. S. 'Minnesota' for week ending October 30th, 1875," in US Naval Enlistment Rendezvous, 1855–1891.

9. Gonnoud telephone interview, 2 June 2002.

10. Quinton Studer, telephone interview, 25 June 2008.

11. Burton Second Endorsement, 13 November 1943.

12. Carol La Vo, "The Short Life of the Squalus," *Naval History* (Spring 1988).

13. Gerald F. "Bud" Loughman, personal interview, 26 December 1997; *"Don't worry"*—Ralph "Shorty" Enzweiler, personal interview, 3 May 2009.

14. Jacobsen letter No. 11.

15. Jacobsen letter No. 2; Joanne Lord, telephone interview, 5 March 2017; *Macaw* log, 16 July 1943.

16. "Lakatoi," Naval History and Heritage Command, history.navy.mil/research/ histories/ship-histories/danfs/1/lakatoi.html; Andy Kravetz, "World War II Vet's Diary Helps Family Piece Together His Story of Survival," *Peoria (IL) Journal Star,* posted online 11 November 2013; Lord telephone interview, 5 March 2017.

17. Howard Rechel, personal interview, 11 June 2002.

18. Jacobsen letter No. 2; Eugene Van Buskirk, personal interview, 14 January 2005; Gonnoud telephone interview, 18 November 2014; Dave Wallington, telephone interview, 6 March 2011.

4. Off to War

1. Pat D'Angelo, "Commodore Andrew R. Mack," in *The History of the U. S. S.* Neshoba (San Angelo, TX: Newsphoto Publishing, 1946), cited in rpadden.com/216/comdormack .htm.

2. "DRYDOCK CO.," *Oakland Tribune,* 11 October 1931; "Joseph A. Moore, 82," *Oakland Tribune,* 1 July 1956; "Fading Pioneer," *Oakland Tribune,* 3 December 1961; "Drydock Razing Begins," *Oakland Tribune,* 6 January 1969; "U. S. Maritime Commission," by Frank A. Gerhardt, usmaritimecommission.de.

3. "U. S. Merchant Marine in World War II," usmm.org/casualty.html.

4. "History of Richmond: World War II and the Shipyards (1940–1945)," ci.richmond. ca.us/112/History-of-Richmond.

5. "U. S. Merchant Marine Casualties during World War II," usmm.org/casualty.html.

6. *"Proceed"*—USS *Triangulum* war diary, 28 August 1943.

7. Calculation based on comparative positions of *Ganymede* and *Lipan* as recorded in their 28 August 1943 war diary entries.

8. Jacobsen letter No. 8. The *President Coolidge* had hit two mines, both "friendly," in the entrance channel at Espiritu Santo, Convoy PW 2294's destination, and sunk almost ten months before. PW 2294 would come within a stone's throw of steaming right over it. But as Jacobsen noted (also in letter No. 8): "Only our Captain, Exec & Navigator knew our course and our destination. We were never told where we were going until we got there." Thus the wild rumormongering.

9. Howard Rechel, personal interview, 11 June 2002; Jacobsen letter No. 8.

10. Dave Wallington, personal interview, 11 June 2004.

11. Nord Lester, personal interview, 8 December 1999.

12. Jacobsen letters Nos. 6 and 13.

13. Jacobsen letter No. 6.

14. Don Srack, personal interview, 28 October 2001.

15. Jacobsen letter No. 8.

16. Srack personal interviews, 28 October 2001 and 25 June 2002.

17. Jacobsen letter No. 8.

18. Clyde Isbell, personal interview, 21 April 2002.

19. *"normal complement"*—"USS MACAW SHIP'S ORGANIZATION," item 103.

20. Jacobsen letter No. 8.

21. Rechel personal interview, 11 June 2002; Robert Gonnoud, telephone interview, 21 February 2015; Dan Weber, personal interview, 24 April 2002; Joseph Throgmorton, telephone interview, 24 April 2011.

22. Jacobsen letter No. 11.

23. Jacobsen letter No. 8.

24. Jacobsen letter No. 9.

25. Jacobsen letters Nos. 5, 8, and 10.

26. Quinton Studer, telephone interview, 25 June 2008; Robert Gonnoud, telephone interview, 2 June 2002.

27. Jacobsen letter No. 8.

28. Jacobsen letter No. 9. V-6 was a World War II–era Naval Reserve program through which members were exempted from the Selective Service, allowed to retain their highest wartime rating, and guaranteed GI Bill benefits.

29. *"Some of these guys"*—Dave Wallington, telephone interview, 7 May 2010; *"chuga-lugged it"*—Quinton Studer, telephone interview, 14 March 2009; *"introducing"*—Macaw log, 23 July 1943; Rechel telephone interview, 11 June 2002; Quinton Studer, personal interview, 10 January 2008; *chosen to overlook it*—Robert Gonnoud, telephone interview, 8 May 2015.

30. Rechel personal interview, 11 June 2002.

31. *"On a watch aboard ship"*—Jacobsen letter No. 10.

32. *three billion trees*—Joseph M. Speakman, "Into the Woods: The First Year of the Civilian Conservation Corps," *Prologue* 38, no. 3 (fall 2006), archives.gov/publications/prologue/2006/fall/ccc.html.

33. Martha Bolke and Penny Goll, personal interview, 28 June 2013; Martha Bolke and Marsha Nowaczyk, personal interview, 22 September 2014.

34. Jacobsen letter No. 10. "Barney Google and Snuffy Smith," created by Billy DeBeck, debuted under the title *Take Barney Google F'rinstance* in 1919 and was still running more than a hundred years later.

35. William Smith and Gordon Smith, personal interview, 5 November 2012.

36. Jacobsen letter No. 1.

37. Jacobsen letter No. 8.

38. Gonnoud telephone interview, 2 June 2002; Burton to Elizabeth Burton, 22 December 1943.

39. Joseph Throgmorton, telephone interview, 9 February 2014.

40. Gonnoud telephone interview, 21 February 2015.

41. Gonnoud telephone interviews, 2 June 2002 and 18 November 2014.

42. Jacobsen letter No. 14; Srack personal interview, 28 October 2001.

43. Jacobsen letter No. 14. Miss Saylor's Coffee-ets were candies made by a confectioner in Alameda, across the Oakland Estuary from Moore Dry Dock.

44. Jacobsen letter No. 13.

45. Srack personal interviews, 28 October 2001 and 25 June 2002.

46. Gonnoud telephone interviews, 21 February and 8 May 2015.

47. Gonnoud telephone interview, 2 June 2002.

48. Jacobsen letter No. 14; Gonnoud telephone interview, 18 November 2014; Harold Hayes, personal interview, 18 September 2012; Jacobsen letter No. 14; Gonnoud telephone interview, 18 November 2014; Stanley Libera, telephone interview, 13 February 2015.

5. Perilous Passage

1. "RECORD of PROCEEDINGS into a BOARD of INVESTIGATION . . . into the grounding of the U. S. S. FLIER (SS250) at Midway Islands, T. H. on January 16, 1944": Crowley, 8 and 9; "RECORD of PROCEEDINGS into a BOARD of INVESTIGATION . . . into the loss of the U. S. S. MACAW (ASR-11) at Midway Islands, T. H. on February 13, 1944": Connolly, 5.

2. *Flier* Investigation: Crowley, 9.

3. U. S. S. *Clamp* (ARS-33) War Diary, January 1944; *Flier* Investigation: Crowley, 9.

4. Al Dobbins, telephone interview, 24 August 2011.

5. *Clamp* War Diary, January 1944.

6. Ibid.; *Flier* Investigation: Crowley, 9; Al Dobbins, telephone interview, 11 February 2012.

7. *Flier* Investigation: Crowley, 9; Dobbins telephone interview, 11 February 2012.

8. *Flier* Investigation: Crowley, 9.

6. South Pacific

1. Jacobsen letters Nos. 6 and 8; Dave Wallington, personal interview, 11 June 2004.

2. Quinton Studer, personal interview, 10 January 2008.

3. Gerald F. "Bud" Loughman, personal interview, 23 December 1991; Loughman to Jack McCarthy, 3 November 1943.

4. Wallington personal interview, 11 June 2004; Robert Gonnoud, telephone interview, 8 May 2015; Robert Gonnoud, telephone interview, 25 August 2015.

5. Jack Vangets, telephone interview, 7 May 2002.

6. Dan Srack, personal interview, 28 October 2001; Dan Weber, personal interview, 24 April 2002; Eugene Van Buskirk, personal interview, 14 January 2005.

7. Jacobsen letter No. 2.

8. Stanley Libera, telephone interview, 7 February 2013.

9. Jacobsen No. 8; Robert Gonnoud, telephone interview, 2 June 2002; Howard Rechel, personal interview, 11 June 2002.

10. The word "banzai," ironically enough, means "May you live ten thousand years."

11. George Fox, personal interview, 27 March 2006.

12. Jacobsen letter No. 6.

13. René Pierre Millot, *Missions in the World Today* (Westerleigh, UK: Hawthorn, 1961), 66; Judith A. Bennett, *Natives and Exotics: World War II and Environment in the Southern Pacific* (Honolulu: University of Hawai'i Press, 2009), 67.

14. Jacobsen letter No. 10.

15. Studer telephone interview, 10 January 2008.

16. Gonnoud telephone interview, 2 June 2002.

17. Gonnoud telephone interview, 18 November 2014.

18. Gerald F. "Bud" Loughman, personal interview, 30 December 1991.

19. Jacobsen No. 5.

20. Weber personal interview, 24 April 2002; Gerald F. "Bud" Loughman, personal interview, 29 November 1997; Gonnoud telephone interview, 2 June 2002; Howard Rechel, personal interview, 11 June 2002; Eugene Van Buskirk, personal interview, 14 January 2005; Joseph Throgmorton, telephone interview, 19 September 2008; Ralph "Shorty" Enzweiler, personal interview, 3 May 2009.

21. Dan Srack, personal interview, 28 October 2001; Dave Wallington, telephone interview, 26 April 2010.

22. Jacobsen letter No. 1.

23. Studer telephone interview, 10 January 2008; Van Buskirk personal interview, 14 January 2005.

24. Loughman personal interview, 30 December 1991. Assuming the island in question was Funafuti, Loughman overstated by forty feet the minimum depth to which Burton would have had to descend.

25. Rechel personal interview, 11 June 2002.

26. Loughman personal interview, 30 December 1991.

27. Wallington, personal interview, 11 June 2004; Wallington telephone interviews, 26 April and 7 May 2010; Rechel personal interview, 11 June 2002.

28. Jacobsen letter No. 10; Robert Gonnoud, telephone interview, 21 February 2015.

29. Jack Vangets, telephone interview, 7 May 2002, and personal interview, 13 June 2004. Bob Jacobsen disputed the accuracy of this story, maintaining that there was no brig on the *Macaw*, and specifically no porthole communicating with a brig. But in fact there was a makeshift brig. Vangets was not the only *Macaw* sailor confined to it. The ship's log mentions others. Radar operator Harold Hayes (personal interview, 18 September 2012), who was not confined to it, recalled a storage room used as a brig and said it had a porthole. Vangets said he thinks he may have been allowed to return to the crew's quarter at night to sleep—sixty years later he wasn't sure.

30. Van Buskirk personal interview, 14 January 2005.

31. Gonnoud telephone interview, 21 February 2015; Melei Telavi, "War Years," in *Tuvalu—A History* (Funafuti: University of the South Pacific and the Tuvalu Ministry of Social Services, 1983); CINCPAC Press Release No. 168, 13 November 1943; Van Buskirk personal interview, 14 January 2005.

32. Rechel personal interview, 11 June 2002.

7. The Loneliness of the Long-Distance Runner

1. Robert Gonnoud, telephone interviews, 2 June 2002 and 21 February 2015.

2. Gonnoud telephone interview, 2 June 2002.

3. Gonnoud telephone interviews, 21 February and 8 May 2015.

4. Jacobsen letter No. 3.

5. Gerald F. "Bud" Loughman, personal interview, 23 December 1991; Lloyd George Fox, personal interview, 27 March 2006; Jacobsen letter No. 9; Quinton Studer, personal interview, 10 January 2008.

6. Jacobsen letter No. 5. An AKA was an attack cargo ship. AKAs carried troops and supplies and provided gunfire support for amphibious landings.

7. Gonnoud telephone interview, 2 June 2002; Howard Rechel, personal interview, 11 June 2002.

8. Joseph Throgmorton, telephone interview, 4 June 2008.

9. Ralph "Shorty" Enzweiler, personal interview, 3 May 2009. It should be noted that Hollywood's portrayal of Bligh over the years as a cold-hearted tyrant may be less than entirely accurate.

10. Eugene Van Buskirk, personal interview, 14 January 2005.

11. Harold Hayes, personal interview, 18 September 2012.

12. Quinton Studer, telephone interview, 14 March 2009.

13. Dave Wallington, telephone interview, 6 March 2011. A 4-F was a draft reject. Thirty percent of draft registrants during World War II were deemed unfit for military service on account of physical defects.

14. Myron Froehlich, personal interview, 21–22 January 2004.

15. Stanley Libera, telephone interviews, 2 March 2011, 7 February 2013, and 4 July 2015.

16. Stanley Libera, telephone interview, 9 May 2015.

17. The *California* was sunk that morning and Mennemeyer reported as lost in action. His family was duly notified, and both the *St. Louis Post-Dispatch* and the *St. Louis Star and Times* listed him among the St. Louis–area men lost in the first week or so of the war. About a month later came better news, that he was alive.

18. Stanley Libera, telephone interview, 30 November 1999.

19. "Submarines on hand Nov 1943," from War Diary of COMSUBPAC (J. H. Brown, Jr., Acting), as submitted in memo [FF12–10/A12–1(1)/(05) Serial 001891] to Commander-in-Chief, US Fleet, 12 December 1943.

20. Just how successful, and how significant, the *Tarpon*'s ninth patrol had been became clear only after the war, with the release of enemy naval records. The one mysteriously unrecognizable ship the *Tarpon* sank during it, about seventy-five miles off the coast of Japan, turned out to be German, the *Michel*, a merchant raider, basically a warship disguised as a cargo vessel. The *Michel* had taken refuge in the Pacific and sunk three Allied vessels there, after the German high command decided that operating in the Atlantic had become too dangerous for surface vessels.

21. Charles Lockwood, Third Endorsement to SPEARFISH Report of Seventh War Patrol, 11 August 1943, p. 1.

22. Rechel personal interview, 11 June 2002.

23. Gonnoud telephone interview, 2 June 2002.

24. Jacobsen letter No. 9.

25. Jacobsen letter No. 15.

26. Clyde Isbell, personal interview, 21 April 2002; Jacobsen letter No. 7; Dave Wallington, personal interview, 11 June 2004.

27. Jacobsen letter No. 5.

28. Jacobsen letter No. 5. Webb was at Pearl Harbor at least twice, once during and once after his time aboard the *Macaw*. Jacobsen was there with him both times, and it is not clear from what he wrote of Webb's Pearl Harbor raffle scam exactly when he alleges Webb engaged in it, whether during the earlier stay or the later or both.

29. Christmas Day Dinner menu, 25 December 1943; Jacobsen letter No. 7.

30. Van Buskirk personal interview, 14 January 2005.

8. Midway

1. "Plate Tectonics and the Hawaiian Hot Spot," geology.com/usgs/hawaiian-hot-spot/.

2. "Rescue Miracle," soundingsonline.com/features/in-depth/234599-rescue-miracle-miles-from-civilization; George H. Read, *The Last Cruise of the* Saginaw (Cambridge, MA: Riverside, 1912), 9.

3. John Cameron, *John Cameron's Odyssey* (New York: Macmillan, 1928), 240–97; "Afloat and Ashore. Poor Castaways. Rescue of the Captain of the Missing Wandering Minstrel," *Daily Alta California* 80, no. 112, 21 April 1889.

4. Lorena A. Barba, "Flying without Flapping: The Wandering Albatross and the Mechanics of Dynamic Soaring," *BU*, blogs.bu.edu/bioaeria12012/2012/11/17/flying-without-flapping/.

5. Robert Louis Stevenson and Lloyd Osbourne, *The Wrecker* (London: Cassell, 1892), 206.

6. Elliot Carlson, *Joe Rochefort's War: The Odyssey of the Codebreaker Who Outwitted Yamamoto at Midway* (Annapolis, MD: Naval Institute Press, 2011).

7. Jonathan Parshall and Anthony Tully, *Shattered Sword: The Untold Story of the Battle of Midway* (Washington, DC: Potomac, 2005).

8. Loughman to Capt. J. A. Connolly, memorandum, 15 February 1944; Jacobsen letter No. 2.

9. Dave Wallington, telephone interview, 6 March 2011.

10. Don Srack, personal interview, 25 June 2002; Jacobsen letter No. 2.

11. "Average Water Temperature in Midway Island," weather-and-climate.com/average-monthly-water-temperature,Midway-Island,Hawaii; Don Srack, personal interview, 28 October 2001; Loughman to William Vaughn, ca. 1 March 1944; Myron Froehlich, telephone interview, 23 May 2002.

12. Dave Wallington, telephone interview, 6 March 2011; Jacobsen letter No. 5.

13. Wallington telephone interview, 6 March 2011; "RECORD of PROCEEDINGS into a BOARD of INVESTIGATION . . . into the loss of the U. S. S. MACAW (ASR-11) at Midway Islands, T. H. on February 13, 1944": Connolly, 6; Robert Gonnoud, telephone interview, 2 June 2002.

14. *Macaw* Investigation: Connolly, 6; Wallington telephone interview, 6 March 2011; Clyde Isbell, personal interviews, 21 April 2002 and 30 April 2004; Quinton Studer, personal interview, 10 January 2008.

15. *Macaw* Investigation: Duff, 55.

16. Jacobsen letter No. 4.

17. Jacobsen letter No. 15.

18. Ibid.

19. "War Diary of Midway Islands for January, 1944," 19–20.

20. Jacobsen letter No. 3. As noted previously, the diving bell, that is, the McCann chamber, was tossed overboard, but by Mother Nature, not by design.

21. Jacobsen letter No. 6.

22. Nord Lester to author, 29 July 1999.

23. *Macaw* Investigation: Curtis, 18.

24. Ibid., 19.

25. *Macaw* Investigation: Connolly, 9.

26. Ibid.

27. Jacobsen letter No. 2.

28. Stanley Libera, telephone interviews, 21 January 2004 and 17 November 2013.

29. Harold Hayes, personal interview, 18 September 2012.

30. Jacobsen letter No. 16; Dan Weber, personal interview, 24 April 2002; Don Srack, personal interview, 25 June 2002; Howard Rechel, personal interview, 11 June 2002. Williamson's year of birth varies from one document to the next. It was either 1909, 1910, or 1911.

31. Gloria Knecht, personal interview, 1 February 2013. Ernst's cousin and fellow immigrant Holmuth Rentschler became a brewmaster for Budweiser.

32. Jacobsen letter No. 11; Hayes personal interview, 18 September 2012; Wallington personal interview, 11 June 2004; Gonnoud telephone interview, 2 June 2002; Eugene Van Buskirk, personal interview, 15 January 2005; Dave Wallington, telephone interview, 11 June 2010, respectively; first quotation by Wallington, second by Van Buskirk; Jacobsen letter No. 2.

33. *Macaw* log.

34. George Washington Manning, telephone interview, 13 June 2016.

35. Jacobsen letter No. 11.

36. Charlotte Bellsmith, telephone interview, 26 June 1999.

37. Don Srack, personal interview, 28 October 2001; Gerald F. "Bud" Loughman, personal interview, 26 December 1997; Dora Mae Mikesell, personal interview, 13 June 2004.

38. Dave Wallington, telephone interview, 7 May 2010; Pre-navy details: Brenda Carter, telephone interview, 14 October 2010; Brenda Carter and Terry Wainscott, personal interview, 21 September 2008; Peggy Handley, telephone interview, 14 October 2010. Navy details: Rechel personal interview, 11 June 2002; Jim Wainscott, telephone interview, 13 October 2008; Jacobsen letter No. 10; Eugene Van Buskirk, personal interview, 14 January 2005; *Macaw* war diary, 3 September 1943.

39. Jacobsen letter No. 6.

40. Jacobsen letter No. 16; Hayes personal interview, 18 September 2012.

9. Emergency Exit

1. "RECORD of PROCEEDINGS into a BOARD of INVESTIGATION . . . into the loss of the U. S. S. MACAW (ASR-11) at Midway Islands, T. H. on February 13, 1944": Connolly, 9.

2. Ibid.

3. Ibid., 10.

4. *Macaw* Investigation: Curtis, 19. Connolly, in his narrative entry for 0700, has the *Macaw* itself identifying its heading as 70 degrees true. It may have shifted between the times the two readings were made, or one or both may have been less than entirely accurate.

5. Ibid.

6. *Macaw* Investigation: Connolly, 10. [Material in brackets interpolated by author.]

7. Ibid.

8. *Macaw* Investigation: Curtis, 19.

9. *Macaw* Investigation: Dease, 57.

10. Monthly Aerological Record, NAS Midway, 1–13 February 1944 (transcribed by hand, apparently by Bud Loughman).

11. Loughman, "NARRATIVE OF U. S. S. MACAW," 3.

12. *Burton ordered them there.*—Ibid.; Nord Lester, telephone interview, 12 July 1999.

13. *Macaw* Investigation: Connolly, 9.

14. Ibid., 10.

15. Lester survivor statement, 17 February 1944. The recompression room, on the main deck amidship, contained a pair of hyperbaric tanks for treating divers suffering decompression sickness, aka the bends.

16. Horsman and Ehlers survivor statements, February 1944.

17. Ehlers survivor statement.

18. Re size and location of searchlights: *Macaw* Investigation: Connolly, 10–11.

19. Ibid., 11.

20. The 1944 Shafroth NOB Midway inspection report gives the height of the tower as 170 feet; the "Midway Mission" report (undated, inferentially ca. 1944–45) gives a figure of 200 feet; *Macaw* Investigation: Connolly, 11.

21. Loughman, "NARRATIVE," 3.

22. *Macaw* Investigation: Edmunds, 62; Loughman to Jack McCarthy, 30 March 1944; Edmunds, "Administrative Report on the deaths of DAUGHERTY, Howard E., S2c, LEHMBECKER, LeRoy B., S1c, and SAMED, Ernest D., S1c on 13 February 1944" (NOB 1504, NA38/P6, Serial 0108); *Macaw* Investigation: Short, 61.

23. Loughman, "NARRATIVE," 3; Gerald F. "Bud" Loughman, personal interview, 1 August 1987; Wainscott survivor statement, February 1944.

24. *Macaw* Investigation: Connolly, 11.

25. Ehlers survivor statement.

26. *three-tenths of 1 percent*—Loughman, "NARRATIVE," 3; quoted matter from Loughman to McCarthy, 30 March 1944.

27. Ehlers and Wainscott survivor statements; Loughman to McCarthy, 30 March 1944; Gerald F. "Bud" Loughman, personal interview, 26 December 1997.

28. Mathers survivor statement, 15 February 1944; Loughman to McCarthy, 30 March 1944; Stanley Libera, telephone interview, 2 March 2011; Loughman, "NARRATIVE," 3.

29. Loughman to McCarthy, 30 March 1944.

30. Loughman, "NARRATIVE," 3.

31. Stanley Libera, personal interview, 3 July 2011; Williamson survivor statement, 15 February 1944; Lester survivor statement; Horsman survivor statement.

32. Howard Rechel, personal interview, 11 June 2002; Mathers survivor statement; Loughman, "NARRATIVE," 3; Lester telephone interview, 12 July 1999.

33. Kumler survivor statement, 15 February 1944.

34. Gerald F. "Bud" Loughman, personal interview, 23 December 1991; Williamson survivor statement; Libera telephone interview, 2 March 2011.

35. Koepke survivor statement, February 1944.

36. Libera telephone interviews, 2 March 2011 and 9 May 2015.

37. Ehlers survivor statement.

38. Williamson survivor statement.

39. Loughman to McCarthy, 30 March 1944.

40. Loughman, "NARRATIVE," 3.

41. Koepke survivor statement.

42. Wainscott survivor statement.

43. Manning survivor statement (undated).

44. Ibid.

45. Manning and Libera survivor statements.

46. Libera telephone interview, 2 March 2011.

47. Knecht survivor statement, February 1944.

48. Mathers survivor statement.

49. Wainscott survivor statement.

50. Lester survivor statement; Loughman to McCarthy, 30 March 1944; Loughman, "NARRATIVE," 3.

51. Loughman to Betty Burton, 22 February 1944.

52. Loughman to McCarthy, 30 March 1944.

53. Nord Lester, telephone interview, 12 July 1999.

54. Lester survivor statement.

55. Williamson survivor statement.

56. Horsman survivor statement.

57. Rechel personal interview, 11 June 2002.

58. Libera telephone interview, 2 March 2011; personal interview, 3 July 2011; and telephone interviews, 7 February 2013 and 9 May 2015. These quotations are not in chronological order.

59. Knecht survivor statement.

60. Manning survivor statement.

61. Jacobsen letter No. 16.

62. Kumler survivor statement.

63. Koepke survivor statement.

10. Business on Great Waters

1. Nord Lester, telephone interview, 12 July 1999.

2. Ibid.; Gerald F. "Bud" Loughman, personal interviews, 1 August 1987 and 23 December 1991.

3. Koepke survivor statement, February 1944.

4. "RECORD of PROCEEDINGS into a BOARD of INVESTIGATION . . . into the loss of the U. S. S. MACAW (ASR-11) at Midway Islands, T. H. on February 13, 1944": Connolly, 11–12.

5. Comm. G. E. Short, "War Diary of Midway Islands for January 1944," NA38/A12–1, Serial 088, 5 February 1944.

6. Gene Lehmbecker, telephone interview, 27 September 2011; Shirley Hirschey, telephone interview, 27 June 2006.

7. Vicki Cannon, personal interview, 25 June 2011.

8. Robert Pitta, telephone interview, 5 October 2018.

9. *"wealthy and wild"*—Ibid; "S. F. Dope Ring Drive," *San Francisco Chronicle,* 19 March 1946; "Four More Are Arrested in S. F. Dope Case," *San Francisco Chronicle,* 20 March 1946; Robert Pitta, telephone interview, 8 November 2018; James Pitta, telephone interviews, 7 October 2018 and 9 July 2019.

10. *Boats of the United States Navy, NAVSHIPS 250–452* (Washington, DC: US Government Printing Office, May 1967), 47–48.

11. "Astronomical Twilight—Astronomical Dawn and Dusk," timeanddate.com/astronomy/astronomical-twilight.html.

12. Manning survivor statement (undated).

13. *Macaw* Investigation, Connolly, 12.

14. Gerald F. "Bud" Loughman, personal interview, 31 December 1991.

15. Kumler survivor statement, 15 February 1944.

16. "Diseases and Conditions: Hypothermia," mayoclinic.org/diseases-conditions/hypothermia/basics/definition/con-20020453.

17. Loughman to McCarthy, 30 March 1944.

18. Manning survivor statement.

19. Administrative Report on the deaths of DAUGHERTY, Howard E., S2c, LEHMBECKER, LeRoy B., S1c, and SAMED, Ernest D., S1c on 13 February 1944" (NOB 1504, NA38/P6, Serial 0108).

20. "Hopkins Sailor Was Drowned Assisting in Rescue Work," *Hennepin County Review,* ca. March 1944 (date unknown), 16.

21. *worked to disfigure it*—Ralph "Shorty" Enzweiler, telephone interview, 11 November 2009; Jacobsen letter No. 4.

11. Aftermath

1. "RECORD of PROCEEDINGS into a BOARD of INVESTIGATION . . . into the loss of the U. S. S. MACAW (ASR-11) at Midway Islands, T. H. on February 13, 1944": Finding of Facts, 67–72; Opinions, 73–74.

2. Midway Mission (Enclosure "A" serial co 011100), undated (ca. 1944–45), 102.

3. *Macaw* Investigation: Opinions, 29.

4. *Macaw* Investigation: Curtis, 23.

5. *Macaw* Investigation: Duff, 55.

6. Lester identified as himself the man at the right end of the second row in the full-crew shot. The same man appears in the back row of the sinking survivors shot. However, at least two wartime rosters of the men in the full-crew photo, one from Bud Loughman's files, one from Don Srack via his wife, who transcribed a list he sent her, name that man as Knecht. Comparison of the photos taken that day with photos of Knecht taken later in life suggests that it was indeed Knecht.

7. George Fox, personal interview, 27 March 2006; Jacobsen letter No. 4; Howard Rechel, personal interview, 11 June 2002.

8. "Midway Mission," 505.

9. Ralph "Shorty" Enzweiler, personal interview, 3 May 2009.

10. Quinton Studer, personal interview, 10 January 2008; Stanley Libera, personal interview, 3 July 2011.

11. Gerald F. "Bud" Loughman, personal interview, 31 December 1991.

12. Harold Hayes, personal interview, 18 September 2012.

13. Fox personal interview, 27 March 2006.

14. Gerald F. "Bud" Loughman, personal interview, 30 December 1991.

15. Robert Gonnoud, telephone interview, 25 August 2015.

16. Jacobsen letter No. 1; Dan Weber, personal interview, 24 April 2002.

17. Anthony Tomkovicz, telephone interview, 12 April 2010.

18. Jacobsen letter No. 12.

19. Jacobsen letter No. 5.

20. Dave Wallington, personal interview, 11 June 2004.

21. Jack Vangets, telephone interview, 7 May 2002.

22. William Herman Smith with his son, Gordon, and Gordon's wife, Sharon Smith, personal interview, 5 November 2012; Gordon Smith, telephone interview, ca. May 2013.

23. James Alls, telephone interview, 14 April 2015.

24. Garneta Ehlers, personal interview, 14 June 2004.

25. Lisa McKeon, telephone interview, 5 December 2015.

26. "Miss June Cole Is Engaged to Charles Arnall Scott," *El Paso (TX) Herald-Post,* 3 October 1949; Scott survivor statement, 14 February 1944; Charlotte Bellsmith, telephone interview, 26 June 1999.

27. Jim Wainscott, telephone interview, 13 October 2008.
Joanne Lord, telephone interview, 5 March 2017.

28. "Augie Paul Koepke," *Palm Beach (FL) Post,* 8 May 1984.

29. Don Manning, telephone interview, 13 June 2016.

30. Gloria Knecht and her daughter Lois, personal interview, 1 February 2013.

31. Weber personal interview, 24 April 2002.

32. Rechel personal interview, 11 June 2002.

33. Eugene Van Buskirk, personal interview,14 January 2005.

34. Fox, personal interview, 27 March 2006.

35. Jack Vangets, telephone interview, 7 May 2002.

36. Joseph Throgmorton, telephone interview, 2 January 2008.

37. Susan Hayes, email to author, 28 Jun 2012; Alice Hayes, telephone interview, 21 July 2012; Harold Hayes personal interview, 18 September 2012.

38. *Wantz*—Nolde's Bakery ad in the *Petersburg (VA) Progress-Index,* 9 July 1959; *Miller*—Jane Anne Martin, telephone interview, 22 April 2017; Karylee Feldman, telephone interview, 4 March 2017.

39. Anthony Tomkovicz, telephone interview, 12 April 2010; Nord Lester, personal interview, 8 December 1999; *Horsman*—"Hearing Friday for Lake Plans," *Brownwood (TX) Bulletin,* 31 October 1974.

40. Henry Burke, telephone interview, 8 February 2012; Robert Gonnoud, telephone interviews, 2 June 2002 and 8 May 2015.

41. "Hall of Valor," valor.militarytimes.com/hero/307891.

42. Gene Lehmbecker, telephone interview, 18 March 2006.

43. Shirley Hirschey, telephone interview, 27 June 2006.

44. Dallas Bogan, "Campbell County Had 150 War Dead during WWII," History of Campbell County, Tennessee, tngenweb.org/campbell/hist-bogan/wardead.html (originally published ca. 2003 in the *LaFollette [TN] Press*).

45. James Pitta, telephone interview, 9 July 2019.

46. Traci Burton, personal interview, 30 Jun 2010.

47. Garneta Ehlers, personal interview, 14 June 2004.

48. William Herman Smith personal interview, 5 November 2012.

49. Don Srack, personal interview, 28 October 2001; Fox, personal interview, 27 March 2006.

50. Jacobsen letter No. 5.

51. Jacobsen letter No. 13.

52. Jacobsen letter No. 9.

53. Jacobsen letter No. 15.

54. Joseph Throgmorton, telephone interviews, 4 June 2008 and 24 April 2011.

55. *almost two miles—Flier* Investigation: Crowley, 2–3.

56. "Fading Pioneer," *Oakland Tribune,* 3 December 1961; "Steel Scrap to Former Foe," *Oakland Tribune,* 25 August 1963.

57. Jacobsen letter No. 14.

58. Mike Severns and Pauline Fiene-Severns, *Diving Hawaii and Midway* (North Clarendon, VT: Tuttle, 2002), 220–21.

Bibliography

Anderson, Genny. "Coral Reef Formation." marinebio.net/marinescience/04benthon/crform.htm.

Articles for the Government of the United States Navy, 1930. Washington, DC: Dept. of the Navy—Bureau of Navigation/US Government Printing Office, 1932. ibiblio.org/hyperwar/USN/ref/Rocks&Shoals/index.html.

Barba, Lorena A. "Flying without Flapping: The Wandering Albatross and the Mechanics of Dynamic Soaring." *BU.* blogs.bu.edu/bioaerial2012/2012/11/17/flying-without-flapping/.

Bennett, Judith A. *Natives and Exotics: World War II and Environment in the Southern Pacific.* Honolulu: University of Hawai'i Press, 2009.

Blair, Clay. *Silent Victory: The US Submarine War against Japan.* Philadelphia: Lippincott, 1975.

Boats of the United States Navy, NAVSHIPS 25-452. Washington, DC: US Government Printing Office, May 1967.

Budiansky, Stephen. *Battle of Wits: The Complete Story of Codebreaking in World War II.* New York: Touchstone, 2002.

Cameron, John. *John Cameron's Odyssey.* New York: Macmillan, 1928.

Campbell, Douglas A. *Eight Survived: The Harrowing Story of the USS Flier and the Only Downed World War II Submariners to Survive and Evade Capture.* Guilford, CT: Globe Pequot, 2010.

Carlson, Elliot. *Joe Rochefort's War: The Odyssey of the Codebreaker Who Outwitted Yamamoto at Midway.* Annapolis, MD: Naval Institute Press, 2011.

Coletta, Paolo E., ed. *United States Navy and Marine Corps Bases, Domestic.* Westport, CT: Greenwood, 1985.

Cook, James. *Captain Cook's Journal. First Voyage.* Project Gutenberg Australia. gutenberg.net.au/ebooks/e00043.html#ch8.

"Coral Anatomy and Structure." NOAA Coral Reef Conservation Program. http://coralreef.noaa.gov/aboutcorals/coral101/anatomy/.

Cornell Lab of Ornithology. "Laysan Albatross." www.allaboutbirds.org/guide/Laysan_Albatross/overview#.

Cudahy, Brian J. *Box Boats: How Container Ships Changed the World.* New York: Fordham University Press, 2006.

Damage Control Book: U.S.S. Macaw (ASR11). Washington, DC: Bureau of Ships, Navy Dept., 1942.

Degan, Patrick. *Flattop Fighting in World War II: The Battles between American and Japanese Aircraft Carriers.* Jefferson, NC: McFarland, 2003.

Echoes. Hopkins (MN) High School Yearbook, 1940.

Farrell, Andrew. "Island Wrecks, V." *Pacific Marine Review* 17 (September 1920).

General Information Book: U.S. Submarine Rescue Vessels ASR-10 & 11. Mare Island, CA: US Navy Yard, 1943.

Guttman, Jon. "The Last Raider." *World War II Magazine.* Leesburg, VA: Weider History Group, 19 August 1997. historynet.com/the-last-raider-july-97-world-war-ii-feature .htm.

Hartney, John D. *The Secret Blue Collar War: A History of the Floating Dry Docks in World War II.* Madison, WI: Insty-Prints, 1995.

Hone, Thomas, ed. *The Battle of Midway: The Naval Institute's Guide to the U.S. Navy's Greatest Victory.* Annapolis, MD: U.S. Naval Institute Press, 2013.

Isom, Dallas Woodbury. *Midway Inquest: Why the Japanese Lost the Battle of Midway.* Bloomington: Indiana University Press, 2007.

Joesting, Edward. *Kauai, the Separate Kingdom.* Honolulu: University of Hawai'i Press, 1988.

Jourdan, David W. *The Search for the Japanese Fleet: USS* Nautilus *and the Battle of Midway.* Lincoln, NE: Potomac, 2015.

Lal, Brij V., and Kate Fortune, eds. *The Pacific Islands: An Encyclopedia,* Vol. 1. Honolulu: University of Hawai'i Press, 2000.

"Maritime History: A Brief History of Midway Atoll." Papahānaumokuākea Marine National Monument. papahanaumokuakea.gov/about/.

"Midway Mission (Enclosure 'A' serial co 011100): Naval Operating Base, Naval Air Station, Submarine Base, PT base, plane refueling base, and cable station." Undated (ca. 1944–45). USN document in custody of NARA San Bruno.

Miller, John, Jr. "The War in the Pacific—Guadalcanal: The First Offensive." U.S. Army in World War II. ibiblio.org/hyperwar/USA.

Millot, René Pierre. *Missions in the World Today.* Westerleigh, UK: Hawthorn, 1961.

Morgan, Troy D., and Spencer C. Tucker. "Guadalcanal." *The War.* pbs.org/thewar/.

Olsen, Edvert. "The Midway Tragedy." *Mid-Pacific Magazine* 15, no. 1 (January 1918).

Parshall, Jonathan, and Anthony Tully. *Shattered Sword: The Untold Story of the Battle of Midway.* Washington, DC: Potomac, 2005.

Read, George H. *The Last Cruise of the* Saginaw. Cambridge, MA: Riverside, 1912.

"RECORD OF PROCEEDINGS of a BOARD OF INVESTIGATION Convened on Board the U.S.S. BUSHNELL by Order of the Commander Submarine Force, U.S. Pacific Fleet To inquire into the grounding of the U.S.S. FLIER (SS250) at Midway Islands, T.H. on January 16, 1944."

"RECORD OF PROCEEDINGS of a BOARD OF INVESTIGATION Convening on Board the U.S.S. BUSHNELL by Order of the Commander Submarine Force, U.S. Pacific Fleet To inquire into the loss of the U.S.S. MACAW (ASR-11) at Midway Islands, T.H. on February 13, 1944."

Rubin, Ken. "The Formation of the Hawaiian Islands." Hawaii Center for Volcanology. soest.hawaii.edu/GG/HCV/haw_formation.html.

Severns, Mike, and Pauline Fiene-Severns. *Diving Hawaii and Midway*. North Clarendon, VT: Tuttle, 2002.

Shafroth, John F. "Shafroth Report: Inspector General's Report of Inspection of Naval Operating Base, Midway, 14-17 June 1944" (CINCPAC file Pac-RGP-rp, S3-1/EG12-1), appendix 11(1). USN document in custody of NARA San Bruno.

Speakman, Joseph M. "Into the Woods: The First Year of the Civilian Conservation Corps." *Prologue* 38, no. 3 (fall 2006).

Speulda-Drews, Lou Ann. *Midway Atoll National Wildlife Refuge: Historic Preservation Plan 2010*. Honolulu: USDI Fish and Wildlife Service, Region 1, December 2010.

Spofford, Ainsworth Rand, ed. *An American Almanac and Treasury of Facts, Statistical, Financial, and Political, for the Year 1886*. Washington, DC: American News Company, 1886.

Stevenson, Robert Louis, and Lloyd Osbourne. *The Wrecker*. London: Cassell, 1892.

Sturma, Michael. *The USS* Flier: *Death and Survival on a World War II Submarine*. Lexington: University Press of Kentucky, 2008.

Telavi, Melei. "War Years." In *Tuvalu—A History*. Funafuti: University of the South Pacific and the Tuvalu Ministry of Social Services, 1983.

Thomas, Nicholas. *Cook: The Extraordinary Voyages of Captain James Cook*. New York: Walker, 2003.

Williams, Greg H. *The Liberty Ships of World War II*. Jefferson, NC: McFarland, 2014.

Suggestions for Further Reading

Cameron, John. *John Cameron's Odyssey*. New York: Macmillan, 1928.

Campbell, Douglas A. *Eight Survived: The Harrowing Story of the USS* Flier *and the Only Downed World War II Submariners to Survive and Evade Capture*. Guilford, CT: Lyons, 2010.

Carlson, Elliot. *Joe Rochefort's War: The Odyssey of the Codebreaker Who Outwitted Yamamoto at Midway*. Annapolis, MD: Naval Institute Press, 2011.

Cudahy, Brian J. *Box Boats: How Container Ships Changed the World*. New York: Fordham University Press, 2006.

Hartney, John Donald. *The Secret Blue Collar War: A History of the Floating Dry Docks in World War II*. Madison, WI: Insty-Prints, 1995.

Hughes, R. J. *Surviving the* Flier. Muncie, IN: Phoenix Flair, 2010.

Parshall, Jonathan, and Anthony Tully. *Shattered Sword: The Untold Story of the Battle of Midway*. Washington, DC: Potomac, 2005.

Read, George H. *The Last Cruise of the* Saginaw. Cambridge, MA: Riverside, 1912.

Stevenson, Robert Louis, and Lloyd Osbourne. *The Wrecker*. London: Cassell, 1892.

Sturma, Michael. *The USS* Flier: *Death and Survival on a World War II Submarine*. Lexington: University Press of Kentucky, 2008.

Thomas, Nicholas. *Cook: The Extraordinary Voyages of Captain James Cook*. New York: Walker, 2003.

Williams, Greg H. *The Liberty Ships of World War II*. Jefferson, NC: McFarland, 2014.

Wouk, Herman. *The Caine Mutiny*. New York: Doubleday, 1951.

Index

ABS, 39

ABSD, 38–39

ABSD-1, 38–40, 45, 78, 167

ABSD-2, 39

Adams, Benjamin, 62

Adams, Eddie, 171

Admiral Kidd Commissioned Officers Club, 178

Advanced Base Sectional Dock, 38–39. *See also* ABSD-1; ABSD-2

aircraft carrier, 27, 39–40, 43, 52, 87, 98–101, 165, 167, 172

AKA, 81

Akagi, 100–101

Alameda, CA, 34–35, 83

Albacore, USS, 182–83

albatross, 48, 96. *See also* gooney bird

Albin, Joseph, 11, 17, 19

Albuquerque, NM, 178

Aleutians, 4, 87

Alls, James, 7–8, 26, 169–70

American Locomotive Company, 44

Anderson, Virgil, 14

Apamama, 26, 103

Appleby, J. C., 58–59

Aqua Velva, 49

Arashi, 165

Arizona, USS, 85–86

ARS, 25

ASR, 8, 25, 32–34, 87. *See also* submarine rescue vessel

Associated Press, 55

Astaire, Fred, 54

Atlanta, USS, 70

Australia, 25, 38, 42, 68, 106, 117, 169

Autin, Adam, 114

B-25B *Mitchell* medium bomber, 52

Balabac Strait, 170

Banchero, George, 6–7, 25

Banks, Neill K., 87

banzai attack, 68

battleships, 39, 53, 66, 85, 87, 98, 149, 165, 168

battle stations, 67, 78, 86

Beijing, China, 27

Bennion, Mervyn S., 86

Besugo, USS, 86, 177

Billis, Luther, 57

Biss, Dan, 172

Black Cat Café, 89

Block Recreation Center, 92

board of inquiry. *See* board of investigation

board of investigation: grounding of the *Flier,* 103, 168; loss of the *Macaw,* 8, 14, 108, 160, 163

Boeing, 168

Bolke, Albert, 50, 89, 113, 129, 137–38, 141–42, 147, 163, 172, 174

Bonneville Dam, 41

Borneo, 170

bosun's chair, 24
Bradford Island, 150
breeches buoy, 24
Bremerton, WA, 38
Brisbane, Australia, 38
Brooks, N. C., 94
Brooks Channel, 2–4, 120, 151, 175, 181
Brooks Islands and Shore. *See* Midway
    Atoll
Brown, Tom E., 114, 131, 134, 137–38,
    144–47, 154, 164, 175, 179, 180
Buda air compressor, 117–18, 122
Burbank Daily Review, 55
Bureau of Navigation, 28
Bureau of Yards and Docks, 38
Burton, Elizabeth P. W. "Betty," 27, 80,
    139, 178
Burton, Paul W., 8–16, 18–22, 27–33,
    43–46, 48–49, 53, 60, 62, 65, 67, 72–77,
    79–83, 85–88, 90, 92, 104–6, 109, 113,
    120, 123, 127, 130–31, 133, 139–40,
    145, 160–64, 168–71, 175–75, 178–82
Burton, Traci, 178
Bushnell, USS, 103, 160

Cahl, James F. P., 6–7, 21, 23, 26, 62
Caine Mutiny, The (Wouk), 81, 83, 168
California, 27, 34, 40, 45, 47, 54–55, 76,
    84–85, 92, 96, 104, 109, 112, 149, 170,
    173, 175, 177, 183–84
California, USS, 85
Cameron, John, 96–97
Camp Rusk, 51
Cannon, Vickie (née Daugherty), 177
captain's mast, 77
CCC, 50–51
chart room, 10, 81, 120–21, 123, 127
Chicago Bridge & Iron Co., 40
Civilian Conservation Corps, 50–51
Clamp, USS, 25–26, 59–62, 103–4, 107–8
Cleveland, SS, 111
Commercial Pacific Cable Co., 97
Congress, 38, 40, 80, 95
Connolly, Joseph A., 8–12, 14, 19, 22,
    24–25, 58, 107–8, 116–18, 121–22,

124–27, 147, 152–54, 160–62, 170,
    181–82
Contractor's Tower, 147. *See also* signal
    tower
Convoy PW 2294, 40–41, 66, 183
Cook, James, 83, 106, 117
coral, 1–2, 18, 23, 25, 59, 71, 93–94, 96–97,
    106–8, 118, 122, 138, 146, 157, 163–64;
    reef formation, 93–94
Coral Sea, Battle of the, 69, 99
Cottrell, Melvin C., 63, 89, 91
Crocker, G. F. J., 21
Crosby, Bing, 54
Crowley, John D., 4–7, 16–17, 19, 23–24,
    26, 58–62, 103, 168–70, 181–82
cruiser, 43, 52, 69–70, 101
Cunniff, Jack, 92
Curtis, Lebbeus, 25, 106–8, 116–18,
    121–22, 163, 182, 184
Cushing, USS, 70

Daggy, Waite, 6–8
Damage Control Book, 21
Daugherty, Howard Eugene, 148–49,
    154–57, 177
Daugherty, Lonzo, 149, 177
Daugherty, Robert, 177
Dauntless dive bomber, 67
Dear John letters, 83–84, 110, 167
Depression, the, 27, 80, 148
Despatch Oven Co., 148
destroyer, 18, 28, 33, 38, 69, 81, 87, 98,
    101, 165, 168, 182–83
Disposition No. 2, 66
Dobbins, Al, 60–62
Dodd, Loudon, 97
Doolittle, James, 52
dry dock, 38–39, 42, 54, 68, 99, 103, 167
DuBois, Monsieur, 36
Duff, Ivan "Frank," 104, 156, 163
Dungarees Navy, 45
Dunn, William A., 12, 14, 21–22, 44, 102

Eastern Island, 2–3, 25, 124, 142, 147
Edmunds, Charles D., 126–27

Efate, 36
Ehlers, Garneta, 112, 178
Ehlers, Herman H., 10, 15, 19, 48, 82, 112,
    123–24, 128, 132–33, 138, 144–45, 147,
    163, 170–71, 178
Ehlers, Vernon, 113
Ehlers, Viola, 113
Electric Boat, 86
Ellice Islands (Tuvalu), 72
Ellis Island, 111
Emperor Chain, 94
English, Bob, 28
Enterprise, USS, 52, 100–101
Enzweiler, Ralph, 50, 74, 83, 164
Espiritu Santo, xiv, 38, 44, 68, 70, 78,
    167
evaporators, 45

Falcon, USS, 34, 59, 87, 175
Farmers State Bank, 112
fathometer, 5, 174
filariasis, 70
1st Marine Division, 68. *See also* marines;
    US Marine Corps
Fisher Body, 172, 175
Fitch, Howard W., 74
Flier, USS, 1, 3–14, 17, 20–26, 28, 58–62,
    87, 90, 103, 105, 116, 154, 156, 160,
    162, 168–70, 182
Flint, MI, 77, 84, 112, 175
Florikan, USS, 25–26, 58–62, 87–88, 103,
    168
flying bridge, 14, 17, 44, 46, 49, 80,
    134–37, 139–42, 156, 158, 180
Flying Clipper service, 98
Ford Island, 88
4-F, 84
Fox, Lloyd George, 69–70, 80, 164–66,
    173–74, 178
Fremantle, Australia, 169
Freon, 49
Frey, Edward, 104
Froehlich, Myron J., 83–84, 102
Fulton, USS, 168
Funafuti, 30, 71–75, 77–79, 92, 94, 110

Funk, William R., 44, 48–49, 77, 112,
    130–31, 137–38, 144

Gaideczka, Peter, 8
Ganymede, SS, 66
Garibaldi, OR, 9, 183
Gaylord, 25–26, 58, 107, 119
General Electric Co., 47
general quarters. *See* battle stations
General Seigel, 96–97
George F. Elliott, USS, 35–36
Gerber, Clyde, 6–7, 25
GI Bill, 80, 173, 175
Gilbert Islands, 26, 59, 72–73
Glenn Curtis, SS, 67
Golden Gate Bridge, 42
Gonnoud, Robert, 9–10, 13, 15–16, 23, 30,
    32, 37, 47–48, 53, 55–57, 65, 67, 71–72,
    74, 77–80, 82, 88, 103, 166–68, 175
gooney bird, 96–97, 164, 165, 171. *See also*
    albatross
Graaff, John P., 13
Grand Coulee Dam, 41
Great Lakes Naval Training Center, 149
Gritton, George R., 16–17, 21
Guadalcanal, Battle of, 35, 53–55, 68–70
Guam, 98
Guano Islands Act, 72, 94
Gwinn, Kenneth, 6
gyrocompass, 14

Haddonfield, NJ, 178
Halford, William, 95
Hannah, Claude W. "Toby," 70, 92
Hannah, Hoyt, 70
Hardy, R. M., 147
Hawaii, 1, 26, 43, 51, 79, 89–90, 93, 95,
    147, 149, 167, 171, 185
Hawaiian Islands, 93–94
Hawaiian Ridge, 94
Hayes, Harold H., 11–12, 57, 84, 110, 114,
    165, 174
Henreid, Paul, 172
Hiryu, 101
H. L. Hunley, 33

Holiday Inn (1942), 54
Hollywood, 54, 110, 174
Holmes, Jasper, 99
Honolulu, 90, 95, 98
Honolulu Advertiser, 167
Hoover, John, 73
Hoover administration, 27
Hoover Dam, 41
Hope, AR, 55
Hope Star, 55
Hopkins, MN, 148
Hopkins High School, 148
Hornet, USS, 52, 100
Horsman, Lewill E., 106–7, 112, 130,
    139–42, 147, 163–64, 175
Housatonic, USS, 33
hundred-fathom curve, 4, 156
Hunley, Horace L., 33
Hutchenson, Shirley, 148, 176

I-7, 87
inclinometer, 60
inquest, 12, 32. *See also* board of
    investigation
Iowa, USS, 168
Iroquois, 97
Isbell, Clyde, 18, 46, 89, 103, 174
Iwo Jima, 167

Jacobsen, Robert, 10–11, 18, 20, 35, 37,
    42–45, 47–49, 52–53, 55–57, 64–68,
    70–71, 74–77, 80–83, 89–90, 92, 101,
    104–6, 110, 112, 114, 133, 144, 164,
    167, 179, 181, 183
Jersey City, NJ, 34, 111
Jewell, Dean F., 77
JN-25, 99
Jones, Albert H., 14, 162, 166
Jorgensen, Adolph, 96

Kaga, 100–101
Kaiser, Henry J., 41
Kaiser shipyards, 41
Kamehameha, King, 95
Kane, Elisha K., 147

Kankakee, USS, 54
Kansas State Agricultural College, 54
Kauai, 95
Keehn, George, 167
Kelly, Leo, 35
Kido Butai, 99–100
Kilauea, 95
Kingsbury, Gilbert, 171
Kingsley, Lewis A., 112–13, 137, 141, 143
Kirishima, 165
Kiska Island, 87
Knecht, Ernst A., 111
Knecht, Erwin R., 111, 136–37, 140–41,
    143, 153, 155–56, 164, 173
Knickerbocker Ice Co., 111
Koepke, Augie P., 35–37, 47, 63, 69, 89–90,
    112, 114, 131–34, 136, 138, 140,
    144–47, 163–64, 171–72, 175–76
Kumler, Charles H., 15–16, 21, 113, 124,
    131, 138, 144, 147, 154, 171
Kumler, Harry, 15–16
Kure Atoll, 94–95
Kuril-Kamchatka Trench, 93

Lackawanna, USS, 94
Lakatoi, 36
Lashuay, Sadie, 177
Laysan albatross, 96. *See also* gooney bird
LCM, 127, 155–56
LCT, 73
Lehmbecker, Elizabeth, 157, 176
Lehmbecker, Frank, 157, 176
Lehmbecker, Gene, 176
Lehmbecker, LeRoy B., 148–49, 154–56,
    176
Leonis, Vincent, 35
Lester, Nord E., 14, 17, 44, 106–7, 112,
    120, 122, 130, 139–41, 145–46, 153,
    163–64, 175, 179–80
Lexington, USS, 98–99
Leyte, 167
Lia, Joseph, 6
Libera, Stanley, 57, 66, 84–86, 89, 109, 114,
    129–32, 135–36, 142–43, 163, 165, 171
Liberty ship, 40–42, 66–67, 183

Library of Congress, 178
Liddell, James, 7
Lightner, John, 63
Lipan, USS, 42, 66
Lockwood, Charles A., 28–29, 87,
    168–69
Loicano, Gloria, 111
Loughman, Gerald F. "Bud," 10, 12–13, 16,
    29–30, 34, 43–44, 48–49, 53, 64, 72,
    75–76, 79–81, 88, 91, 102, 109, 111,
    113, 120–22, 126–31, 133, 137–41,
    145–46, 153–54, 156–57, 159, 164–66,
    170, 176, 178–80
Lucky Lager, 75, 89
Luders, Ernst, 104
Luganville, 68

Maas, Bert E., 10–11, 18, 89
MacArthur, Douglas, 170
Macaw, USS: assignment to Task Group
    116.11, 38; attempted salvage of,
    25–26, 101–9; boredom on, 48, 79–80;
    bull sessions aboard, 49–51, 80–81;
    commissioning of, 15; commissioning
    party for, 34–35; construction of, 34;
    convoy role of, 38, 41–43, 67–68; crime
    and punishment on, 49, 77; current
    inhabitants of, 184–85; current
    location of, 184; demolition of, 184;
    diversions on, 48; drinking on, 48–49;
    encounter with SS *Philip Kearny,* 43;
    equator-crossing festivities on, 63–66;
    at Espiritu Santo, 68; food on, 47–48,
    83, 92; at Funafuti, 71–78; grounding of,
    8–17; hygiene on, 44–46; investigation
    into the loss of, 8, 12, 14, 160–64, 169;
    navigational mishaps of, 71–74, 88–89;
    near self-destruction by depth charge
    of, 67–68; overcrowding on, 45, 79; at
    Pearl Harbor, 83–92; propulsion of, 44;
    pumping capacity of, 21; race relations
    on, 64–66; sartorial standards on,
    45–46; seasickness on, 43–44; shortage
    of fresh water on, 45; sinking of,
    115–45; sleeping quarters on, 46–47,
    102–3; torpedo practice by, 10, 88, 114;
    at Wallis Island, 70–71
Mack, Andrew R., 45
Magazine Loch, 83
Manning, Don, 173
Manning, George W., 112, 135–36, 140,
    143–44, 152–53, 155–56, 173
Mare Island, 28, 95, 169
marines, 31, 41, 68–69, 71–72, 98, 124,
    142, 159. *See also* US Marine Corps
Marshall Islands, 148
Mathers, Lawrence, 110, 129–30, 137,
    144–47, 173
McCann rescue chamber, 22, 34, 103, 184
McCarthy, Jack, 64, 129, 133, 139
McClusky, C. Wade, 100–101, 165
McIntosh, Dessa O., 55
Medal of Honor, 86
Meiji Seamount, 93
Mennemeyer, Ralph J., 10–11, 18, 37, 47,
    85, 114
merchant marine, 41
Middaugh, Hugh A., 36
Middlebrook Islands. *See* Midway Atoll
Midway, Battle of, 1, 7, 9, 98–101, 164–65
Midway, USS, 172
Midway Atoll: appropriation of, 94; buoys
    at, 2–3, 5, 11, 13–17, 19, 61, 104, 109,
    115, 139–46, 153, 160–62, 179–81, 183;
    civilian development of, 95, 97–98;
    climate of, 3, 102; currents at, 2, 4, 11,
    14, 119–20, 163; depredations by
    Japanese sailors at, 97; description of in
    Robert Louis Stevenson novel, 97;
    discovery of, 94; early dredging at,
    95; geology of, 93–94; postwar
    developments at, 184–85; prewar
    history of, 94–98; recreational facilities
    at, 164; topography of, 1–4; water level
    in, 119, 163; water temperature at, 102,
    154
"Midway Mission," 161
Midway Naval Air Station, 4, 124
Miller, Stephen, 64, 80, 133, 174
Minneapolis, MN, 148

Minneapolis Tribune, 148
Minnesota Aircraft School, 148
Miss Saylor's Coffee-ets, 56
Mitsubishi "Betty" bomber, 35
Monaghan, USS, 87
Monterey, CA, 38, 43
Moore Dry Dock Co., 34–35, 40, 83, 183–84
Moreell, Ben, 38
Morgan City, LA, 40
Moses, 96
Muti, Albert, 56, 63, 175

National Oceanic and Atmospheric
    Administration, 185
Nauru, 73
Nautilus, USS, 165–66, 168
naval air station, 4, 51, 124, 147, 148
Naval Reserve Training Center, 178
Naval War College, 27
Navy Cross, 29
New Caledonia, 36
New Hebrides, 36, 38, 42, 68
New London, CT, 1, 28, 171
Nimitz, Chester W., 9, 99
Niuafo'ou, 67
NOB 1504, 1, 8, 106, 126, 151
NOB Midway, 148, 150
North Sea, 33–34

Oakland, CA, 34, 36, 40–41, 70, 76–77, 83,
    150, 167, 183
Oakland Estuary, 15, 34, 83
Oakley, Thomas B., 88
Ocean Island, 95
O'Hara, Maureen, 172
Okinawa, 170, 175
Osbourne, Lloyd, 97

Pacific Mail Steamship Company, 95
Pago Pago, 67
Pallikulo Bay, 68
Panama Canal, 1, 39–40, 172
Pan American Airways, 98
Papahanaumokuakea Marine National
    Monument, 185

Paramount Studios, 54
Parks, Rush A., 47, 77
PB2Y *Coronado* seaplane, 125, 147
PBY *Catalina* seaplane, 98
PC-602, USS, 58, 60
Pearl Harbor, 1, 8, 25, 28, 29, 38, 42, 58,
    62, 67, 78–79, 90, 103, 105, 148, 156,
    160, 165, 168–69, 184; arrival at, 83, 86;
    assignment to, 167, 173–75; attack on,
    40, 48, 51–52, 54, 66, 85, 98, 149, 183;
    Christmas at, 92; cryptanalysis office
    at, 99; departure from, 92; German
    POWs at, 167; navigational
    misadventures at, 88; personnel
    transfers at, 84–85, 88–89, 92, 114, 150;
    picnic at, 89; reception of mail at,
    83–84; submarine base at, 86–87;
    torpedo practice at, 88
Pennsylvania, USS, 53–54, 149
Peregrine, USS, 172
Perth, Australia, 169–70
Phelps, Fannie, 149
Philadelphia, PA, 27, 31, 178
Philip Kearny, SS, 43
Philippines, 167–68, 170
photosynthetic dinoflagellates, 93
Pierson, Charles E. "Chuck," 92
pilothouse, 9–10, 13–17, 80, 118, 120–21,
    123–34, 136–41, 144, 146–47, 154, 161,
    171, 180, 182
Pitta, Amaro, 150
Pitta, Edward A., 149–53, 155–56, 177
Pitta, James, 150
Pitta, Joe, 177
Pitta, Manuel, 150
polliwogs, 63–65
polyps, 93–94
Pope, Charles D., 62
porpoises, 26, 48
PT boat, 26, 69, 72, 159

Queeg, Philip F., 81, 83

range light, 2–3, 15, 162
rearming boat, 148–49, 153–56

Rechel, Howard, 36–37, 43, 76, 78, 82, 142–43, 164, 173
Red Cross, 55
Red Oak Victory, SS, 183
Redondo Reflex, 175
Red Sea, 25
reef formation, 93–94
Regular Navy, 48, 114
revocation of qualification, 32–33
Reynolds, William, 94
Richmond, CA, 40–41, 183
Rochefort, Joseph, 99
Roosevelt, Franklin D., 27, 42
Roosevelt, Theodore, 97–98
Rosie the Riveter/World War II Home Front National Historical Park, 183
Royal Navy, 25

S-4, USS, 33
S-5, USS, 33
S-51, USS, 33
Saginaw, USS, 95
Salt Lake City, USS, 52
Samad, David, 149, 177
Samed, Ernest D., 149–53, 155–57, 177
Samoa, 67
San Diego, CA, 36, 44, 140, 148, 171, 175, 178
Sand Island, 1–4, 96–98, 119, 125, 155, 164
San Francisco, 19, 67, 76, 94, 98, 110, 112, 149–51, 157, 164, 173, 175
San Francisco, USS, 70
San Francisco Bay, 28, 38, 40, 42–43, 46, 49, 55, 95, 112, 150
Saratoga, USS, 27
Sargo, USS, 66, 84–85, 89
Sazanami, 98, 182–83
S-boat, 4
Schnitzer Brothers, 183
Scott, Charles A., 112, 131, 135, 140, 152–53, 156, 164, 171
Sea Bees, 184
Seal, USS, 170
Searaven, USS, 170

searchlight platform, 78, 80, 133, 136, 161
seasickness, 43–44, 61, 112, 146, 153–54, 175
semaphore, 1, 5, 46, 67
Shackle, USS, 184
shakedown cruise, 38, 43
Shakespeare, William, 80, 133, 174
Sharp, George A., 34, 59–60, 62, 87, 168, 175
shellbacks, 63–64
Shoho, 98
Shokaku, 99
Sicard, Montgomery, 95
sick bay, 49
signal tower, 1, 4, 8, 124–27, 147
Sitkoh Bay, USS, 167
Smith, Gordon, 168
Smith, William H., 23–24, 51–53, 69, 81, 168, 178
Solace, USS, 70
Solomon Islands, 28, 68
Song Dynasty, 38
Soryu, 100–101
Southern California Edison, 184
South Pacific (1958), 57
South Pacific, 30, 54, 67, 70, 83, 87
South Side (of Chicago), 50, 172
Spanish Main, The (1945), 172
Sparks, Bosun, 25
Spearfish, USS, 87
Spit Island, 147
Sprout Brook, NY, 41
Squalus, USS, 34, 59, 87, 175
Srack, Donald, 45, 55–56, 102, 110, 113, 170, 178, 181
Stalingrad, Battle of, 55
Station Hypo, 99
Stevenson, Robert Louis, 96
Stout, John R., 18, 76–77
St. Peter's Catholic Church, 111
St. Peter's Grammar School, 111
Struthers Wells-Titusville Corp., 13
Studer, Quinton, 9, 19, 32, 48–49, 64, 71, 75, 84, 103, 110, 165

submarines, 1–2, 4, 8, 10–11, 17–18, 22–24, 26–29, 32–34, 41, 58, 60, 62, 66–67, 79, 81, 84–87, 98, 107, 165, 167–68, 173, 182
submarine bases, 1–2, 83, 103, 156, 169, 174, 184
Submarine Division 42, 32
Submarine Division 45, 92
Submarine Division 362, 178
submarine escape training tank, 28
submarine rescue vessel, 8, 32–34, 36, 88, 170, 175; development of, 33–34; prewar deployment of, 34; unglamorous status of, 32, 88. *See also* ASR
submarine service: appeal of, 66, 85; danger of, 85; denial of, 113; expulsion from, 29, 32, 87, 181; preferential treatment of, 47; reposting within, 89, 170; status within, 32, 88
Submarine Squadron 5, 178
Sumner, USS, 78–79
Swan Island, 147

taking the range, 2, 15
Talbot, John G., 95
Tarawa, 73, 78–79, 97, 110, 113
Tarawa, Battle of, 73, 79
Tarpon, USS, 28–30, 32, 86, 88, 177, 179
Task Group 116.11, 38, 40
TBY radio, 125
tectonic plate, 93–94
Tennessee, USS, 66, 85–86
Terminal Island, 36
Terror, USS, 73–74
Thames River, 1
Throgmorton, Joseph, 46, 53, 82, 174, 180
Tiburon Peninsula, 40
Tingle, Lieutenant Colonel, 124
Token, USS, 41–42, 66
Tomkovicz, Anthony, 53–54, 63, 149, 167, 174
Topeka, KS, 54
Topeka Daily Capital, 54
torpedo plane, 100

torpedo practice, 10, 88, 114
Towhee, USS, 172
Treasure Island (Stevenson), 96
Treasure Island, 55–56
tuberculosis, 70, 149
tugboat, 15, 32, 42, 58, 88, 97
Tumult, USS, 41–43, 66
Turner, Nathan, 92
Tuvalu (Ellice Islands), 72
Typhoon Cobra, 168

US Army, 36, 177
US Army Corps of Engineers, 175
US Fish and Wildlife Service, 185
Ushio, 98, 183
US Marine Corps, 175. *See also* 1st Marine Division; marines
US Maritime Commission, 40
US Naval Academy, 4, 27, 30–31, 75, 87, 180
US Naval Reserve, 170, 178
US Treasury Department, 176

Van Buskirk, Eugene, 37, 66, 75, 77–78, 83, 89, 92, 114, 173
Van Der Heyden, Violet, 26
Vangets, Jack, 43, 63, 65, 77–78, 92, 168, 174
Vaughn, Robert, 44, 64–66, 109, 113, 133–36, 138, 141, 156–57, 176
Vaughn, William, 157
Verkennes, Joseph, 77–78, 112, 139, 163, 175
Voke, Dora Mae, 113
Voke, Walter E., 113
volcanoes, 67, 93–94, 156

Wade, Edward J., 34–35, 43–44, 88, 111–12, 114, 129, 135, 140, 152–53, 155–56, 175–76
Waikiki, 89, 167
Wainscott, Curtis, 88, 113–14, 126–27, 133–34, 136, 138, 144–47, 163, 171–72
WaKeeney, KS, 54
Wake Island, 52, 125, 147

Waldron, John, 100
Wallington, Dave, 13, 24, 37, 43–44, 49, 64, 74, 76–78, 83–84, 89, 92, 102–3, 112, 114, 167–68, 175
Wallis Island, 70–71
Wandering Minstrel, 95–97
Wantz, William H., 49, 64, 174
Washington, DC, 7, 28, 52, 168–69
Washington Naval Treaty of 1922, 98
Webb, Lyle M., 54–57, 90, 167, 175
Weber, Daniel, 19, 21, 46, 66, 110, 167, 171, 173
Western State College of Colorado, 110
West Virginia, USS, 85–86
Whitmarsh, Donald, 83–84, 110, 140–43, 152
Williamson, Richard B., 78, 110, 130–32, 141–43, 147, 167, 173

Windle, Worth T., 9–17, 19, 21, 90, 162, 175
Wingrove, Warden, 30, 71–72, 88–89
WLW-WSAI, 171
Wogan, Helen, 178
Wogan, Thomas L., 28–32, 86, 88, 177–78, 181
World War I, 33, 38, 55, 111, 149
Wouk, Herman, 81, 168
Wrecker, The (Stevenson and Osbourne), 97

Yokohama, Japan, 95, 184
Yorktown, USS, 99–101
YT-188, 4–5, 11

Zeigler, Vernon, 167
Zero, 100–101
Zuikaku, 99
Zuroweste, Frank, 46